1990 Supplement
To Seventh Editions

MODERN CRIMINAL PROCEDURE

Cases — Comments — Questions

and

BASIC CRIMINAL PROCEDURE

Cases — Comments — Questions

By

Yale Kamisar

*Henry K. Ransom Professor of Law,
University of Michigan*

Wayne R. LaFave

*David C. Baum Professor of Law,
University of Illinois*

Jerold H. Israel

*Alene and Allan F. Smith Professor of Law,
University of Michigan*

AMERICAN CASEBOOK SERIES®

WEST PUBLISHING CO.
ST. PAUL, MINN.
1990

Mod. & Basic Crim.Proc., 7th Ed. (K, L & I) ACB
1990 Supp.

Preface

This supplement contains all significant United States Supreme Court cases since the end of the 1988–89 Term—the cut-off date for the principal books. This volume also contains selected provisions of the U.S. Constitution (App. A); selected federal statutory provisions, e.g., the Bail Reform Act, the Speedy Trial Act and the recently amended Wire and Electronic Communications Interception Act (App. B); the Federal Rules of Criminal Procedure (App. C); and proposed amendments to the Rules (App. D).

YALE KAMISAR
WAYNE LaFAVE
JEROLD H. ISRAEL

July, 1990

*

Table of Contents

Table of Cases

The principal cases are in bold type. Cases cited or discussed in the text are roman type. References are to pages. Cases cited in principal cases and within other quoted materials are not included.

1990 Supplement
To Seventh Editions

MODERN CRIMINAL PROCEDURE

Cases — Comments — Questions

and

BASIC CRIMINAL PROCEDURE

Cases — Comments — Questions

*

Part Two

POLICE PRACTICES

Chapter 5

ARREST, SEARCH AND SEIZURE

SECTION 1. THE EXCLUSIONARY RULE

7th ed., p. 145; end of Note 6, add:

Even if there has been direct U.S. involvement in the foreign search, the Fourth Amendment may be inapplicable for yet another reason. In *United States v. Verdugo–Urquidez,* ___ U.S. ___, 110 S.Ct. 1056, 108 L.Ed.2d 222 (1990), the opinion of the Court, per Rehnquist, C.J., declares that the phrase "the people" in the Fourth Amendment (and the First, Second, Ninth and Tenth Amendments) "refers to a class of persons who are part of a national community or who have otherwise developed sufficient connection with this community to be considered part of that community." The defendant in the instant case was deemed not to be such a person; he was a Mexican citizen and resident who, to be sure, just two days before the search of his residence in Mexico had been turned over to U.S. authorities by Mexican police, but "this sort of presence—lawful but involuntary—is not the sort to indicate any substantial connection with our country." (The Court added it was an open question whether even the illegal aliens in *Lopez–Mendoza,* 7th ed., p. 143, were such persons, though their situation was different from the defendant's here because they "were in the

United States voluntarily and presumably had accepted some societal obligations.") The three dissenters agreed, as Blackmun, J., put it, "that when a foreign national is held accountable for purported violations of United States criminal laws, he has effectively been treated as one of 'the governed' and therefore is entitled to Fourth Amendment protections." Because the two concurring Justices placed great emphasis upon the inapplicability of the Fourth Amendment's warrant clause to the search in the instant case (Kennedy, J., stressing this was not a case in which "the full protections of the Fourth Amendment would apply" because of the "absence of local judges or magistrates available to issue warrants"; Stevens, J., that "American magistrates have no power to authorize such searches"), the application of *Verdugo–Urquidez* to a foreign search of an alien's property made even without probable cause is not entirely clear.

SECTION 2. PROTECTED AREAS AND INTERESTS

7th ed., p. 161; end of fn. i, add:

Thomas was questioned and distinguished in *United States v. Colyer,* 878 F.2d 469 (D.C.Cir. 1989), holding there was no search where a drug dog in the public corridor of a train "alerted" to a particular sleeper compartment.

1

SECTION 4. SEARCH WARRANTS

7th ed., p. 206; in lieu of first paragraph of Note 6, add:

6. *Seizure of items not named in the search warrant.* In HORTON v. CALIFORNIA, ___ U.S. ___, 110 S.Ct. 2301, ___ L.Ed. 2d ___ (1990), a police officer's affidavit established probable cause to search defendant's home for the proceeds of a robbery (including three specified rings) and for the weapons used in that robbery, but the magistrate issued a warrant only for the proceeds. They were not found in execution of the warrant, but the guns were; they were seized. The defendant claimed this seizure did not come within Justice Stewart's plurality decision in *Coolidge v. New Hampshire,* 403 U.S. 443, 91 S.Ct. 2022, 29 L.Ed.2d 564 (1971), that items found in "plain view" may be seized "where it is immediately apparent to the police that they have evidence before them," because he also required "that the discovery of evidence in plain view must be inadvertent." The Court in *Horton,* 7–2, disagreed. STEVENS, J., explained:

"Justice Stewart concluded that the inadvertence requirement was necessary to avoid a violation of the express constitutional requirement that a valid warrant must particularly describe the things to be seized. He explained:

'The rationale of the exception to the warrant requirement, as just stated, is that a plain-view seizure will not turn an initially valid (and therefore limited) search into a "general" one, while the inconvenience of procuring a warrant to cover an inadvertent discovery is great. But where the discovery is anticipated, where the police know in advance the location of the evidence and intend to seize it, the situation is altogether different. The requirement of a warrant to seize imposes no inconvenience whatever, or at least none which is constitutionally cognizable in a legal system that regards warrantless searches as *"per se*

unreasonable" in the absence of "exigent circumstances."

'If the initial intrusion is bottomed upon a warrant that fails to mention a particular object, though the police know its location and intend to seize it, then there is a violation of the express constitutional requirement of "Warrants . . . particularly describing . . . [the] things to be seized." '

"We find two flaws in this reasoning. First, evenhanded law enforcement is best achieved by the application of objective standards of conduct, rather than standards that depend upon the subjective state of mind of the officer. The fact that an officer is interested in an item of evidence and fully expects to find it in the course of a search should not invalidate its seizure if the search is confined in area and duration by the terms of a warrant or a valid exception to the warrant requirement. If the officer has knowledge approaching certainty that the item will be found, we see no reason why he or she would deliberately omit a particular description of the item to be seized from the application for a search warrant. Specification of the additional item could only permit the officer to expand the scope of the search. On the other hand, if he or she has a valid warrant to search for one item and merely a suspicion concerning the second, whether or not it amounts to probable cause, we fail to see why that suspicion should immunize the second item from seizure if it is found during a lawful search for the first. The hypothetical case put by Justice White in his dissenting opinion in *Coolidge* is instructive:

'Let us suppose officers secure a warrant to search a house for a rifle. While staying well within the range of a rifle search, they discover two photographs of the murder victim, both in plain sight in the bedroom. Assume also that the discovery of the one photograph was inadvertent but finding the other was anticipated. The Court would permit the seizure of only one of the photographs. But in terms of the "minor" peril to Fourth Amendment values there is surely no difference between these two photographs: the interference with possession is the same in each case and the officers' appraisal of the photograph they expected to see is no less reliable than their judgment about the other. And in both situations the actual inconvenience and danger to evidence remain identical if the officers must depart and secure a warrant.'

"Second, the suggestion that the inadvertence requirement is necessary to prevent the police from conducting general searches, or from converting specific warrants into general warrants, is not persuasive because that interest is already served by the requirements that no warrant issue unless it 'particularly describ[es] the place to be searched and the persons or things to be seized,' and that a warrantless search be circumscribed by the exigencies which justify its initiation. Scrupulous adherence to these requirements serves the interests in limiting the area and duration of the search that the inadvertence requirement inadequately protects. Once those commands have been satisfied and the officer has a lawful right of access, however, no additional Fourth Amendment interest is furthered by requiring that the discovery of evidence be inadvertent. If the scope of the search exceeds that permitted by the terms of a validly issued warrant or the character of the relevant exception from the warrant requirement, the subsequent seizure is unconstitutional without more."

BRENNAN, J., joined by Marshall, J. dissenting, responded that "these flaws are illusory. First, the majority explains that it can see no reason why an officer who 'has knowledge approaching certainty' that an item will be found in a particular location 'would deliberately omit a particular description of the item to be seized from the application for a search warrant.' But to the individual whose possessory interest has been invaded, it matters not *why* the

police officer decided to omit a particular item from his application for a search warrant. When an officer with probable cause to seize an item fails to mention that item in his application for a search warrant—for whatever reason—and then seizes the item anyway, his conduct is *per se* unreasonable. Suppression of the evidence so seized will encourage officers to be more precise and complete in future warrant applications.

"Furthermore, there are a number of instances in which a law enforcement officer might deliberately choose to omit certain items from a warrant application even though he has probable cause to seize them, knows they are on the premises, and intends to seize them when they are discovered in plain view. For example, the warrant application process can often be time-consuming, especially when the police attempt to seize a large number of items. An officer interested in conducting a search as soon as possible might decide to save time by listing only one or two hard-to-find items, such as the stolen rings in this case, confident that he will find in plain view all of the other evidence he is looking for before he discovers the listed items. Because rings could be located almost anywhere inside or outside a house, it is unlikely that a warrant to search for and seize the rings would restrict the scope of the search. An officer might rationally find the risk of immediately discovering the items listed in the warrant—thereby forcing him to conclude the search immediately—outweighed by the time saved in the application process.

"The majority also contends that, once an officer is lawfully in a house and the scope of his search is adequately circumscribed by a warrant, 'no additional Fourth Amendment interest is furthered by requiring that the discovery of evidence be inadvertent.' Put another way, ' "the inadvertence rule will in no way reduce the number of places into which [law enforcement officers] may lawfully look." ' The majority is correct, but it has asked the wrong question. It is true that the inadvertent discovery requirement furthers no privacy interests. The requirement in no way reduces the scope of a search or the number of places into which officers may look. But it does protect possessory interests. Cf. *Illinois v. Andreas,* [7th ed., p. 256] ('The plain-view doctrine is grounded on the proposition that once police are lawfully in a position to observe an item first-hand, its owner's privacy interest in that item is lost; *the owner may retain the incidents of title and possession* but not privacy') (emphasis added). The inadvertent discovery requirement is essential if we are to take seriously the Fourth Amendment's protection of possessory interests as well as privacy interests. The Court today eliminates a rule designed to further possessory interests on the ground that it fails to further privacy interests. I cannot countenance such constitutional legerdemain."

SECTION 6. WARRANTLESS SEARCHES OF PREMISES, VEHICLES, AND CONTAINERS

7th ed., p. 224; in lieu of Note 3(b), add:

(b) *When the officers are acting for their own protection.* The question of when a "protective sweep" is permissible reached the Court in MARYLAND v. BUIE, ____ U.S. ____, 110 S.Ct. 1093, 108 L.Ed.2d 276 (1990), where the state court had required full probable cause of a dangerous situation. By analogy to *Terry v. Ohio,* 7th ed., p. 269, and *Michigan v. Long,* 7th ed., p. 291, the Court opted for a less demanding reasonable suspicion test. The state had argued for a "bright-line rule" to the effect that "police should be permitted to conduct a protective sweep whenever they make an in-home arrest for a violent crime"; the Court responded that *Terry* requires individualized suspicion, but then adopted a two-part sweep rule which included another kind of bright line. Specifically, the Court (7–2), per White, J., concluded:

"We agree with the State, as did the court below, that a warrant was not required. We also hold that as an incident to the arrest the officers could, as a precautionary matter and without probable cause or reasonable suspicion, look in closets and other spaces immediately adjoining the place of arrest from which an attack could be immediately launched. Beyond that, however, we hold that there must be articulable facts which, taken together with the rational inferences from those facts, would warrant a reasonable prudent officer in believing that the area to be swept harbors an individual posing a danger to those on the arrest scene. * * *

"We should emphasize that such a protective sweep, aimed at protecting the arresting officers, if justified by the circumstances, is nevertheless not a full search of the premises, but may extend only to a cursory inspection of those spaces where a person may be found. The sweep lasts no longer than is necessary to dispel the reasonable suspicion of danger and in any event no longer than it takes to complete the arrest and depart the premises."

The Court remanded for application of this test. The facts, as stated in the Supreme Court opinions, are these: Two men (one wearing a red running suit) committed an armed robbery of a restaurant on Feb. 3; warrants for them (Buie and Allen) were issued that day, and Buie's home was immediately placed under surveillance. On Feb. 5, after a police department secretary called the residence and verified that Buie was there, 6 or 7 officers proceeded to the house and fanned out through the first and second floors. Officer Rozar said he would "freeze" the basement so that no one could come up; he drew his weapon and twice shouted into the basement for anyone there to come out, and Buie then emerged from the basement. He was arrested, searched and handcuffed by Rozar. Once Buie was outside the house, Officer Frolich entered the basement, noticed a red running suit in plain view and seized it. Rozar testified he was not worried about any possible danger when he arrested Buie; Frolich said he entered the basement "in case there was someone else" down there, though he "had no idea who lived there." What should the result be on remand?

7th ed., pp. 226–227; delete Notes 3 and 4:

7th ed., p. 231; before Note 4, add:

3a. Assuming no such exigent circumstances, is it permissible for police to engage in a subterfuge which causes an occupant to remove the evidence to another place where warrantless search is permissible? See *State v. Hendrix,* 782 S.W.2d 833 (Tenn.1989) (proper for police to telephone residence with anonymous false "tip" that police were on their way there with search warrant, causing defendant to leave with drugs in car, which was then stopped and searched). What if the telephoning police had falsely reported a gas leak and likely explosion?

7th ed., p. 239, before Note 4, add:

Would the result in *Welsh* have been different if the police were in immediate hot pursuit? See *State v. Bolte,* 560 A.2d 644 (N.J.1989) (rejecting state's argument answer is yes because "citizens should not be encouraged to elude arrest by retreating into their homes").

7th ed., p. 256; before Note 3, add:

Is *Johns* distinguishable from *Sanders* because, as one court put it, *United States v. Barrett,* 890 F.2d 855 (6th Cir.1989), *Sanders* applies only when "the police had probable cause to believe that containers held contraband before the containers were placed within automobiles," in the sense that the police must have had probable cause as to one or more specifically identified containers prior to their placement within a vehicle?

7th ed., p. 269; after Note 3, add:

4. In *Florida v. Wells,* ___ U.S. ___, 110 S.Ct. 1632, 109 L.Ed.2d 1 (1990), all members of the Court agreed that the inventory of a locked suitcase found in an impounded vehicle was unlawful under *Bertine* because "the Florida Highway Patrol had no policy whatever with respect to the opening of closed containers encountered during an inventory search." The Chief Justice, for five members of the Court, went on to say that the state court erred in saying *Bertine* requires a policy either mandating or barring inventory of all containers:

"But in forbidding uncanalized discretion to police officers conducting inventory searches, there is no reason to insist that they be conducted in a totally mechanical 'all or nothing' fashion. * * * A police officer may be allowed sufficient latitude to determine whether a particular container should or should not be opened in light of the nature of the search and characteristics of the container itself. Thus, while policies of opening all containers or of opening no containers are unquestionably permissible, it would be equally permissible, for example, to allow the opening of closed containers whose contents officers determine they are unable to ascertain from examing the containers' exteriors. The allowance of the exercise of judgment based on concerns related to the purposes of an inventory search does not violate the Fourth Amendment."

Brennan and Marshall, JJ., concurring, declined to join the majority opinion because, in "pure dictum given the disposition of the case," it "goes on to suggest that a State may adopt an inventory policy that vests individual police officers with *some* discretion to decide whether to open such containers." Blackmun, J., concurring, agreed that the Fourth Amendment did not impose an "all or nothing" requirement, so that a state "probably could adopt a policy which requires the opening of all containers that are not locked, or a policy which requires the opening of all containers over or under a certain size, even though these policies do not call for the opening of all or no containers," but objected it was "an entirely different matter, however, to say, as this majority does, that an individual policeman may be afforded discretion in conducting an inventory search." Stevens, J., concurring separately, agreed with the Blackmun opinion.

5. Consider *Ex parte Boyd,* 542 So.2d 1276 (Ala.1989): "We are unaware of any case, federal or state, that presents the issue of whether a search can be valid as an inventory notwithstanding a four-day lapse of time between the impoundment and the inventory. We are of the opinion that the Fourth Amendment requires that, without a demonstrable justification based upon exigent circumstances other than the mere nature of automobiles, the inventory be conducted either contemporaneously with the impoundment or as soon thereafter as would be safe, practical, *and* satisfactory in light of the objectives for which this exception to the Fourth Amendment warrant requirement was created. In other words, to be valid, there must be a sufficient temporal proximity between the impoundment and the inventory. * * * The justifications for the intrusion—protecting the owner's property, protecting the police from false claims or disputes, and protecting the police from danger—are simply not served, however, when the inventory is inexcusably postponed; in that circumstance, the inventory becomes unreasonable."

SECTION 7. STOP AND FRISK

7th ed., p. 280; after Note 4, add:

5. What then of questioning travelers during the regular stop of a bus or train? Compare *Bostick v. State,* 554 So.2d 1153 (Fla.1989) (a seizure if the officer "stood in a position that partially blocked the only possible exit from the bus," as then there "is no place to which a reasonable traveler might leave and no place to which he or she might walk away"); with *United States v. Savage,* 889 F.2d 1113 (D.C.Cir.1989) (passenger in roomette questioned by officers standing at door in corridor; no

seizure, as "nothing in the record indicates that the detectives prevented Savage from leaving his compartment," and "detectives' positions were compelled by the location in which they were conducting their interview; there was no other place for them to stand").

7th ed., p. 283; in lieu of Note 3, but incorporating fns. h and i (all but first sentence), add:

3. ALABAMA v. WHITE, ____ U.S. ____, 110 S.Ct. 2412, ____ L.Ed.2d ____ (1990), involved these facts: "On April 22, 1987, at approximately 3 p.m., Corporal B.H. Davis of the Montgomery Police Department received a telephone call from an anonymous person, stating that Vanessa White would be leaving 235–C Lynwood Terrace Apartments at a particular time in a brown Plymouth station wagon with the right taillight lens broken, that she would be going to Dobey's Motel, and that she would be in possession of about an ounce of cocaine inside a brown attaché case. Corporal Davis and his partner, Corporal P.A. Reynolds, proceeded to the Lynwood Terrace Apartments. The officers saw a brown Plymouth station wagon with a broken right taillight in the parking lot in front of the 235 building. The officers observed respondent leave the 235 building, carrying nothing in her hands, and enter the station wagon. They followed the vehicle as it drove the most direct route to Dobey's Motel. When the vehicle reached the Mobile Highway, on which Dobey's Motel is located, Corporal Reynolds requested a patrol unit to stop the vehicle. The vehicle was stopped at approximately 4:18 p.m., just short of Dobey's Motel. Corporal Davis asked respondent to step to the rear of her car, where he informed her that she had been stopped because she was suspected of carrying cocaine in the vehicle. He asked if they could look for cocaine and respondent said they could look. The officers found a locked brown attaché case in the car and, upon request, respondent provided the combination to the lock." In up-

holding the stop, the Court, per White, J., reasoned:

"The opinion in [*Illinois v.*] *Gates* [7th ed., p. 175] recognized that an anonymous tip alone seldom demonstrates the informant's basis of knowledge or veracity inasmuch as ordinary citizens generally do not provide extensive recitations of the basis of their everyday observations and given that the veracity of persons supplying anonymous tips is 'by hypothesis largely unknown, and unknowable.' This is not to say that an anonymous caller could never provide the reasonable suspicion necessary for a *Terry* stop.[h] But the tip in *Gates* was not an exception to the general rule, and the anonymous tip in this case is like the one in *Gates:* '[it] provides virtually nothing from which one might conclude that [the caller] is either honest or his information reliable; likewise, the [tip] gives absolutely no indication of the basis for the [caller's] predictions regarding [Vanessa White's] criminal activities.' * * *

"As there was in *Gates,* however, in this case there is more than the tip itself. The tip was not as detailed, and the corroboration was not as complete, as in *Gates,* but the required degree of suspicion was likewise not as high. * * *

"Reasonable suspicion is a less demanding standard than probable cause not only in the sense that reasonable suspicion can be established with information that is different in quantity or content than that required to establish probable cause, but also in the sense that reasonable suspicion can arise from information that is less reliable than that required to show probable cause.[i] * * * Reasonable suspicion, like probable cause, is dependent upon both the content of information possessed by police and its degree of reliability. Both factors—quantity and quality—are considered in the 'totality of the circumstances—the whole picture' that must be taken into account when evaluating whether there is reasonable suspicion. Thus, if a tip has a relatively low degree of reliability, more information will be required to establish the requisite quantum of suspicion than would be required if the tip were more reliable. The *Gates* Court applied its totality of the circumstances approach in this manner, taking into account the facts known to the officers from personal observation, and giving the anonymous tip the weight it deserved in light of its indicia of reliability as established through independent police work. The same approach applies in the reasonable suspicion context, the only difference being the level of suspicion that must be established. Contrary to the court below, we conclude that when the officers stopped respondent, the anonymous tip had been sufficiently corroborated to furnish reasonable suspicion that respondent was engaged in criminal activity and that the investigative stop therefore did not violate the Fourth Amendment.

"It is true that not every detail mentioned by the tipster was verified, such as the name of the woman leaving the building or the precise apartment from which she left; but the officers did corroborate that a woman left the 235 building and got into the particular vehicle that was described by the caller. With respect to the time of departure predicted by the informant, Corporal Davis testified that the caller gave a particular time when the woman would be leaving, but he did not state what that time was. He did testify that, after the call, he and his partner proceeded to the Lynwood Terrace Apartments to put the 235 building under surveillance. Given the fact that the officers proceeded to the indicated address immediately after the call and that respondent emerged not too long thereafter, it appears from the record before us that respondent's departure from the building was within the time frame predicted by the caller. As for the caller's prediction of respondent's destination, it is true that the officers stopped her just short of Dobey's Motel and did not know whether she would have pulled in or continued on past it. But given that the four-mile route driven by respondent was the most direct route possible to Dobey's Motel, but nevertheless involved several turns, we think respondent's destination was significantly corroborated.

"The Court's opinion in *Gates* gave credit to the proposition that because an informant is shown to be right about some things, he is probably right about other facts that he has alleged, including the claim that the object of the tip is engaged in criminal activity. Thus, it is not unreasonable to conclude in this case that the independent corroboration by the police of significant aspects of the informer's predictions imparted some degree of reliability to the other allegations made by the caller.

"We think it also important that, as in *Gates,* 'the anonymous [tip] contained a range of details relating not just to easily obtained facts and conditions existing at the time of the tip, but to future actions of third parties ordinarily not easily predicted.' The fact that the officers found a car precisely matching the caller's description in front of the 235 building is an example of the former. Anyone could have 'predicted' that fact because it was a condition presumably existing at the time of the call. What was important was the caller's ability to predict respondent's *future behavior,* because it demonstrated inside information—a special familiarity with respondent's affairs. The general public would have had no way of knowing that respondent would shortly leave the building, get in the described car, and drive the most direct route to Dobey's Motel. Because only a small number of people are generally privy to an individual's itinerary, it is reasonable for police to believe that a person with access to such information is likely to also have access to reliable information about that individual's illegal activities. When significant

aspects of the caller's predictions were verified, there was reason to believe not only that the caller was honest but also that he was well informed, at least well enough to justify the stop."

STEVENS, J., for the three dissenters, objected: "Anybody with enough knowledge about a given person to make her the target of a prank, or to harbor a grudge against her, will certainly be able to formulate a tip about her like the one predicting Vanessa White's excursion. In addition, under the Court's holding, every citizen is subject to being seized and questioned by any officer who is prepared to testify that the warrantless stop was based on an anonymous tip predicting whatever conduct the officer just observed. Fortunately, the vast majority of those in our law enforcement community would not adopt such a practice. But the Fourth Amendment was intended to protect the citizen from the overzealous and unscrupulous officer as well as from those who are conscientious and truthful. This decision makes a mockery of that protection."

7th ed., p. 292; end of Note 5, add:

Cf. *Arizona v. Hicks,* 7th ed., p. 225; and *Ybarra v. Illinois,* 7th ed., p. 203.

SECTION 9. ADMINISTRATIVE INSPECTIONS AND REGULATORY SEARCHES: MORE ON BALANCING THE NEED AGAINST THE INVASION OF PRIVACY

7th ed., p. 312; in lieu of Notes 6–7, add:

6. *Interior checkpoints.*

MICHIGAN DEP'T OF STATE POLICE v. SITZ
—— U.S. ——, 110 S.Ct. 2481, —— L.Ed. 2d —— (1990).

CHIEF JUSTICE REHNQUIST delivered the opinion of the Court. ＊ ＊ ＊

Under the guidelines, [for a sobriety checkpoint pilot program established by the Department], checkpoints would be set up at selected sites along state roads. All vehicles passing through a checkpoint would be stopped and their drivers briefly examined for signs of intoxication. In cases where a checkpoint officer detected signs of intoxication, the motorist would be directed to a location out of the traffic flow where an officer would check the motorist's driver's license and car registration and, if warranted, conduct further sobriety tests. Should the field tests and the officer's observations suggest that the driver was intoxicated, an arrest would be made. All other drivers would be permitted to resume their journey immediately.

The first—and to date the only—sobriety checkpoint operated under the program was conducted in Saginaw County with the assistance of the Saginaw County Sheriff's Department. During the hour-and-fifteen-minute duration of the checkpoint's operation, 126 vehicles passed through the checkpoint. The average delay for each vehicle was approximately 25 seconds. Two drivers were detained for field sobriety testing, and one of the two was arrested for driving under the influence of alcohol. A third driver who drove through without stopping was pulled over by an officer in an observation vehicle and arrested for driving under the influence.

On the day before the operation of the Saginaw County checkpoint, respondents filed a complaint in the Circuit Court of Wayne County seeking declaratory and injunctive relief from potential subjection to the checkpoints. Each of the respondents "is a licensed driver in the State of Michigan . . . who regularly travels throughout the State in his automobile." During pretrial proceedings, petitioners agreed to delay further implementation of the checkpoint program pending the outcome of this litigation.

After the trial, [the] court ruled that the Michigan program violated the Fourth Amendment * * *. On appeal, the

Michigan Court of Appeals affirmed * * *.

To decide this case the trial court performed a balancing test derived from our opinion in *Brown v. Texas* [7th ed., p. 285]. * * *

As characterized by the Court of Appeals, the trial court's findings with respect to the balancing factors were that the State has "a grave and legitimate" interest in curbing drunken driving; that sobriety checkpoint programs are generally "ineffective" and, therefore, do not significantly further that interest; and that the checkpoints' "subjective intrusion" on individual liberties is substantial. * * *

In this Court respondents seek to defend the judgment in their favor by insisting that the balancing test derived from *Brown v. Texas* was not the proper method of analysis. Respondents maintain that the analysis must proceed from a basis of probable cause or reasonable suspicion and rely for support on language from our decision last Term in *Treasury Employees v. Von Raab,* [7th ed., p. 319]. We said in *Von Raab:*

"Where a Fourth Amendment intrusion serves special governmental needs, beyond the normal need for law enforcement, it is necessary to balance the individual's privacy expectations against the Government's interests to determine whether it is impractical to require a warrant or some level of individualized suspicion in the particular context."

Respondents argue that there must be a showing of some special governmental need "beyond the normal need" for criminal law enforcement before a balancing analysis is appropriate, and that petitioners have demonstrated no such special need.

But it is perfectly plain from a reading of *Von Raab,* which cited and discussed with approval our earlier decision in *United States v. Martinez–Fuerte,* 428 U.S. 543, 96 S.Ct. 3074, 49 L.Ed.2d 1116 (1976), that it was in no way designed to repudiate our prior cases dealing with police stops of motorists on public highways. *Martinez–Fuerte,* which utilized a balancing analysis in approving highway checkpoints for detecting illegal aliens, and *Brown v. Texas,* are the relevant authorities here.

Petitioners concede, correctly in our view, that a Fourth Amendment "seizure" occurs when a vehicle is stopped at a checkpoint. * * * The question thus becomes whether such seizures are "reasonable" under the Fourth Amendment.

It is important to recognize what our inquiry is *not* about. No allegations are before us of unreasonable treatment of any person after an actual detention at a particular checkpoint. See *Martinez–Fuerte* ("claim that a particular exercise of discretion in locating or operating a checkpoint is unreasonable is subject to post-stop judicial review"). As pursued in the lower courts, the instant action challenges only the use of sobriety checkpoints generally. We address only the initial stop of each motorist passing through a checkpoint and the associated preliminary questioning and observation by checkpoint officers. Detention of particular motorists for more extensive field sobriety testing may require satisfaction of an individualized suspicion standard.

No one can seriously dispute the magnitude of the drunken driving problem or the States' interest in eradicating it. Media reports of alcohol-related death and mutilation on the Nation's roads are legion. The anecdotal is confirmed by the statistical. "Drunk drivers cause an annual death toll of over 25,000 and in the same time span cause nearly one million personal injuries and more than five billion dollars in property damage." * * *

Conversely, the weight bearing on the other scale—the measure of the intrusion on motorists stopped briefly at sobriety checkpoints—is slight. We reached a similar conclusion as to the intrusion on motorists subjected to a brief stop at a highway checkpoint for detecting illegal aliens. See *Martinez–Fuerte.* We see virtually no difference between the levels of intrusion on law-abiding motorists from the brief stops necessary to the effectuation of these two types of checkpoints, which to the average motorist would seem identical save for the nature of the questions the checkpoint officers might ask. The trial court and the Court of Appeals, thus, accurately gauged the "objective" intrusion, measured by the duration of the seizure and the intensity of the investigation, as minimal.

With respect to what it perceived to be the "subjective" intrusion on motorists, however, the Court of Appeals found such intrusion substantial. The court first affirmed the trial court's finding that the guidelines governing checkpoint operation minimize the discretion of the officers on the scene. But the court also agreed with the trial court's conclusion that the checkpoints have the potential to generate fear and surprise in motorists. This was so because the record failed to demonstrate that approaching motorists would be aware of their option to make U-turns or turnoffs to avoid the checkpoints. On that basis, the court deemed the subjective intrusion from the checkpoints unreasonable.

We believe the Michigan courts misread our cases concerning the degree of "subjective intrusion" and the potential for generating fear and surprise. The "fear and surprise" to be considered are not the natural fear of one who has been drinking over the prospect of being stopped at a sobriety checkpoint but, rather, the fear and surprise engendered in law abiding motorists by the nature of the stop. This was made clear in *Martinez–Fuerte.* Comparing checkpoint stops to roving patrol stops considered in prior cases, we said,

"we view checkpoint stops in a different light because the subjective intrusion—the generating of concern or even fright on the part of lawful travelers—is appreciably less in the case of a checkpoint stop. In [*United States v.*] *Ortiz,* [422

U.S. 891, 95 S.Ct. 2585, 45 L.Ed.2d 623 (1975),] we noted:

" '[T]he circumstances surrounding a checkpoint stop and search are far less intrusive than those attending a roving-patrol stop. Roving patrols often operate at night on seldom-traveled roads, and their approach may frighten motorists. At traffic checkpoints the motorist can see that other vehicles are being stopped, he can see visible signs of the officers' authority, and he is much less likely to be frightened or annoyed by the intrusion.' " a

Here, checkpoints are selected pursuant to the guidelines, and uniformed police officers stop every approaching vehicle. The intrusion resulting from the brief stop at the sobriety checkpoint is for constitutional purposes indistinguishable from the checkpoint stops we upheld in *Martinez–Fuerte.*

The Court of Appeals went on to consider as part of the balancing analysis the "effectiveness" of the proposed checkpoint program. Based on extensive testimony in the trial record, the court concluded that the checkpoint program failed the "effectiveness" part of the test, and that this failure materially discounted petitioners' strong interest in implementing the program. We think the Court of Appeals was wrong on this point as well.

The actual language from *Brown v. Texas,* upon which the Michigan courts based their evaluation of "effectiveness," describes the balancing factor as "the degree to which the seizure advances the public interest." This passage from *Brown* was not meant to transfer from politically accountable officials to the courts the decision as to which among reasonable alternative law enforcement techniques should be employed to deal with a serious public danger. Experts in police science might disagree over which of several methods of apprehending drunken drivers is preferrable as an ideal. But for purposes of Fourth Amendment analysis, the choice among such reasonable alternatives remains with the governmental officials who have a unique understanding of, and a responsibility for, limited public resources, including a finite number of police officers. *Brown*'s rather general reference to "the degree to which the seizure advances the public interest" was derived, as the opinion makes clear, from the line of cases culminating in *Martinez–Fuerte.* Neither *Martinez–Fuerte* nor *Delaware v. Prouse,* 440 U.S. 648, 99 S.Ct. 1391, 59 L.Ed.2d 660 (1979), however, the two cases cited by the Court of Appeals as providing the basis for its "effectiveness" review, supports the searching examination of "effectiveness" undertaken by the Michigan court.

In *Delaware v. Prouse,* we disapproved random stops made by Delaware Highway Patrol officers in an effort to apprehend unlicensed drivers and unsafe vehicles. We observed that *no* empirical evidence indicated that such stops would be an effective means of promoting roadway safety and said that "[i]t seems common sense that the percentage of all drivers on the road who are driving without a license is very small and that the number of licensed drivers who will be stopped in order to find one unlicensed operator will be large indeed." We observed that the random stops involved the "kind of standardless and unconstrained discretion [which] is the evil the Court has discerned when in previous cases it has insisted that the discretion of the official in the field be circumscribed, at least to some extent." We went on to state that our holding did not "cast doubt on the permissibility of roadside truck weigh-stations and inspection checkpoints, at which some vehicles may be subject to further detention for safety and regulatory inspection than are others." b

---

a. However, the Court held in *Ortiz* that vehicle *searches* at a permanent checkpoint could be undertaken only upon probable cause.

b. The Court in *Prouse* also said it was not prohibiting driver's license checks by methods "that involve less intrusion or that do not involve

Unlike *Prouse,* this case involves neither a complete absence of empirical data nor a challenge to random highway stops. During the operation of the Saginaw County checkpoint, the detention of each of the 126 vehicles that entered the checkpoint resulted in the arrest of two drunken drivers. Stated as a percentage, approximately 1.5 percent of the drivers passing through the checkpoint were arrested for alcohol impairment. In addition, an expert witness testified at the trial that experience in other States demonstrated that, on the whole, sobriety checkpoints resulted in drunken driving arrests of around 1 percent of all motorists stopped. By way of comparison, the record from one of the consolidated cases in *Martinez–Fuerte,* showed that in the associated checkpoint, illegal aliens were found in only 0.12 percent of the vehicles passing through the checkpoint. The ratio of illegal aliens detected to vehicles stopped (considering that on occasion two or more illegal aliens were found in a single vehicle) was approximately 0.5 percent. We concluded that this "record . . . provides a rather complete picture of the effectiveness of the San Clemente checkpoint", and we sustained its constitutionality. We see no justification for a different conclusion here.

In sum, the balance of the State's interest in preventing drunken driving, the extent to which this system can reasonably be said to advance that interest, and the degree of intrusion upon individual motorists who are briefly stopped, weighs in favor of the state program. We therefore hold that it is consistent with the Fourth Amendment. The judgment of the Michigan Court of Appeals is accordingly reversed, and the cause is remanded for further proceedings not inconsistent with this opinion.[c]

the unconstrained exercise of discretion," and listed as "one possible alternative" the "questioning of all oncoming traffic at roadblock-type stops."

JUSTICE STEVENS, with whom JUSTICE BRENNAN and JUSTICE MARSHALL join as to Parts I and II, dissenting. * * *

I

There is a critical difference between a seizure that is preceded by fair notice and one that is effected by surprise. That is one reason why a border search, or indeed any search at a permanent and fixed checkpoint, is much less intrusive than a random stop. A motorist with advance notice of the location of a permanent checkpoint has an opportunity to avoid the search entirely, or at least to prepare for, and limit, the intrusion on her privacy.

No such opportunity is available in the case of a random stop or a temporary checkpoint, which both depend for their effectiveness on the element of surprise. A driver who discovers an unexpected checkpoint on a familiar local road will be startled and distressed. She may infer, correctly, that the checkpoint is not simply "business as usual," and may likewise infer, again correctly, that the police have made a discretionary decision to focus their law enforcement efforts upon her and others who pass the chosen point.

This element of surprise is the most obvious distinction between the sobriety checkpoints permitted by today's majority and the interior border checkpoints approved by this Court in *Martinez–Fuerte.* The distinction casts immediate doubt upon the majority's argument, for *Martinez–Fuerte* is the only case in which we have upheld suspicionless seizures of motorists. But the difference between notice and surprise is only one of the important reasons for distinguishing between permanent and mobile checkpoints. With respect to the former, there is no room for discretion in either the timing or the location of the stop—it is a permanent part of the land-

c. The concurring opinion of Blackmun, J., and the dissenting opinion of Brennan, J., joined by Marshall, J., are omitted.

scape. In the latter case, however, although the checkpoint is most frequently employed during the hours of darkness on weekends (because that is when drivers with alcohol in their blood are most apt to be found on the road), the police have extremely broad discretion in determining the exact timing and placement of the roadblock.

There is also a significant difference between the kind of discretion that the officer exercises after the stop is made. A check for a driver's license, or for identification papers at an immigration checkpoint, is far more easily standardized than is a search for evidence of intoxication. A Michigan officer who questions a motorist at a sobriety checkpoint has virtually unlimited discretion to detain the driver on the basis of the slightest suspicion. A ruddy complexion, an unbuttoned shirt, bloodshot eyes or a speech impediment may suffice to prolong the detention. Any driver who had just consumed a glass of beer, or even a sip of wine, would almost certainly have the burden of demonstrating to the officer that her driving ability was not impaired.

Finally, it is significant that many of the stops at permanent checkpoints occur during daylight hours, whereas the sobriety checkpoints are almost invariably operated at night. A seizure followed by interrogation and even a cursory search at night is surely more offensive than a daytime stop that is almost as routine as going through a toll gate. Thus we thought it important to point out that the random stops at issue in *Ortiz* frequently occurred at night.

These fears are not, as the Court would have it, solely the lot of the guilty. To be law abiding is not necessarily to be spotless, and even the most virtuous can be unlucky. Unwanted attention from the local police need not be less discomforting simply because one's secrets are not the stuff of criminal prosecutions. Moreover,

those who have found—by reason of prejudice or misfortune—that encounters with the police may become adversarial or unpleasant without good cause will have grounds for worrying at any stop designed to elicit signs of suspicious behavior. Being stopped by the police is distressing even when it should not be terrifying, and what begins mildly may by happenstance turn severe.

For all these reasons, I do not believe that this case is analogous to *Martinez–Fuerte*. In my opinion, the sobriety checkpoints are instead similar to—and in some respects more intrusive than—the random investigative stops that the Court held unconstitutional in [*United States v.*] *Brignone–Ponce*[, 422 U.S. 873, 95 S.Ct. 2574, 45 L.Ed.2d 607 (1975),] d and *Prouse*. In the latter case the Court explained:

"We cannot agree that stopping or detaining a vehicle on an ordinary city street is less intrusive than a roving-patrol stop on a major highway and that it bears greater resemblance to a permissible stop and secondary detention at a checkpoint near the border. In this regard, we note that *Brignoni–Ponce* was not limited to roving-patrol stops on limited-access roads, but applied to any roving-patrol stop by Border Patrol agents on any type of roadway on less than reasonable suspicion. We cannot assume that the physical and psychological intrusion visited upon the occupants of a vehicle by a random stop to check documents is of any less moment than that occasioned by a stop by border agents on roving patrol. Both of these stops generally entail law enforcement officers signaling a moving automobile to pull over to the side of the roadway, by means of a possibly unsettling show of authority. Both interfere with freedom of movement, are inconvenient, and consume time. Both may create substantial anxiety."

d. Holding that a roving patrol could stop motorists near the border for brief inquiry into

their residential status only upon individualized reasonable suspicion.

We accordingly held that the State must produce evidence comparing the challenged seizure to other means of law enforcement, so as to show that the seizure

"is a sufficiently productive mechanism to justify the intrusion upon Fourth Amendment interests which such stops entail. On the record before us, that question must be answered in the negative. Given the alternative mechanisms available, both those in use and those that might be adopted, we are unconvinced that the incremental contribution to highway safety of the random spot check justifies the practice under the Fourth Amendment."

II

* * *

The Court's analysis of [the degree to which the sobriety checkpoint seizures advance the public interest] resembles a business decision that measures profits by counting gross receipts and ignoring expenses. The evidence in this case indicates that sobriety checkpoints result in the arrest of a fraction of one percent of the drivers who are stopped, but there is absolutely no evidence that this figure represents an increase over the number of arrests that would have been made by using the same law enforcement resources in conventional patrols. Thus, although the *gross* number of arrests is more than zero, there is a complete failure of proof on the question whether the wholesale seizures

have produced any *net* advance in the public interest in arresting intoxicated drivers.

Indeed, the position adopted today by the Court is not one endorsed by any of the law enforcement authorities to whom the Court purports to defer. The Michigan police do not rely, as the Court does, on the *arrest rate* at sobriety checkpoints to justify the stops made there. Colonel Hough, the commander of the Michigan State Police and a leading proponent of the checkpoints, admitted at trial that the arrest rate at the checkpoints was "very low." Instead, Colonel Hough and the State have maintained that the mere *threat* of such arrests is sufficient to deter drunk driving and so to reduce the accident rate. * * * There is, obviously, nothing wrong with a law enforcement technique that reduces crime by pure deterrence without punishing anybody; on the contrary, such an approach is highly commendable. One cannot, however, prove its efficacy by counting the arrests that were made. One must instead measure the number of crimes that were avoided. Perhaps because the record is wanting, the Court simply ignores this point.

The Court's sparse analysis of this issue differs markedly from Justice Powell's opinion for the Court in *Martinez–Fuerte.* He did not merely count the 17,000 arrests made at the San Clemente checkpoint in 1973; he also carefully explained why those arrests represented a net benefit to the law enforcement interest at stake.[15] Common sense, moreover, suggests that immigration checkpoints are more neces-

15. "Our previous cases have recognized that maintenance of a traffic-checking program in the interior is necessary because the flow of illegal aliens cannot be controlled effectively at the border. We note here only the substantiality of the public interest in the practice of routine stops for inquiry at permanent checkpoints, a practice which the Government identifies as the most important of the traffic-checking operations. These checkpoints are located on important highways; in their absence such highways would offer illegal aliens a quick and safe route into the interior. Routine checkpoint inquiries apprehend many smugglers and illegal aliens who succumb to the lure of such highways. And the

prospect of such inquiries forces others onto less efficient roads that are less heavily traveled, slowing their movement and making them more vulnerable to detection by roving patrols.

"A requirement that stops on major routes inland always be based on reasonable suspicion would be impractical because the flow of traffic tends to be too heavy to allow the particularized study of a given car that would enable it to be identified as a possible carrier of illegal aliens. In particular, such a requirement would largely eliminate any deterrent to the conduct of well-disguised smuggling operations, even though smugglers are known to use these highways regularly."

sary than sobriety checkpoints: there is no reason why smuggling illegal aliens should impair a motorist's driving ability, but if intoxication did not noticeably affect driving ability it would not be unlawful. Drunk driving, unlike smuggling, may thus be detected absent any checkpoints. A program that produces thousands of otherwise impossible arrests is not a relevant precedent for a program that produces only a handful of arrests which would be more easily obtained without resort to suspicionless seizures of hundreds of innocent citizens.

III

[M]y objections to random seizures or temporary checkpoints do not apply to a host of other investigatory procedures that do not depend upon surprise and are unquestionably permissible. These procedures have been used to address other threats to human life no less pressing than the threat posed by drunken drivers. It is, for example, common practice to require every prospective airline passenger, or every visitor to a public building, to pass through a metal detector that will reveal the presence of a firearm or an explosive. Permanent, nondiscretionary checkpoints could be used to control serious dangers at other publicly operated facilities. Because concealed weapons obviously represent one such substantial threat to public safety, I would suppose that all subway passengers could be required to pass through metal detectors, so long as the detectors were permanent and every passenger was subjected to the same search. Likewise, I would suppose that a State could condition access to its toll roads upon not only paying the toll but also taking a uniformly administered breathalyzer test. That requirement might well keep all drunken drivers off the highways that serve the fastest and most dangerous traffic. This procedure would not be subject to the

constitutional objections that control this case: the checkpoints would be permanently fixed, the stopping procedure would apply to all users of the toll road in precisely the same way, and police officers would not be free to make arbitrary choices about which neighborhoods should be targeted or about which individuals should be more thoroughly searched.
* * *

7th ed., p. 316; end of Note 8, add:

But see *United States v. $124,570 U.S. Currency,* 873 F.2d 1240 (9th Cir.1989) (*Davis* rationale unavailable where airport detection system significantly "distorted" by customs officials offering inspectors rewards for discovery of large amounts of cash).

SECTION 10. CONSENT SEARCHES

7th ed., p. 331; after first paragraph in Note 11, add:

In *United States v. Mines,* 883 F.2d 801 (9th Cir.1989), the defendant consented to search of his luggage upon being told the agents were conducting a narcotics investigation. Inside defendant's bag the police found a machine gun, which they turned over to reveal it was without serial numbers, a fact which led to a determination the gun was illegally possessed because not registered. In response to defendant's reliance on *Arizona v. Hicks,* 7th ed., p. 225, the court asserted the instant case was distinguishable because (i) consent searches, unlike the warrantless search on exigent circumstances in *Hicks,* need not be "strictly circumscribed by the exigencies," and (ii) the search here "occurred not in a private apartment but in a public place—an airport—where expectations of privacy are sharply reduced." Are these reasons convincing? Is the result correct?

7th ed., p. 331; in lieu of *Matlock* case and Note 6 following, add:

ILLINOIS v. RODRIGUEZ

___ U.S. ___, 110 S.Ct. ___, ___ L.Ed.2d ___ (1990).

JUSTICE SCALIA delivered the opinion of the Court. * * *

On July 26, 1985, police were summoned to the residence of Dorothy Jackson on South Wolcott in Chicago. They were met by Ms. Jackson's daughter, Gail Fischer, who showed signs of a severe beating. She told the officers that she had been assaulted by respondent Edward Rodriguez earlier that day in an apartment on South California. Fischer stated that Rodriguez was then asleep in the apartment, and she consented to travel there with the police in order to unlock the door with her key so that the officers could enter and arrest him. During this conversation, Fischer several times referred to the apartment on South California as "our" apartment, and said that she had clothes and furniture there. It is unclear whether she indicated that she currently lived at the apartment, or only that she used to live there.

The police officers drove to the apartment on South California, accompanied by Fischer. They did not obtain an arrest warrant for Rodriguez, nor did they seek a search warrant for the apartment. At the apartment, Fischer unlocked the door with her key and gave the officers permission to enter. They moved through the door into the living room, where they observed in plain view drug paraphernalia and containers filled with white powder that they believed (correctly, as later analysis showed) to be cocaine. They proceeded to the bedroom, where they found Rodriguez asleep and discovered additional containers of white powder in two open attaché cases. The officers arrested Rodriguez and seized the drugs and related paraphernalia.

Rodriguez was charged with possession of a controlled substance with intent to deliver. He moved to suppress all evidence seized at the time of his arrest, claiming that Fischer had vacated the apartment several weeks earlier and had no authority to consent to the entry. The Cook County Circuit Court granted the motion, holding that at the time she consented to the entry Fischer did not have common authority over the apartment. The Court concluded that Fischer was not a "usual resident" but rather an "infrequent visitor" at the apartment on South California, based upon its findings that Fischer's name was not on the lease, that she did not contribute to the rent, that she was not allowed to invite others to the apartment on her own, that she did not have access to the apartment when respondent was away, and that she had moved some of her possessions from the apartment. The Circuit Court also rejected the State's contention that, even if Fischer did not possess common authority over the premises, there was no Fourth Amendment violation if the police *reasonably believed* at the time of their entry that Fischer possessed the authority to consent.

* * *

The Fourth Amendment generally prohibits the warrantless entry of a person's home, whether to make an arrest or to search for specific objects. The prohibition does not apply, however, to situations in which voluntary consent has been obtained, either from the individual whose property is searched, or from a third party who possesses common authority over the premises, see *United States v. Matlock*, [415 U.S. 164, 94 S.Ct. 988, 39 L.Ed.2d 242 (1974)]. The State of Illinois contends that that exception applies in the present case.

As we stated in *Matlock*, "[c]ommon authority" rests "on mutual use of the property by persons generally having joint access or control for most purposes."[a]

a. Where there is such "common authority," the Court went on to say in *Matlock*, "it is reasonable to recognize that any of the co-inhabitants has the right to permit the inspection in his own right and that the others have assumed the

The burden of establishing that common authority rests upon the State. On the basis of this record, it is clear that burden was not sustained. The evidence showed that although Fischer, with her two small children, had lived with Rodriguez beginning in December 1984, she had moved out on July 1, 1985, almost a month before the search at issue here, and had gone to live with her mother. She took her and her children's clothing with her, though leaving behind some furniture and household effects. During the period after July 1 she sometimes spent the night at Rodriguez's apartment, but never invited her friends there, and never went there herself when he was not home. Her name was not on the lease nor did she contribute to the rent. She had a key to the apartment, which she said at trial she had taken without Rodriguez's knowledge (though she testified at the preliminary hearing that Rodriguez had given her the key). On these facts the State has not established that, with respect to the South California apartment, Fischer had "joint access or control for most purposes." To the contrary, the Appellate Court's determination of no common authority over the apartment was obviously correct.

[R]espondent asserts that permitting a reasonable belief of common authority to validate an entry would cause a defendant's Fourth Amendment rights to be "vicariously waived." We disagree.

We have been unyielding in our insistence that a defendant's waiver of his trial rights cannot be given effect unless it is "knowing" and "intelligent." We would assuredly not permit, therefore, evidence seized in violation of the Fourth Amendment to be introduced on the basis of a trial court's mere "reasonable belief"—

derived from statements by unauthorized persons—that the defendant has waived his objection. But one must make a distinction between, on the one hand, trial rights that *derive* from the violation of constitutional guarantees and, on the other hand, the nature of those constitutional guarantees themselves. * * *

What Rodriguez is assured by the trial right of the exclusionary rule, where it applies, is that no evidence seized in violation of the Fourth Amendment will be introduced at his trial unless he consents. What he is assured by the Fourth Amendment itself, however, is not that no government search of his house will occur unless he consents; but that no such search will occur that is "unreasonable." There are various elements, of course, that can make a search of a person's house "reasonable"—one of which is the consent of the person or his cotenant. The essence of respondent's argument is that we should impose upon this element a requirement that we have not imposed upon other elements that regularly compel government officers to exercise judgment regarding the facts: namely, the requirement that their judgment be not only responsible but correct.[b]

[I]n order to satisfy the "reasonableness" requirement of the Fourth Amendment, what is generally demanded of the many factual determinations that must regularly be made by agents of the government—whether the magistrate issuing a warrant, the police officer executing a warrant, or the police officer conducting a search or seizure under one of the exceptions to the warrant requirement—is not that they always be correct, but that they always be reasonable. As we put it in *Brinegar v. United States,* [7th ed., p. 178]:

risk that one of their number might permit the common area to be searched."

b. In an omitted portion of the opinion, illustrations were given: (i) the probable cause requirement for a warrant, as to which the magistrate may act on "seemingly reliable but factually inaccurate information"; (ii) the war-

rant requirement, as to which the officer may be reasonably mistaken as to the warrant's scope, *Maryland v. Garrison,* 7th ed., p. 200; and (iii) the search incident to arrest doctrine, where the officer may be reasonably mistaken as to the person to be arrested, *Hill v. California,* 7th ed., p. 325.

"Because many situations which confront officers in the course of executing their duties are more or less ambiguous, room must be allowed for some mistakes on their part. But the mistakes must be those of reasonable men, acting on facts leading sensibly to their conclusions of probability."

We see no reason to depart from this general rule with respect to facts bearing upon the authority to consent to a search. Whether the basis for such authority exists is the sort of recurring factual question to which law enforcement officials must be expected to apply their judgment; and all the Fourth Amendment requires is that they answer it reasonably. The Constitution is no more violated when officers enter without a warrant because they reasonably (though erroneously) believe that the person who has consented to their entry is a resident of the premises, than it is violated when they enter without a warrant because they reasonably (though erroneously) believe they are in pursuit of a violent felon who is about to escape.

Stoner v. California, [7th ed., p. 332] is in our view not to the contrary. There, in holding that police had improperly entered the defendant's hotel room based on the consent of a hotel clerk, we stated that "the rights protected by the Fourth Amendment are not to be eroded . . . by unrealistic doctrines of 'apparent authority.'" It is ambiguous, of course, whether the word "unrealistic" is descriptive or limiting—that is, whether we were condemning as unrealistic all reliance upon apparent authority, or whether we were condemning only such reliance upon apparent authority as is unrealistic. Similarly ambiguous is the opinion's earlier statement that "there [is no] substance to the claim that the search was reasonable because the police, relying upon the night clerk's expressions of consent, had a reasonable basis for the belief that the clerk had authority to consent to the search." Was there no substance to it because it failed as a matter of law, or because the

facts could not possibly support it? At one point the opinion does seem to speak clearly:

"It is important to bear in mind that it was the petitioner's constitutional right which was at stake here, and not the night clerk's nor the hotel's. It was a right, therefore, which only the petitioner could waive by word or deed, either directly or through an agent."

But as we have discussed, what is at issue when a claim of apparent consent is raised is not whether the right to be free of searches has been *waived,* but whether the right to be free of *unreasonable* searches has been *violated.* Even if one does not think the *Stoner* opinion had this subtlety in mind, the supposed clarity of its foregoing statement is immediately compromised, as follows:

"It is true that the night clerk clearly and unambiguously consented to the search. But there is nothing in the record to indicate that *the police had any basis whatsoever to believe that* the night clerk had been authorized by the petitioner to permit the police to search the petitioner's room."

The italicized language should have been deleted, of course, if the statement two sentences earlier meant that an appearance of authority could never validate a search. In the last analysis, one must admit that the rationale of *Stoner* was ambiguous—and perhaps deliberately so. It is at least a reasonable reading of the case, and perhaps a preferable one, that the police could not rely upon the obtained consent because they knew it came from a hotel clerk, knew that the room was rented and exclusively occupied by the defendant, and could not reasonably have believed that the former had general access to or control over the latter. * * *

As *Stoner* demonstrates, what we hold today does not suggest that law enforcement officers may always accept a person's invitation to enter premises. Even when the invitation is accompanied by an explicit assertion that the person lives there, the surrounding circumstances could conceivably be such that a reasonable person would doubt its truth and not act upon it without further inquiry. As with other factual determinations bearing upon search and seizure, determination of consent to enter must "be judged against an objective standard: would the facts available to the officer at the moment . . . 'warrant a man of reasonable caution in the belief'" that the consenting party had authority over the premises? If not, then warrantless entry without further inquiry is unlawful unless authority actually exists. But if so, the search is valid.

In the present case, the Appellate Court found it unnecessary to determine whether the officers reasonably believed that Fischer had the authority to consent, because it ruled as a matter of law that a reasonable belief could not validate the entry. Since we find that ruling to be in error, we remand for consideration of that question. The judgment of the Illinois Appellate Court is reversed and remanded for further proceedings not inconsistent with this opinion.

JUSTICE MARSHALL, with whom JUSTICE BRENNAN and JUSTICE STEVENS join, dissenting. * * *

Unlike searches conducted pursuant to the recognized exceptions to the warrant requirement, third-party consent searches are not based on an exigency and therefore serve no compelling social goal. Police officers, when faced with the choice of relying on consent by a third party or securing a warrant, should secure a warrant, and must therefore accept the risk of error should they instead choose to rely on consent. * * *

Acknowledging that the third party in this case lacked authority to consent, the majority seeks to rely on cases suggesting that reasonable but mistaken factual judgments by police will not invalidate otherwise reasonable searches. The majority reads these cases as establishing a "general rule" that "what is generally demanded of the many factual determinations that must regularly be made by agents of the government—whether the magistrate issuing a warrant, the police officer executing a warrant, or the police officer conducting a search or seizure under one of the exceptions to the warrant requirement—is not that they always be correct, but that they always be reasonable."

The majority's assertion, however, is premised on the erroneous assumption that third-party consent searches are generally reasonable. The cases the majority cites thus provide no support for its holding. In *Brinegar v. United States,* for example, the Court confirmed the unremarkable proposition that police need only probable cause, not absolute certainty, to justify the arrest of a suspect on a highway. As *Brinegar* makes clear, the possibility of factual error is built into the probable cause standard, and such a standard, by its very definition, will in some cases result in the arrest of a suspect who has not actually committed a crime. Because probable cause defines the reasonableness of searches and seizures outside of the home, a search is reasonable under the Fourth Amendment whenever that standard is met, notwithstanding the possibility of "mistakes" on the part of police. In contrast, our cases have already struck the balance against warrantless home intrusions in the absence of an exigency. Because reasonable factual errors by law enforcement officers will not validate unreasonable searches, the reasonableness of the officer's mistaken belief that the third party had authority to consent is irrelevant. * * * [c]

---

c. As for the other illustrations given by the majority, the dissenters explained that "*Hill* should be understood no less than *Brinegar* as simply a gloss on the meaning of 'probable cause,'" while *Garrison* "was premised on the [fact that] searches based on warrants are generally reasonable," and "like *Brinegar,* thus tells us nothing about the reasonableness under the Fourth Amendment of a warrantless arrest."

Mod. & Basic Crim.Proc., 7th Ed. (K., L. & I.) ACB—2
1990 Supp.

7th ed., p. 334; in lieu of all of Note 4 in column 2, add:

State v. Leach, 782 P.2d 1035 (Wash.1989) (co-owner's prior consent to search of travel agency not effective against defendant, who was arrested there but remained present during the search, as where "the police have obtained consent to search from an individual possessing, at best, equal control over the premises, that consent remains valid against a cohabitant, who also possesses equal control, only while the cohabitant is absent," and "should the cohabitant be present and able to object, the police must also obtain the cohabitant's consent").

Chapter 8

POLICE INTERROGATION AND CONFESSIONS

SECTION 3. THE *MIRANDA* "REVOLUTION"

APPLYING AND EXPLAINING *MIRANDA*

7th ed., p. 498; add to Note 8:

ILLINOIS v. PERKINS, ___ U.S. ___, 110 S.Ct. 2394, ___ L.Ed.2d ___ (1990), resolved the controversy described in Note 8 over whether the use of "jail plants" to elicit incriminating statements from incarcerated suspects constitutes "custodial interrogation" within the meaning of *Miranda.* "The interests protected by *Miranda* are not implicated in these cases," held the Court, per KENNEDY, J.; "*Miranda* warnings are not required when the suspect is unaware that he is speaking to a law enforcement officer and gives a voluntary statement."

The case arose as follows: Respondent Perkins, who was suspected of committing the Stephenson murder, was incarcerated on charges unrelated to the murder. The police placed Charlton (who had been a fellow inmate of Perkins in another prison) and Parisi (an undercover officer) in the same cellblock with Perkins. The secret government agents were instructed to engage Perkins in casual conversation and to report anything he said about the Stephenson murder. The cellblock consisted of 12 separate cells that opened onto a common room. When Charlton met Perkins in the prison he introduced Parisi by his alias. Parisi suggested that the three of them escape. There was further conversation. Parisi asked Perkins if he had ever

"done" anybody. Perkins replied that he had and proceeded to describe his involvement in the Stephenson murder in detail.

In an opinion joined by six other Justices, Kennedy, J., explained why Perkins' statements were not barred by *Miranda:*

"The essential ingredients of a 'police-dominated atmosphere' and compulsion are not present when an incarcerated person speaks freely to someone that he believes to be a fellow inmate. Coercion is determined from the perspective of the suspect. [When] a suspect considers himself in the company of cellmates and not officers, the coercive atmosphere is lacking. * * *

"It is the premise of *Miranda* that the danger of coercion results from the interaction of custody and official interrogation. We reject the argument that *Miranda* warnings are required whenever a suspect is in custody in a technical sense and converses with someone who happens to be a government agent. [When] the suspect has no reason to think that the listeners have official power over him, it should not be assumed that his words are motivated by the reaction he expects from his listeners. '[W]hen the agent carries neither badge nor gun and wears not "police blue," but the same prison gray' as the suspect, there is no '*interplay* between police interrogation and police custody.' Kamisar, *Brewer v. Williams, Massiah and Miranda: What is 'Interrogation?' When Does it Matter?*, 67 Geo.L.J. 1, 67, 63 (1978). [The] only difference between this case and *Hoffa* [7th ed., p. 369] is that the suspect here was incarcerated, but de-

21

tention, whether or not for the crime in question, does not warrant a presumption that the use of an undercover agent to speak with an incarcerated suspect makes any confession thus obtained involuntary.

* * *

"This Court's Sixth Amendment decisions in [the *Massiah* line of cases, see 7th ed. at pp. 431, 575–95] also do not avail respondent. We held in those cases that the government may not use an undercover agent to circumvent the Sixth Amendment right to counsel once a suspect has been charged with the crime. After charges have been filed, the Sixth Amendment prevents the government from interfering with the accused's right to counsel. In the instant case no charges had been filed on the subject of the interrogation, and our Sixth Amendment precedents are not applicable." [a]

Only MARSHALL, J., dissented, maintaining that "[t]he conditions that require the police to apprise a defendant of his constitutional rights—custodial interrogation conducted by an agent of the police—were present in this case. Because [respondent] received no *Miranda* warnings before he was subjected to custodial interrogation, his confession was not admissible." Continued Justice Marshall:

"Because Perkins was interrogated by police while he was in custody, *Miranda* required that the officer inform him of his rights. In rejecting that conclusion, the Court finds that 'conversations' between undercover agents and suspects are devoid of the coercion inherent in stationhouse interrogations conducted by law enforcement officials who openly represent the State. *Miranda* was not, however, concerned solely with police *coercion*. It dealt

with *any* police tactics that may operate to compel a suspect in custody to make incriminating statements without full awareness of his constitutional rights. [Thus,] when a law enforcement agent structures a custodial interrogation so that a suspect feels compelled to reveal incriminating information, he must inform the suspect of his constitutional rights and give him an opportunity to decide whether or not to talk. * * *

"Custody works to the State's advantage in obtaining incriminating information. The psychological pressures inherent in confinement increase the suspect's anxiety, making him likely to seek relief by talking with others. Dix, *Undercover Investigations and Police Rulemaking,* 53 Texas L.Rev. 203, 230 (1975). The inmate is thus more susceptible to efforts by undercover agents to elicit information from him. Similarly, where the suspect is incarcerated, the constant threat of physical danger peculiar to the prison environment may make him demonstrate his toughness to other inmates by recounting or inventing past violent acts. 'Because the suspect's ability to select people with whom he can confide is completely within their control, the police have a unique opportunity to exploit the suspect's vulnerability. In short, the police can insure that if the pressures of confinement lead the suspects to confide in anyone, it will be a police agent.' W. White, *Police Trickery in Inducing Confessions,* 127 U.Pa.L.Rev. 581, 605 (1979). In this case, the police deceptively took advantage of Perkins' psychological vulnerability by including him in a sham escape plot, a situation in which he would feel compelled to demonstrate his willingness to shoot a prison guard by

a. Brennan, J., concurred in the judgment of the Court, "agree[ing] that when a suspect does not know that his questioner is a police agent, such questioning does not amount to 'interrogation' in an 'inherently coercive' environment so as to require application of *Miranda* "—"the only issue raised at this stage of the litigation." But he went on to say that "the deception and manipulation practiced on respondent raise a substan-

tial claim that the confession was obtained in violation of the Due Process Clause." For "the deliberate use of deception and manipulation by the police appears to be incompatible 'with a system that presumes innocence and assures that a conviction will not be secured by inquisitional means' and raises serious concerns that respondent's will was overborne."

revealing his past involvement in a murder. See App. 49 (agent stressed that a killing might be necessary in the escape and then asked Perkins if he had ever murdered someone).

"Thus, the pressures unique to custody allow the police to use deceptive interrogation tactics to compel a suspect to make an incriminating statement. The compulsion is not eliminated by the suspect's ignorance of his interrogator's true identity. The Court therefore need not inquire past the bare facts of custody and interrogation to determine whether *Miranda* warnings are required. * * *

"Even if *Miranda*, as interpreted by the Court, would not permit such obviously compelled confessions, the ramifications of today's opinion are still disturbing. The exception carved out of the *Miranda* doctrine today may well result in a proliferation of departmental policies to encourage police officers to conduct interrogations of confined suspects through undercover agents, thereby circumventing the need to administer *Miranda* warnings. Indeed, if *Miranda* now requires a police officer to issue warnings only in those situations in which the suspect might feel compelled 'to speak by the fear of reprisal for remaining silent or in the hope of more lenient treatment should he confess,' presumably it allows custodial interrogation by an undercover officer posing as a member of the clergy or a suspect's defense attorney. Although such abhorrent tricks would play on a suspect's need to confide in a trusted adviser, neither would cause the suspect to 'think that the listeners have official power over him.' The Court's adoption of the 'undercover agent' exception to the *Miranda* rule thus is necessarily also the adoption of a substantial loophole in our jurisprudence protecting suspects' Fifth Amendment rights."

———

7th ed., p. 498; after Note 8, add new Note:

8(a). *More on "custodial interrogation" and the "booking question exception" to Miranda.* Consider PENNSYLVANIA v. MUNIZ, ___ U.S. ___, 110 S.Ct. 2638, ___ L.Ed.2d ___ (1990) (also discussed at Supp., p. 26. The case arose as follows:

Respondent Muniz was arrested for driving while intoxicated. Without advising him of his *Miranda* rights, Officer Hosterman asked Muniz to perform three standard field sobriety tests. Muniz performed poorly and then admitted that he had been drinking. Muniz was taken to a Booking Center. Following its routine practice for receiving persons suspected of driving under the influence, the Booking Center videotaped the ensuing proceedings. Muniz was told that his action and voice were being recorded, but again he was not advised of his *Miranda* rights. Officer Hosterman first asked Muniz his name, address, height, weight, eye color, date of birth, and current age (the "first seven questions" or the seven "booking" questions). Both the delivery and content of his answers were incriminating. Next the officer asked Muniz what the Court called "the sixth birthday question": "Do you know what the date was of your sixth birthday?" Muniz responded, "No, I don't."

The officer then requested Muniz to perform the same sobriety tests that he had been asked to do earlier during the initial roadside stop. While performing the tests, Muniz made several audible and incriminating statements. Finally, Muniz was asked to submit to a breathalyzer test. He refused. At this point, for the first time, Muniz was advised of his *Miranda* rights. Both the video and audio portions of the videotape were admitted into evidence, along with the arresting officer's testimony that Muniz failed the roadside sobriety tests and made incriminating statements at the time. Muniz was convicted of driving while intoxicated.

The Court excluded only Muniz's response to the "sixth birthday question" (by a 5–4 vote). BRENNAN, J., wrote the opinion of the Court, except as to the grounds for admitting Muniz's answers to the first seven questions or "booking" questions.

Some of the issues raised by the case were relatively easy. Muniz's answers to direct questions were not barred by *Miranda* "merely because the slurred nature of his speech was incriminating." Under *Schmerber v. California* (discussed at pp. 37, 597, 692–93 & 697–98 of the 7th ed.) and its progeny, "any slurring of speech and other evidence of lack of muscular coordination revealed by Muniz's responses * * * constitute nontestimonial components of those responses." Muniz's incriminating utterances during the physical sobriety tests were also admissible because "not prompted by an interrogation within the meaning of *Miranda*." Officer Hosterman's conversation with Muniz concerning the tests "consisted primarily of carefully scripted instructions as to how the tests were to be performed," instructions "not likely to be perceived as calling for any verbal response" and thus "not 'words or actions' constituting custodial interrogation." a

More difficult issues were whether Muniz's response to the sixth birthday question should be allowed into evidence and whether Muniz's answers to the first seven questions asked him at the Booking Center (the seven "booking" questions) were admissible—and if not, *why* not.

In contrast to a number of other questions Muniz was asked, the sixth birthday question, observed the Court, per Bren-

nan, J., "required a testimonial response. When Officer Hosterman asked Muniz if he knew the date of his sixth birthday and Muniz, for whatever reason, could not remember or calculate that date, he was [placed in a predicament the self-incrimination clause was designed to prevent]. By hypothesis, the inherently coercive environment created by the custodial interrogation precluded the option of remaining silent. Muniz was left with the choice of incriminating himself by admitting that he did not then know the date of his sixth birthday, or answering untruthfully by reporting a date that he did not then believe to be accurate (an incorrect guess would be incriminating as well as truthful). [The] incriminating inference of impaired mental facilities stemmed, not just from the fact that Muniz slurred his response, but also from a testimonial aspect of that response."

REHNQUIST, C.J., joined by White, Blackmun and Stevens, JJ., disagreed:

"The sixth birthday question here was an effort on the part of the police to check how well Muniz was able to do a simple mathematical exercise. Indeed, had the question related only to the date of his birthday, it presumably would have come under the 'booking exception' to *Miranda* to which the Court refers elsewhere in its opinion. [See discussion below.] [If] the police may require Muniz to use his body in order to demonstrate the level of his physical coordination, there is no reason why they should not be able to require him to speak or write in order to determine his mental coordination. That was all that was sought here. Since it was permissible for the police to extract and

---

a. "Similarly," added the Court, "*Miranda* does not require suppression of the statements Muniz made when asked to submit to a breathalyzer examination." The officer who requested Muniz to take the breathalyzer test "carefully limited her role to providing Muniz with relevant information about [the] test and the implied consent law. She questioned Muniz only as to whether he understood her instructions and wished to submit to the test. These

limited and focused inquiries were necessarily 'attendant to' the legitimate police procedure [and] not likely to be perceived as calling for any incriminating response."

The Court noted that "Muniz does not and cannot challenge the introduction into evidence of his refusal to submit to the breathalyzer test." See *South Dakota v. Neville* (fn. a, 7th ed., p. 489).

examine a sample of Schmerber's blood to determine how much that part of his system had been affected by alcohol, I see no reason why they may not examine the functioning of Muniz's mental processes for the same purpose."

Eight members of the Court agreed that the answers to the "booking" questions were admissible, but they differed as to the reason. Four Justices (Rehnquist, C.J., joined by White, Blackmun and Stevens, JJ.) did not consider the questions "testimonial." Thus, they did not address the issue whether, even if the questions were "testimonial," they came under a "booking exception" to *Miranda*. The other four Justices (Brennan, J., joined by O'Connor, Scalia and Kennedy, JJ.,) believed the first seven questions were "testimonial" and did amount to "custodial interrogation" within the meaning of *Miranda.* Nonetheless, they concluded that Muniz's answers were admissible because of a "routine booking question" exception to *Miranda* —one that permits questions "to secure the 'biographical data necessary to complete booking or pretrial services.' " The state court had found that the first seven questions were "requested for record-keeping purposes only"; thus, "the questions appear reasonably related to the police's administrative concerns."

Only MARSHALL, J., would have kept out the answers to the first seven questions. He rejected both the Brennan group's and the Rehnquist group's rationales for admitting Muniz's answers to these questions;

"[The questions] sought 'testimonial' responses for the same reason the sixth birthday question did: because the content of the answers would indicate Muniz's state of mind. The booking questions, like the sixth birthday question, required Muniz to (1) answer correctly, indicating lucidity,

(2) answer incorrectly, implying that his mental facilities were impaired, or (3) state that he did not know the answer, also indicating impairment. Muniz's initial incorrect response to the question about his age and his inability to give his address without looking at his license, like his inability to answer the sixth birthday question, in fact gave rise to the incriminating inference that his mental facilities were impaired."

As for the Brennan group's rationale for admitting Muniz's answers—the questions fell within a "routine booking question" exception to *Miranda*—even if such an exception was appropriate in some instances, responded Marshall, J., the exception "should not extend to booking questions [asked in circumstances, such as the instant case, which] the police should know are reasonably likely to elicit incriminating responses."

More generally, Justice Marshall balked at creating "yet another exception" to *Miranda* because "[s]uch exceptions undermine *Miranda*'s fundamental principle that the doctrine should be clear so that it can be easily applied by both police and courts." Continued Marshall:

"The plurality's position, were it adopted by a majority of the Court, would necessitate difficult, time-consuming litigation over whether particular questions asked during booking are 'routine,' whether they are necessary to secure biographical information, whether that information is itself necessary for recordkeeping purposes, and whether the questions are— despite their routine nature—designed to elicit incriminating testimony. The far better course would be to maintain the clarity of the doctrine by requiring police to preface all direct questioning of a suspect with *Miranda* warnings if they want his responses to be admissible at trial."

Chapter 10
GRAND JURY INVESTIGATIONS

SECTION 1. THE ROLE OF THE INVESTIGATIVE GRAND JURY

7th ed., p. 639; end of fn. b, add:

In *Butterworth v. Smith,* ___ U.S. ___, 110 S.Ct. 1376, 108 L.Ed.2d 572 (1990), the Court sustained a First Amendment challenge to a state statute that imposed a secrecy obligation upon a grand jury witness (extending to the "content, gist, or import" of his testimony) insofar as that obligation extended beyond the point of discharge of the grand jury. The Court reasoned that several of the traditional functions of grand jury secrecy were no longer served by a witness-secrecy requirement following the end of the grand jury's investigation, and those that remained were "not sufficient to overcome [the witness'] First Amendment right to make a truthful statement of information he acquired on his own."

SECTION 3. APPLICATION OF THE PRIVILEGE AGAINST SELF–INCRIMINATION

7th ed., p. 702; after Note 5, add:

6. Consider in light of *Doe II* and *Schmerber* (fn. b, 7th ed., p. 692), *Pennsylvania v. Muniz,* ___ U.S. ___, 110 S.Ct. 2638, ___ L.Ed.2d ___ (1990) (more comprehensively discussed at Supp., p. 23). In *Muniz,* all but Justice Marshall agreed that a drunk-driving arrestee's slurring of his speech in responding to a series of sobriety-test questions was not in itself a "testimonial" communication. Justice Brennan's opinion for the Court noted that the arrestee's slurred speech reveals no more than the "physical manner in which he articulates words," analogous to revealing "the physical properties of the sound of one's voice" through a voiceprint. It accordingly constituted "real or physical evidence" under the doc-trine of *Schmerber,* as did other evidence of lack of muscular coordination.

The Court was sharply divided (5–4), however, in the characterization of the arrestee's answer to the question, "Do you know what was the date of your sixth birthday"? The majority held that the answer to that question was testimonial "because of its content." "The trier of fact," Justice Brennan noted, "could infer from Muniz's answer (that he did not *know* the proper date) that his mental state was confused." Justice Brennan rejected as "addressing the wrong question" the state's contention that this inference concerns "the physiological function of the brain," no different than the "physiological makeup of his blood." He noted: "That the fact to be inferred * * * concern[s] the physical status of Muniz's brain merely describes the way in which the inference is incriminating. The correct question * * * is whether the incriminating inference of mental confusion is drawn from a testimonial act * * * [as defined in *Doe II*]." Here, the suspect clearly was "asked for a response requiring him to communicate an express or implied assertion of fact or belief," and he give such a response as to his knowledge of a particular fact. "The Commonwealth's protest that it had no investigatory interest in the actual date of Muniz's sixth birthday is inappropriate. The critical point is that the Commonwealth had an investigatory interest in Muniz's assertion of belief that was communicated by his answer to the question."

The four dissenters viewed the state's contention as well taken. "The sixth birthday question," Chief Justice Rehnquist noted, "was an effort on the part of the police to check how well Muniz was able to do a simple mathematical exercise." The Court does not question the police authority to require Muniz to perform a series of physical-dexterity tests. "If the police may thus require Muniz to use his body in order to demonstrate the level of physical coordination, there is no reason why they should not be able to require him to speak or write in order to determine his mental coordination." Just as *Schmerber* held it to be permissible under the Fifth Amendment to extract blood to "determine how much of that part of [the body's] system had been affected by alcohol," it should be held permissible here "to examine the functioning of Muniz's mental processes for the same purpose."

7th ed., p. 727; after Note 7, add:

8. The implications of the several doctrines discussed in this section were brought together in an unusual setting in *Baltimore City Department of Social Services v. Bouknight*, ____ U.S. ____, 110 S.Ct. 900, 107 L.Ed.2d 992 (1990). The Supreme Court there rejected a self-incrimination objection to a subpoena directing respondent Bouknight to produce her infant son, an abused child who had previously been declared a ward of the court. The Court noted that the respondent could not claim the privilege based upon "anything an examination of the [child] might reveal," as that would be a claim based upon "the contents or nature of the thing demanded." However, the mother could conceivably claim the privilege because "the act of production would amount to testimony regarding her control over and possession of [the child]." While the state could "readily introduce [other] evidence of Bouknight's continuing control over the child" (including the court order giving her limited custody and her previous statements reflecting control), her "implicit communication of control over [the child] at the moment of production might aid the state in prosecuting Bouknight [for child abuse]." The Court had no need to decide, however, whether "this limited testimonial assertion is sufficiently incriminating and sufficiently testimonial for purposes of the privilege." In receiving conditional custody from the juvenile court, the mother had "assumed custodial duties related to production" (analogous to that of an entity agent) and had done so as part of noncriminal regulatory scheme which included a production component (analogous to regulations sustained under the required records doctrine). The Court added that it had no need in the case before it "to define the precise limitations that may exist upon the State's ability to use the testimonial aspects of Bouknight's act of production in subsequent criminal proceedings," but the "imposition of such limitations," as done in *Braswell*, was not "foreclosed."

Chapter 11

THE SCOPE OF THE EXCLUSIONARY RULES

SECTION 2. THE "FRUIT OF THE POISONOUS TREE"

A. HISTORICAL BACKGROUND AND OVERVIEW

7th ed., p. 753; after Note 5, add new Note 5(a):

5(a). *Confession as the "fruit" of a Payton violation.* In NEW YORK v. HARRIS, ___ U.S. ___, 110 S.Ct. 1640, 109 L.Ed. 2d 13 (1990), a 5–4 majority, per WHITE, J., held that where the police have probable cause to arrest a suspect, the exclusionary rule does not bar the use of a statement made by the suspect outside his home even though the statement is obtained after an in-house arrest in violation of *Payton v. New York,* 7th ed., p. 232. The police had probable cause to believe Harris had killed a woman. They went to his apartment to take him into custody, but did not first obtain an arrest warrant. After being advised of his *Miranda* rights and waiving them, Harris reportedly admitted that he had committed the homicide. He was then taken to the station house, where, after again being advised of his rights and again waiving them, he signed a written inculpatory statement. Since the state did not challenge the trial court's suppression of Harris' statement to the police while still inside his home, the sole issue was the admissibility of the statement he made at the station house. The New York Court of Appeals ruled that the station house statement was the inadmissible fruit of the *Payton* violation, but the Supreme Court reversed:

"Nothing in the reasoning of [*Payton*] suggests that an arrest in a home without a warrant but with probable cause somehow renders unlawful continued custody of the suspect once he is removed from the house. * * * Because the officers had probable cause to arrest Harris for a crime, Harris was not unlawfully in custody when he was removed to the station house, given *Miranda* warnings and allowed to talk. For Fourth Amendment purposes, the legal issue is the same as it would be had the police arrested Harris on his door step, illegally entered his home to search for evidence, and later interrogated Harris at the station house. Similarly, if the police had made a warrantless entry into Harris' home, not found him there, but arrested him on the street when he returned, a later statement made by him after proper warnings would no doubt be admissible.

"[In *Brown, Dunaway* and *Taylor*], evidence obtained from a criminal defendant following arrest was suppressed because the police lacked probable cause. The three cases stand for the familiar proposition that the indirect fruits of an illegal search or arrest should be suppressed when they bear a sufficiently close relationship to the underlying illegality. We have emphasized, however, that attenuation analysis is only appropriate where, as a threshold matter, courts determine that 'the challenged evidence is in some sense the product of illegal governmental activity.' *Crews.* * * *

"Harris's statement taken at the police station was not the product of being in unlawful custody. Neither was it the fruit of having been arrested in the home rather than someplace else. The case is analogous to *Crews.* In that case, we refused to suppress a victim's in-court identification despite the defendant's illegal arrest. The Court found that the evidence was not 'come at by exploitation [of] the defendant's Fourth Amendment rights,' and that it was not necessary to inquire whether the 'taint' of the Fourth Amendment violation was sufficiently attenuated to permit the introduction of the evidence. Here, likewise, the police had a justification to question Harris prior to his arrest; therefore, his subsequent statement was not an exploitation of the illegal entry into Harris' home.

"We do not hold, as the dissent suggests, that a statement taken by the police while a suspect is in custody is always admissible as long as the suspect is in legal custody. Statements taken during legal custody would of course be inadmissible for example, if, they were the product of coercion, if *Miranda* warnings were not given, or if there was a violation of the rule of *Edwards.* We do hold that the station-house statement in this case was admissible because Harris was in legal custody, as the dissent concedes, and because the statement, while the product of an arrest and being in custody, was not the fruit of the fact that the arrest was made in the house rather than someplace else.

"To put the matter another way, suppressing the statement taken outside the house would not serve the purpose of the rule that made Harris's in-house arrest illegal. The warrant requirement for an arrest in the home is imposed to protect the home, and anything incriminating the police gathered from arresting Harris in his home, rather than elsewhere, has been excluded, as it should have been; the purpose of the rule has thereby been vindicated. We are not required by the Constitution to go further and suppress statements later made by Harris in order to deter police from violating *Payton.* ✷ ✷ ✷

Even though we decline to suppress statements made outside the home following a *Payton* violation, the principal incentive to obey *Payton* still obtains: the police know that a warrantless entry will lead to the suppression of any evidence found or statements taken inside the home. If we did suppress statements like Harris', moreover, the incremental deterrent value would be minimal. Given that the police have probable cause to arrest a suspect in Harris' position, they need not violate *Payton* in order to interrogate the suspect. It is doubtful therefore that the desire to secure a statement from a criminal suspect would motivate the police to violate *Payton.* As a result, suppressing a station-house statement obtained after a *Payton* violation will have little effect on the officers' actions, one way or another."

Dissenting JUSTICE MARSHALL, joined by Brennan, Blackmun and Stevens, JJ., deemed *Brown v. Illinois* controlling:

"An application of the *Brown* factors to this case compels the conclusion that Harris' statement at the station house must be suppressed. About an hour elapsed between the illegal arrest and Harris' confession, without any intervening factor other than the warnings required by *Miranda.* This Court has held, however, that '*Miranda* warnings, *alone* and *per se,* . . . cannot assure in every case that the Fourth Amendment violation has not been unduly exploited.' *Brown.* Indeed, in *Brown,* we held that a statement made almost *two* hours after an illegal arrest, and after *Miranda* warnings had been given, was not sufficiently removed from the violation so as to dissipate the taint.

"As to the flagrancy of the violation, petitioner does not dispute that the officers were aware that the Fourth Amendment prohibited them from arresting Harris in his home without a warrant. Notwithstanding the officers' knowledge that a warrant is required for a routine arrest in the home, 'the police * * * made no attempt to obtain a warrant although five days had elapsed between the killing and the arrest and they had developed evidence of probable cause early in their investigation. Indeed, one of the officers testified that it was departmental policy not to get warrants before making arrests in the home. From this statement a reasonable inference can be drawn [that] the department's policy was a device used to avoid restrictions on questioning a suspect until after the police had strengthened their case with a confession. Thus, the police illegality was knowing and intentional, in the language of *Brown,* it "had a quality of purposefulness," and the linkage between the illegality and the confession is clearly established.' [quoting from the court below.] [2]

"In short, the officers decided, apparently consistent with a 'departmental policy,' to violate Harris' Fourth Amendment rights so they could get evidence that they could not otherwise obtain. As the trial court held, 'No more clear violation of [*Payton*], in my view, could be established.' Where, as here, there is a particularly flagrant constitutional violation and little in the way of elapsed time or intervening circumstances, the statement in the police station must be suppressed.

"Had the Court analyzed this case as our precedents dictate that it should, I could end my discussion here—the dispute would reduce to an application of the *Brown* factors to the constitutional wrong and the inculpatory statement that followed. But the majority chooses no such unremarkable battleground. Instead, the Court redrafts our

cases in the service of conclusions they straightforwardly and explicitly reject. Specifically, the Court finds suppression unwarranted on the authority of its newly-fashioned *per se* rule. In the majority's view, when police officers make a warrantless home arrest in violation of *Payton,* their physical exit from the suspect's home *necessarily* breaks the causal chain between the illegality and any subsequent statement by the suspect, such that the statement is admissible regardless of the *Brown* factors.

"[The] majority's *per se* rule in this case fails to take account of our repeated holdings that violations of privacy in the home are especially invasive. Rather, its rule is necessarily premised on the proposition that the effect of a *Payton* violation magically vanishes once the suspect is dragged from his home. But the concerns that make a warrantless home arrest a violation of the Fourth Amendment are nothing so evanescent. A person who is forcibly separated from his family and home in the dark of night after uniformed officers have broken down his door, handcuffed him, and forced him at gunpoint to accompany them to a police station does not suddenly breathe a sigh of relief at the moment he is dragged across his doorstep. Rather, the suspect is likely to be so frightened and rattled that he will say something incriminating. These effects, of course, extend far beyond the moment the physical occupation of the home ends. The entire focus of the *Brown* factors is to fix the point at which those effects are sufficiently dissipated that deterrence is not meaningfully advanced by suppression. The majority's assertion, as though the proposition were axiomatic, that the effects of such an intru-

2. The "restrictions on questioning" to which the court refers are restrictions imposed by New York law. New York law provides that an arrest warrant may not issue until an "accusatory instrument" has been filed against the suspect. The New York courts have held that police officers may not question a suspect in the absence of an attorney once such an accusatory instrument has been filed. These two rules operate to prohibit police from questioning a suspect after arresting him in his home unless his lawyer is

present. If the police comply with *Payton,* the suspect's lawyer will likely tell him not to say anything, and the police will get nothing. On the other hand, if they violate *Payton* by refusing to obtain a warrant, the suspect's right to counsel will not have attached at the time of the arrest, and the police may be able to question him without interference by a lawyer. The lower court's inference that a departmental policy of violating the Fourth Amendment existed was thus fully justified.

sion *must* end when the violation ends is both undefended and indefensible.

* * *

"Perhaps the most alarming aspect of the Court's ruling is its practical consequences for the deterrence of *Payton* violations. Imagine a police officer who has probable cause to arrest a suspect but lacks a warrant. The officer knows if he were to break into the home to make the arrest without first securing a warrant, he would violate the Fourth Amendment and any evidence he finds in the house would be suppressed. Of course, if he does not enter the house, he will not be able to use any evidence inside the house either, for the simple reason that he will never see it. The officer also knows, though, that waiting for the suspect to leave his house before arresting him could entail a lot of waiting, and the time he would spend getting a warrant would be better spent arresting criminals. The officer could leave the scene to obtain a warrant, thus avoiding some of the delay, but that would entail giving the suspect an opportunity to flee.

"More important, the officer knows that if he breaks into the house without a warrant and drags the suspect outside, the suspect, shaken by the enormous invasion of privacy he has just undergone, may say something incriminating. Before today's decision, the government would only be able to use that evidence if the Court found that the taint of the arrest had been attenuated; after the decision, the evidence will be admissible regardless of whether it was the product of the unconstitutional arrest.[5] Thus, the officer envisions the following best-case scenario if he chooses to violate the Constitution: he avoids a major expenditure of time and effort, ensures that the suspect will not escape, and procures the most damaging

evidence of all, a confession. His worst-case scenario is that he will avoid a major expenditure of effort, ensure that the suspect will not escape, and will see evidence in the house (which would have remained unknown absent the constitutional violation) that cannot be used in the prosecution's case-in-chief. The Court thus creates powerful incentives for police officers to violate the Fourth Amendment. In the context of our constitutional rights and the sanctity of our homes, we cannot afford to presume that officers will be entirely impervious to those incentives."

SECTION 3. USE OF ILLEGALLY OBTAINED EVIDENCE FOR IMPEACHMENT PURPOSES

A. The Expansion of a Once-Narrow Exception

7th ed., p. 777; after Note 5, add:

6. In JAMES v. ILLINOIS, ___ U.S. ___, 110 S.Ct. 648, 107 L.Ed.2d 676 (1990), a 5–4 majority, per BRENNAN, J., refused to expand the "impeachment exception" to the exclusionary rule to permit the prosecution to impeach the testimony of *all* defense witnesses with illegally obtained evidence. According to the majority, expanding the impeachment exception to such an extent "would not further the truthseeking value with equal force but would appreciably undermine the deterrent effect of the exclusionary rule."

The case arose as follows: A day after a murder occurred, the police took James, a suspect, into custody. He was found at his mother's beauty salon sitting under a hair dryer; when he emerged, his hair was black and curly. When the police questioned James about his prior hair color, he told them it had been reddish-brown, long, and combed straight back. When questioned later at the police station,

---

5. Indeed, if the officer, as here, works in New York State, the Court's assertion that "[i]t is doubtful therefore that the desire to secure a statement from a criminal suspect would motivate the police to violate *Payton*" takes on a

singularly ironic cast. The court below found as a matter of fact that the officers in this case had intentionally violated *Payton* for *precisely* the reason the Court identifies as "doubtful." See n. 2 and accompanying text.

James stated that he had his hair dyed black and curled at the beauty parlor in order to change his appearance. Because the police lacked probable cause for James' arrest, both statements regarding his hair were suppressed.

At the trial, five eye witnesses testified that the person responsible for the murder had long, "reddish" hair, worn in a slicked-back style and that they had seen James several weeks earlier, at which time he had the aforementioned hair color and style. James did not testify in his own defense. He called as a witness Jewel Henderson, a family friend. She testified that on the day of the shooting James' hair had been black. The state then impeached Henderson's testimony by reporting James' prior admissions that he had reddish hair at the time of the shooting and had dyed and curled his hair the next day in order to change his appearance. James ultimately was convicted of murder.

The Illinois Supreme Court concluded, that, in order to deter "perjury by proxy," the impeachment exception ought to allow the state to impeach the testimony of defense witnesses other than the defendant himself. The U.S. Supreme Court reversed:

"[T]he Illinois Supreme Court held that our balancing approach in *Walder* and its progeny justifies expanding the scope of the impeachment exception to permit prosecutors to use illegally obtained evidence to impeach the credibility of defense witnesses. We disagree. Expanding the class of impeachable witnesses from the defendant alone to all defense witnesses would create different incentives affecting the behavior of both defendants and law enforcement officers. As a result, this expansion would not promote the truthseeking function to the same extent as did creation of the original exception, and yet it would significantly undermine the deterrent effect of the general exclusionary rule. Hence, we believe that this proposed expansion would frustrate rather than further the purposes underlying the exclusionary rule.

"The previously recognized exception penalizes defendants for committing perjury by allowing the prosecution to expose their perjury through impeachment using illegally obtained evidence. Thus defendants are discouraged in the first instance from 'affirmatively resort[ing] to perjurious testimony.' But the exception leaves defendants free to testify truthfully on their own behalf; they can offer probative and exculpatory evidence to the jury without opening the door to impeachment by carefully avoiding any statements that directly contradict the suppressed evidence. The exception thus generally discourages perjured testimony without discouraging truthful testimony.

"In contrast, expanding the impeachment exception to encompass the testimony of all defense witnesses would not have the same beneficial effects. First, the mere threat of a subsequent criminal prosecution for perjury is far more likely to deter a witness from intentionally lying on a defendant's behalf than to deter a defendant, already facing conviction for the underlying offense, from lying on his own behalf. Hence the Illinois Supreme Court's underlying premise that a defendant frustrated by our previous impeachment exception can easily find a witness to engage in 'perjury by proxy' is suspect.[4]

"More significantly, expanding the impeachment exception to encompass the testimony of all defense witnesses likely would chill some defendants from presenting their best defense—and sometimes any defense at all—through the testimony of others. Whenever police obtained evidence illegally, defendants would have to

---

4. The dissent concedes, as it must, that "of course, false testimony can result from faulty recollection" as opposed to intentional lying. Even assuming that Henderson's testimony in this case (as opposed to the detective's contrary testimony) was indeed false, nothing in the record suggests that Henderson intentionally committed perjury rather than honestly provided her best (even if erroneous) perception and recollection of events.

assess prior to trial the likelihood that the evidence would be admitted to impeach the otherwise favorable testimony of any witness they call. Defendants might reasonably fear that one or more of their witnesses, in a position to offer truthful and favorable testimony, would also make some statement in sufficient tension with the tainted evidence to allow the prosecutor to introduce that evidence for impeachment. First, defendants sometimes need to call 'reluctant' or 'hostile' witnesses to provide reliable and probative exculpatory testimony, and such witnesses likely will not share the defendants' concern for avoiding statements that invite impeachment through contradictory evidence. Moreover, defendants often cannot trust even 'friendly' witnesses to testify without subjecting themselves to impeachment, simply due to insufficient care or attentiveness. This concern is magnified in those occasional situations when defendants must call witnesses to testify despite having had only a limited opportunity to consult with or prepare them in advance. For these reasons, we have recognized in a variety of contexts that a party 'cannot be absolutely certain that his witnesses will testify as expected.' As a result, an expanded impeachment exception likely would chill some defendants from calling witnesses who would otherwise offer probative evidence.

"This realization alters the balance of values underlying the current impeachment exception governing defendants' testimony. Our prior cases make clear that defendants ought not be able to 'pervert' the exclusion of illegally obtained evidence into a shield for perjury, but it seems no more appropriate for the State to brandish such evidence as a sword with which to dissuade defendants from presenting a meaningful defense through other witnesses. Given the potential chill created by expanding the impeachment exception, the conceded gains to the truthseeking process from discouraging or disclosing perjured testimony would be offset to some extent by the concomitant loss of probative witness testimony. Thus, the truthseeking rationale supporting the impeachment of defendants in *Walder* and its progeny does not apply to other witnesses with equal force.

"Moreover, the proposed expansion of the current impeachment exception would significantly weaken the exclusionary rule's deterrent effect on police misconduct. This Court has characterized as a mere 'speculative possibility,' *Harris v. New York,* the likelihood that permitting prosecutors to impeach defendants with illegally obtained evidence would encourage police misconduct. Law enforcement officers will think it unlikely that the defendant will first decide to testify at trial and will also open the door inadvertently to admission of any illegally obtained evidence. Hence, the officers' incentive to acquire evidence through illegal means is quite weak.

"In contrast, expanding the impeachment exception to *all* defense witnesses would significantly enhance the expected value to the prosecution of illegally obtained evidence. First, this expansion would vastly increase the number of occasions on which such evidence could be used. Defense witnesses easily outnumber testifying defendants, both because many defendants do not testify themselves and because many if not most defendants call multiple witnesses on their behalf. Moreover, due to the chilling effect identified above, illegally obtained evidence holds even greater value to the prosecution for each individual witness than for each defendant. The prosecutor's access to impeachment evidence would not just deter perjury; it would also deter defendants from calling witnesses in the first place, thereby keeping from the jury much probative exculpatory evidence. For both of these reasons, police officers and their superiors would recognize that obtaining evidence through illegal means stacks the deck heavily in the prosecution's favor. It is thus far more than a 'speculative possibility' that police misconduct will be encouraged by permitting such use of illegally obtained evidence.

"The United States argues that this result is constitutionally acceptable because excluding illegally obtained evidence solely from the prosecution's case in chief would still provide a quantum of deterrence sufficient to protect the privacy interests underlying the exclusionary rule. We disagree. Of course, a police officer might in certain situations believe that obtaining particular evidence through illegal means, resulting in its suppression from the case in chief, would prevent the prosecution from establishing a prima facie case to take to a jury. In such situations, the officer likely would be deterred from obtaining the evidence illegally for fear of jeopardizing the entire case. But much if not most of the time, police officers confront opportunities to obtain evidence illegally after they have already legally obtained (or know that they have other means of legally obtaining) sufficient evidence to sustain a prima facie case. In these situations, a rule requiring exclusion of illegally obtained evidence from only the government's case in chief would leave officers with little to lose and much to gain by overstepping constitutional limits on evidence gathering.[8] Narrowing the exclusionary rule in this manner, therefore, would significantly undermine the rule's ability 'to compel respect for the constitutional guaranty in the only effectively available way—by removing the incentive to disregard it.' So long as we are committed to protecting the people from the disregard of their constitutional rights during the course of criminal investigations, inadmissibility of illegally obtained evidence must remain the rule, not the exception." [a]

8. Indeed, the detectives who unlawfully detained James and elicited his incriminating statements already knew that there were several eyewitnesses to the shooting. Because the detectives likely believed that the exclusion of any statement they obtained from James probably would not have precluded the prosecution from making

Dissenting JUSTICE KENNEDY, joined by Rehnquist, C.J., and O'Connor and Scalia, JJ., maintained that the majority had given the exclusionary rule excessive protection but had afforded the truth-seeking function of the criminal trial inadequate weight:

"To deprive the prosecution of probative evidence acquired in violation of the law may be a tolerable and necessary cost of the exclusionary rule. Implementation of the rule requires us to draw certain lines to effect its purpose of deterring unlawful conduct. But the line drawn by today's opinion grants the defense side in a criminal case broad immunity to introduce whatever false testimony it can produce from the mouth of a friendly witness. Unless petitioner's conviction is reversed, we are told, police would flout the Fourth Amendment, and as a result, the accused would be unable to offer any defense. This exaggerated view leads to a drastic remedy: The jury cannot learn that defense testimony is inconsistent with probative evidence of undoubted value. A more cautious course is available, one that retains Fourth Amendment protections and yet safeguards the truth-seeking function of the criminal trial. * * *

"I agree with the majority that the resolution of this case depends on a balance of values that informs our exclusionary rule jurisprudence. We weigh the 'likelihood [of] deterrence against the costs of withholding reliable information from the truth-seeking process.' The majority adopts a sweeping rule that the testimony of witnesses other than the defendant may never be rebutted with excludable evidence. I cannot draw the line where the majority does.

a prima facie case, an exclusionary rule applicable only to the prosecution's case in chief likely would have provided little deterrent effect in this case.

a. Stevens, J., who joined the opinion of the Court, also wrote a separate opinion.

"The interest in protecting the truth-seeking function of the criminal trial is every bit as strong in this case as in our earlier cases that allowed rebuttal with evidence that was inadmissible as part of the prosecution's case in chief. Here a witness who knew the accused well took the stand to testify about the accused's personal appearance. The testimony could be expected to create real doubt in the mind of jurors concerning the eyewitness identifications by persons who did not know the accused. To deprive the jurors of knowledge that statements of the defendant himself revealed the witness' testimony to be false would result in a decision by triers of fact who were not just kept in the dark as to excluded evidence, but positively misled. The potential for harm to the truth-seeking process resulting from the majority's new rule in fact will be greater than if the defendant himself had testified. It is natural for jurors to be skeptical of self-serving testimony by the defendant. Testimony by a witness said to be independent has the greater potential to deceive. And if a defense witness can present false testimony with impunity, the jurors may find the rest of the prosecution's case suspect, for ineffective and artificial cross-examination will be viewed as a real weakness in the State's case. Jurors will assume that if the prosecution had any proof the statement was false, it would make the proof known. The majority does more than deprive the prosecution of evidence. The State must also suffer the introduction of false testimony and appear to bolster the falsehood by its own silence.

"The majority's fear that allowing the jury to know the whole truth will chill defendants from putting on any defense seems to me far too speculative to justify the rule here announced. No restriction on the defense results if rebuttal of testimony by witnesses other than the defendant is confined to the introduction of excludable evidence that is in direct contradiction of the testimony. If mere 'tension with the tainted evidence' opened the door to introduction of *all* the evidence subject to suppression, then the majority's fears might be justified. But in this context rebuttal can and should be confined to situations where there is direct conflict, which is to say where, within reason, the witness' testimony and the excluded testimony cannot both be true.

"Also missing from the majority's analysis is the almost certain knowledge that the testimony immunized from rebuttal is false. The majority's apparent assumption that defense witnesses protected by today's rule have only truth-telling in mind strikes me as far too sanguine to support acceptance of a rule that controls the hard reality of contested criminal trials. The majority expresses the common sense of the matter in saying that presentation of excluded evidence must sometimes be allowed because it 'penalizes defendants for committing perjury.'

"In some cases, of course, false testimony can result from faulty recollection. But the majority's ironclad rule is one that applies regardless of the witness' motives, and may be misused as a license to perjure. Even if the witness testifies in good faith, the defendant and his lawyer, who offer the testimony, know the facts. Indeed, it is difficult here to imagine the defense attorney's reason for asking Henderson about petitioner's hair color if he did not expect her to cast doubt on the eyewitness identification of petitioner by giving a description of petitioner's hair color contrary to that contained in his own (suppressed) statement.

"The suggestion that the threat of a perjury prosecution will provide sufficient deterrence to prevent false testimony is not realistic. A heightened proof requirement applies in Illinois and other States, making perjury convictions difficult to sustain. Where testimony presented on behalf of a friend or family member is involved, the threat that a future jury will convict the witness may be an idle one.

"The damage to the truth-seeking process caused by the majority's rule is certain to be great whether the testimony is perjured or merely false. In this case there can be little doubt of the falsity, since petitioner's description of his own hair was at issue. And as a general matter the alternative to rebuttal is endorsement of judicial proceedings conducted in reliance on information known to be untrue. Suppressed evidence is likely to consist of either voluntary statements by the defendant himself or physical evidence. Both have a high degree of reliability, and testimony in direct conflict to such evidence most often will represent an attempt to place falsehoods before the jury.

"The suggestion that all this is so far beyond the control of the defendant that he will put on no defense is not supported. As to sympathetic witnesses, such as the family friend here, it should not be too hard to assure the witness does not volunteer testimony in contradiction of the facts. The defendant knows the content of the suppressed evidence. Even in cases where the time for consultation is limited, the defense attorney can take care not to elicit contradicting testimony. And in the case of truly neutral witnesses, or witnesses hostile to the accused, it is hard to see the danger that they will present false testimony for the benefit of the defense.

"The majority's concerns may carry greater weight where contradicting testimony is elicited from a defense witness on cross-examination. In that situation there might be a concern that the prosecution would attempt to produce such testimony as the foundation to put excluded evidence before the jury. We have found that possibility insufficient to justify immunity for a defendant's own false testimony on cross-examination. *Havens.* As to cross-examination of other witnesses, perhaps a different rule could be justified. Rather than wait for an appropriate case to consider this or similar measures, however, the majority opts for a wooden rule immunizing all defense testimony from rebuttal, without regard to knowledge that the testimony introduced at the behest of the defendant is false or perjured.

"I also cannot agree that admission of excluded evidence on rebuttal would lead to the 'disregard [of] constitutional rights' by law enforcement officers that the majority fears. This argument has been raised in our previous cases in this area of the law. To date we have rejected it. Now the spectre appears premised on an assumption that a single slip of the tongue by any defense witness will open the door to any suppressed evidence at the prosecutor's disposal. If this were so, the majority's concern that officers would be left with little to lose from conducting an illegal search would be understandable. And the argument might hold more force if, as the majority speculates, police confront the temptation to seize evidence illegally 'much if not most of the time' after gathering sufficient evidence to present proof of guilt beyond a reasonable doubt in the case in chief. Again, however, I disagree with the predictions.

"It is unrealistic to say that the decision to make an illegal search turns on a precise calculation of the possibilities of rebuttal at some future trial. There is no reason to believe a police officer, unschooled in the law, will assess whether evidence already in his possession would suffice to survive a motion for acquittal following the case in chief. The officer may or may not even know the identity of the ultimate defendant.[3] He certainly will not know anything about potential defense witnesses,

3. In this case, contrary to the impression conveyed by the majority, n. 8, the arresting officers knew almost nothing of the state of a future prosecution case. The officers did know there were several eyewitnesses to the shooting. But these eyewitnesses had made no identification of any suspect. The officers did not know petitioner's real name or his true appearance, but had sought him out at the beauty parlor on an anonymous tip. They could not know what physical evidence, such as the murder weapon, they might find on petitioner, or might lose, to the case in chief as a result of illegal conduct. The suggestion that the officers' calculated assess-

much less what the content of their testimony might be. What he will know for certain is that evidence from an illegal search or arrest (which may well be crucial to securing a conviction) will be lost to the case in chief. Our earlier assessments of the marginal deterrent effect are applicable here. 'Assuming that the exclusionary rule has a deterrent effect on proscribed police conduct, sufficient deterrence flows when the evidence in question is made unavailable to the prosecution in its case in chief.' *Harris.*

"In this case, the defense witness, one Jewel Henderson, testified that petitioner's hair was black on the date of the offense. Her statement, perjured or not, should not have been offered to the jurors without giving them the opportunity to consider the unequivocal and contradicting description by the person whose own hair it was. I would allow the introduction of petitioner's statement that his hair was red on the day of the shootings. The result is consistent with our line of cases from *Walder* to *Havens,* and compelled by their reasoning.[b] * * *

"Where the jury is misled by false testimony, otherwise subject to flat contradiction by evidence illegally seized, the protection of the exclusionary rule is 'perverted into a license to use perjury by way of a defense, free from the risk of confrontation with prior inconsistent utterances.' *Havens.* The perversion is the same where the perjury is by proxy."

ment of a future trial allowed them to ignore the exclusionary rule finds no support in the record and, in fact, is pure speculation.

b. The dissent noted that the prosecution had also used defendant's statement that he went to the beauty parlor to "change his appearance" to suggest that defendant had a guilty mind and an intention to evade capture by disguise. "This," observed the dissent, "goes beyond what was nec-

B. WHAT KINDS OF CONSTITUTIONAL OR OTHER VIOLATIONS ARE ENCOMPASSED WITHIN THE IMPEACHMENT EXCEPTION?

7th ed., p. 777; substitute Note 3 below for old Note 3:

3. *Use of statements obtained in violation of Sixth Amendment right to counsel.* In MICHIGAN v. HARVEY, ___ U.S. ___, 110 S.Ct. 1176, 108 L.Ed.2d 293 (1990), a 5–4 majority, per REHNQUIST, C.J., held that statements obtained in violation of the rule established in *Michigan v. Jackson,* 7th ed., pp. 522–23, may be used to impeach a defendant's false or inconsistent testimony:

"*Michigan v. Jackson* is based on the Sixth Amendment, but its roots lie in this Court's decisions in *Miranda* and succeeding cases. * * * *Edwards* [7th ed., p. 511] added a second layer of protection [to] *Miranda,* [establishing a] prophylactic rule designed to prevent police from badgering a defendant into waiving his previously asserted *Miranda* rights.

"*Jackson* simply superimposed the Fifth Amendment analysis of *Edwards* onto the Sixth Amendment. Reasoning that 'the Sixth Amendment right to counsel at a postarraignment interrogation requires at least as much protection as the Fifth Amendment right to counsel at any custodial interrogation,' [the *Jackson* Court] concluded that the *Edwards* protections should apply when a suspect charged with a crime requests counsel outside the context of interrogation. This rule, like *Edwards,* is based on the supposition that suspects who assert their right to counsel are unlikely to waive that right voluntarily in subsequent interrogations.

essary to rebut Henderson's testimony and raises many of the concerns expressed in the majority opinion." Nonetheless, added the dissent, because of the overwhelming evidence of guilt, it agreed with the court below that "any error as to the additional statements or the effect of the prosecutor's argument had no effect on [the] trial and may be considered harmless."

"We have already decided that although statements taken in violation of only the prophylactic *Miranda* rules may not be used in the prosecution's case-in-chief, they are admissible to impeach conflicting testimony by the defendant. *Harris v. New York; Oregon v. Hass.* * * * There is no reason for a different result in a *Jackson* case, where the prophylactic rule is designed to ensure voluntary, knowing, and intelligent waivers of the Sixth Amendment right to counsel rather than the Fifth Amendment privilege against self-incrimination or 'right to counsel.' We have mandated the exclusion of reliable and probative evidence for *all* purposes only when it is derived from involuntary statements. We have never prevented use by the prosecution of relevant voluntary statements by a defendant, particularly when the violations alleged by a defendant relate only to procedural safeguards that are 'not themselves rights protected by the Constitution,' but are instead measures designed to ensure that constitutional rights are protected. In such cases, we have decided that the 'search for truth in a criminal case' outweighs the 'speculative possibility' that exclusion of evidence might deter future violations of rules not compelled directly by the Constitution in the first place. *Hass.* [The *Hass* case] was decided 15 years ago, and no new information has come to our attention which should lead us to think otherwise now.

"* * * Both *Jackson* and *Edwards* establish prophylactic rules that render some otherwise valid waivers of constitutional rights invalid when they result from police-initiated interrogation, and in neither case should 'the shield provided by [the prophylactic rule] be perverted into a license to use perjury by way of a defense, free from the risk of confrontation with prior inconsistent utterances.' *Harris.*"

Dissenting JUSTICE STEVENS (author of the Court's opinion in *Jackson*), joined by Brennan, Marshall and Blackmun, JJ., maintained that the Court had made it clear that "the constitutional rule recognized in *Jackson* is based on the Sixth Amendment interest in preserving 'the integrity of an accused's choice to communicate with police only through counsel,'" and that "the Court should acknowledge as much and hold that the Sixth Amendment is violated when the fruits of the State's impermissible encounter with the represented defendant are used for impeachment just as it is when the fruits are used in the prosecutor's case in chief":

"[Unlike the situation when evidence is seized in violation of the Fourth Amendment or a statement is obtained in violation of *Miranda*, the] exclusion of statements made by a represented and indicted defendant outside the presence of counsel follows not as a remedy for a violation that has preceded trial but as a necessary incident of the constitutional right itself.[7] '[T]he Sixth Amendment right to counsel exists, and is needed, in order to protect the fundamental right to a fair trial.' It is not implicated, as a general matter, in the absence of some effect of the challenged conduct on the trial process itself. It is thus the use of the evidence for trial, not the method of its collection prior to trial,

---

7. As Professor Schulhofer has commented:

"[T]he *Massiah* 'exclusionary rule' is not merely a prophylactic device; it is not designed to reduce the *risk* of actual constitutional violations and is not intended to deter any pretrial behavior whatsoever. Rather, *Massiah* explicitly permits government efforts to obtain information from an indicted suspect, so long as that information is not used 'as evidence against *him* at his trial.' The failure to exclude evidence, therefore, cannot be considered *collateral* to some more fundamental violation. Instead, it is the admission at trial that in itself

denies the constitutional right." Schulhofer, *Confessions and the Court*, 79 Mich.L.Rev. 865, 889 (1981).

See also Loewy, *Police-Obtained Evidence and the Constitution: Distinguishing Unconstitutionally Obtained Evidence from Unconstitutionally Used Evidence*, 87 Mich.L.Rev. 907, 931 (1989) ("The justification for disallowing such evidence would not be the 'exclusionary rule,' but the sixth amendment's rules governing fair trials"); Wasserstrom & Mertens, *The Exclusionary Rule on the Scaffold: But Was it a Fair Trial?*, 22 Am.Crim.L.Rev. 85, 175 (1984).

that is the gravamen of the Sixth Amendment claim. * * *

"[The] police misconduct in *Walder, Harris, Havens,* and *Hass* all occurred before the defendant had been formally charged, when the unsolved crime was still being investigated and the questioning of a suspect might be expected to produce evidence that is necessary to obtain an indictment. Knowledge that the improper conduct of an interrogation will destroy its use as substantive evidence provides a powerful incentive to follow the dictates of *Miranda* and its progeny with great care.

"Once a defendant is formally charged with an offense, however, the State is no longer merely engaged in the task of determining who committed an unsolved crime; rather, it is preparing to convict the defendant of the crime he allegedly committed. '[T]he government's role shifts from investigation to accusation.' The State has obtained sufficient evidence to establish probable cause and the ethical prosecutor has sufficient admissible evidence to convict. In practice, the investigation is often virtually complete. Any subsequent investigation is a form of discovery. The cost of an illegal interrogation is therefore greatly reduced. The police would have everything to gain and nothing to lose by repeatedly visiting with the defendant and seeking to elicit as many comments as possible about the pending trial. Knowledge that such conversations could not be used affirmatively would not detract from the State's interest in obtaining them for their value as impeachment evidence."

Part Three

THE COMMENCEMENT OF FORMAL PROCEEDINGS

Chapter 12

PRETRIAL RELEASE

SECTION 1. THE RIGHT TO BAIL; PRETRIAL RELEASE PROCEDURES

7th ed., p. 797; end of fn. d, add:

In some localities, arrestees are subject to urinalysis drug tests, and the results are taken into account by the judge in determining the risks which would be involved in releasing the defendant. For description and evaluation of these practices, see Abell, *Pretrial Drug Testing: Expanding Rights and Protecting Public Safety*, 57 Geo.Wash.L.Rev. 943 (1989); Rosen & Goldkamp, *The Constitutionality of Drug Testing at the Bail Stage*, 80 J.Crim.L. & C. 114 (1989).

SECTION 2. PREVENTIVE DETENTION

7th ed., p. 809; in first column, line 30 after "juror" put fn. b:

b. The Act states that this detention hearing, except upon a grant of a continuance, "shall be held immediately upon the person's first appearance before the judicial officer." "Nothing in § 3142(f) indicates that compliance with the first appearance requirement is a precondition to

holding the hearing or that failure to comply with the requirement renders such a hearing a nullity," and thus "a failure to comply with the first appearance requirement does not defeat the Government's authority to seek detention of the person charged." *United States v. Montalvo–Murillo*, ___ U.S. ___, 110 S.Ct. 2072, 109 L.Ed.2d 720 (1990).

SECTION 3. PREVENTING DETENTION; USE OF THE CITATION AND SUMMONS

7th ed., p. 823; end of Note 4, add:

In *State v. Greenslit*, 559 A.2d 672 (Vt.1989), where (unlike *Robinson*) the notice to appear was given for an offense—present use of marijuana—as to which there would likely be evidence on the person, the court ruled "it is the existence of probable cause for the arrest which brings the search within constitutional limits, not merely the act of taking an individual into custody."

Chapter 18

THE SCOPE OF THE PROSECUTION: JOINDER AND SEVERANCE OF OFFENSES AND DEFENDANTS

SECTION 2. FAILURE TO JOIN RELATED OFFENSES

7th ed., p. 998; in lieu of *Vitale* case and through first line of Note 1 following, add:

GRADY v. CORBIN

___ U.S. ___, 110 S.Ct. 2084, ___ L.Ed. 2d ___ (1990).

JUSTICE BRENNAN delivered the opinion of the Court. * * *

For purposes of this proceeding, we take the following facts as true. At approximately 6:35 p.m. on October 3, 1987, respondent Thomas Corbin drove his automobile across the double yellow line of Route 55 in LaGrange, New York, striking two oncoming vehicles. Assistant District Attorney (ADA) Thomas Dolan was called to the scene, where he learned that both Brenda Dirago, who had been driving the second vehicle to be struck, and her husband Daniel had been seriously injured. Later that evening, ADA Dolan was informed that Brenda Dirago had died from injuries sustained in the accident. That same evening, while at the hospital being treated for his own injuries, respondent was served with two uniform traffic tickets directing him to appear at the LaGrange Town Justice Court on October 29, 1987. One ticket charged him with the misdemeanor of driving while intoxicated; the other charged him with failing to keep right of the median. A blood test taken at the hospital that evening indicated a blood alcohol level of 0.19%, nearly twice the level at which it is *per se* illegal to operate a motor vehicle in New York.

Three days later, Assistant District Attorney Frank Chase began gathering evidence for a homicide prosecution in connection with the accident. "Despite his active involvement in building a homicide case against [Corbin], however, Chase did not attempt to ascertain the date [Corbin] was scheduled to appear in Town Justice Court on the traffic tickets, nor did he inform either the Town Justice Court or the Assistant District Attorney covering that court about his pending investigation." Thus, Assistant District Attorney Mark Glick never mentioned Brenda Dirago's death in the statement of readiness for trial and other pretrial pleadings he submitted to respondent and the LaGrange Town Justice Court on October 14, 1987.

Accordingly, when respondent pleaded guilty to the two traffic tickets on October 27, 1987, a date on which no member of the District Attorney's office was present in court,[3] the presiding judge was unaware

---

3. The record does not indicate why the return dates for the traffic tickets were changed from October 29 to October 27. In any event, the District Attorney was not deprived of a meaningful opportunity to participate in this prosecution. If the District Attorney had wanted to prevent

Corbin from pleading guilty to the traffic tickets so that the State could combine all charges into a single prosecution containing the later-charged felony counts, he could have availed himself of [statutory adjournment procedures].

of the fatality stemming from the accident. Corbin was never asked if any others had been injured on the night in question and did not voluntarily incriminate himself by providing such information.[4] The presiding judge accepted his guilty plea, but because the District Attorney's office had not submitted a sentencing recommendation, the judge postponed sentencing until November 17, 1987, when an Assistant District Attorney was scheduled to be present in court. The Assistant District Attorney present at sentencing on that date, Heidi Sauter, was unaware that there had been a fatality, was unable to locate the case file, and had not spoken to ADA Glick about the case. Nevertheless, she did not seek an adjournment so that she could ascertain the facts necessary to make an informed sentencing recommendation. Instead, she recommended a "minimum sentence," and the presiding judge sentenced Corbin to a $350 fine, a $10 surcharge, and a 6–month license revocation.

Two months later, on January 19, 1988, a grand jury investigating the October 3, 1987, accident indicted Corbin, charging him with reckless manslaughter, second-degree vehicular manslaughter, and criminally negligent homicide for causing the death of Brenda Dirago; third-degree reckless assault for causing physical injury to Daniel Dirago; and driving while intoxicated. The prosecution filed a bill of particulars that identified the three reckless or negligent acts on which it would rely to prove the homicide and assault charges: (1) operating a motor vehicle on a public

highway in an intoxicated condition, (2) failing to keep right of the median, and (3) driving approximately 45 to 50 miles per hour in heavy rain, "which was a speed too fast for the weather and road conditions then pending." Respondent moved to dismiss the indictment on statutory and constitutional double jeopardy grounds. After a hearing, the Dutchess County Court denied respondent's motion, ruling that the failure of Corbin or his counsel to inform the Town Justice Court at the time of the guilty plea that Corbin had been involved in a fatal accident constituted a "material misrepresentation of fact" that "was prejudicial to the administration of justice."[6]

Respondent then sought a writ of prohibition barring prosecution on all counts of the indictment. The Appellate Division denied the petition without opinion, but the New York Court of Appeals reversed. The court prohibited prosecution of the driving while intoxicated counts pursuant to New York's statutory double jeopardy provision. The court further ruled that prosecution of the two vehicular manslaughter counts would violate the Double Jeopardy Clause of the Fifth Amendment pursuant to the *Blockburger* test because, as a matter of state law, driving while intoxicated "is unquestionably a lesser included offense of second degree vehicular manslaughter." Finally, relying on the "pointed dictum" in this Court's opinion in *Vitale*, the court barred prosecution of the remaining counts because the bill of particulars expressed an intention to "rely on the prior traffic offenses as the acts neces-

---

Furthermore, the District Attorney's participation in this prosecution amounted to more than a failure to move for an adjournment. ADA Glick filed papers indicating a readiness to proceed to trial, and Assistant District Attorney Heidi Sauter appeared at Corbin's sentencing on behalf of the People of the State of New York.

4. The New York Court of Appeals held that, although an attorney may not misrepresent facts, "a practitioner representing a client at a traffic violation prosecution should not be expected to *volunteer* information that is likely to be highly damaging to his client's position." Because the

Court of Appeals refused to characterize as misconduct the behavior of either Corbin or his attorney, we need not decide whether our double jeopardy analysis would be any different if affirmative misrepresentations of fact by a defendant or his counsel were to mislead a court into accepting a guilty plea it would not otherwise accept.

6. The New York Court of Appeals found no misrepresentations and no misconduct during the guilty plea colloquy on October 27, 1987. We accept its characterization of the proceedings.

sary to prove the homicide and assault charges." Two judges dissented, arguing that respondent had deceived the Town Justice Court when pleading guilty to the traffic tickets. We granted certiorari, and now affirm.

The facts and contentions raised here mirror almost exactly those raised in this Court 10 years ago in *Illinois v. Vitale,* 447 U.S. 410, 100 S.Ct. 2260, 65 L.Ed.2d 228 (1980). Like Thomas Corbin, John Vitale allegedly caused a fatal car accident. A police officer at the scene issued Vitale a traffic citation charging him with failure to reduce speed to avoid an accident. Vitale was convicted of that offense and sentenced to pay a $15 fine. The day after his conviction, the State charged Vitale with two counts of involuntary manslaughter based on his reckless driving. Vitale argued that this subsequent prosecution was barred by the Double Jeopardy Clause.

This Court held that the second prosecution was not barred under the traditional *Blockburger* test because each offense "require[d] proof of a fact which the other [did] not." Although involuntary manslaughter required proof of a death, failure to reduce speed did not. Likewise, failure to slow was not a statutory element of involuntary manslaughter. Thus, the subsequent prosecution survived the *Blockburger* test.

But the Court did not stop at that point. Justice White, writing for the Court, added that, even though the two prosecutions did not violate the *Blockburger* test:

"[I]t may be that to sustain its manslaughter case the State may find it necessary to prove a failure to slow or to rely on conduct necessarily involving such failure; it may concede as much

prior to trial. In that case, because Vitale has already been convicted for conduct that is a necessary element of the more serious crime for which he has been charged, his claim of double jeopardy would be substantial under *Brown* [*v. Ohio,* 432 U.S. 161, 97 S.Ct. 2221, 53 L.Ed.2d 187 (1977)] and our later decision in *Harris v. Oklahoma,* 433 U.S. 682 [97 S.Ct. 2912, 53 L.Ed.2d 1054] (1977)."

We believe that this analysis is correct and governs this case.[7] To determine whether a subsequent prosecution is barred by the Double Jeopardy Clause, a court must first apply the traditional *Blockburger* test. If application of that test reveals that the offenses have identical statutory elements or that one is a lesser included offense of the other, then the inquiry must cease, and the subsequent prosecution is barred.

The State argues that this should be the last step in the inquiry and that the Double Jeopardy Clause permits successive prosecutions whenever the offenses charged satisfy the *Blockburger* test. We disagree. The Double Jeopardy Clause embodies three protections: "It protects against a second prosecution for the same offense after acquittal. It protects against a second prosecution for the same offense after conviction. And it protects against multiple punishments for the same offense." The *Blockburger* test was developed "in the context of multiple punishments imposed in a single prosecution." In that context, "the Double Jeopardy Clause does no more than prevent the sentencing court from prescribing greater punishment than the legislature intended." The *Blockburger* test is simply a "rule of statutory construction," a guide to determining whether the legislature intended multiple punishments.[8]

---

7. We recognized in *Brown v. Ohio* that when application of our traditional double jeopardy analysis would bar a subsequent prosecution, "[a]n exception may exist where the State is unable to proceed on the more serious charge at the outset because the additional facts necessary to sustain that charge have not occurred or have

not been discovered despite the exercise of due diligence." Because ADA Dolan was informed of Brenda Dirago's death on the night of the accident, such an exception is inapplicable here.

8. Justice Scalia's dissent contends that *Blockburger* is not just a guide to legislative in-

Successive prosecutions, however, whether, following acquittals or convictions, raise concerns that extend beyond merely the possibility of an enhanced sentence:

"The underlying idea, one that is deeply ingrained in at least the Anglo–American system of jurisprudence, is that the State with all its resources and power should not be allowed to make repeated attempts to convict an individual for an alleged offense, thereby subjecting him to embarassment, expense and ordeal and compelling him to live in a continuing state of anxiety and insecurity. . . ."

Multiple prosecutions also give the State an opportunity to rehearse its presentation of proof, thus increasing the risk of an erroneous conviction for one or more of the offenses charged. Even when a State can bring multiple charges against an individual under *Blockburger,* a tremendous additional burden is placed on that defendant if he must face each of the charges in a separate proceeding.

Because of these independent concerns, we have not relied exclusively on the *Blockburger* test to vindicate the Double Jeopardy Clause's protection against multiple prosecutions. As we stated in *Brown v. Ohio:*

"The *Blockburger* test is not the only standard for determining whether successive prosecutions impermissibly involve the same offense. Even if two offenses are sufficiently different to permit the imposition of consecutive sentences, successive prosecutions will be barred in some circumstances where the second prosecution requires the relitigation of factual issues already resolved by the first."

Justice Powell, writing for the Court in *Brown,* provided two examples. In *Ashe v. Swenson,* [7th ed., p. 1006], the Court had held that the Double Jeopardy Clause barred a prosecution for robbing a participant in a poker game because the defendant's acquittal in a previous trial for robbing a different participant in the same poker game had conclusively established that he was not present at the robbery. In *In re Nielsen,* 131 U.S. 176, 9 S.Ct. 672, 33 L.Ed. 118 (1889), the Court had held that a conviction for cohabiting with two wives over a 2½-year period barred a subsequent prosecution for adultery with one of the wives on the day following the end of that period. Although application of the *Blockburger* test would have permitted the imposition of consecutive sentences in both cases, the Double Jeopardy Clause nonetheless barred these successive prosecutions.

Furthermore, in the same Term we decided *Brown,* we reiterated in *Harris v. Oklahoma* that a strict application of the *Blockburger* test is not the exclusive means of determining whether a subsequent prosecution violates the Double Jeopardy Clause. In *Harris,* the defendant was first convicted of felony murder after his companion shot a grocery store clerk in the course of a robbery. The State then indicted and convicted him for robbery with a firearm. The two prosecutions were not for the "same offense" under *Blockburger* since, as a statutory matter, felony murder could be established by proof of any felony, not just robbery, and robbery with a

---

tent, but rather an exclusive definition of the term "same offence" in the Double Jeopardy Clause. To support this contention, Justice Scalia asserts that "[w]e have applied the [*Blockburger* test] in virtually every case defining the 'same offense' decided since *Blockburger.*" Every one of the eight cases cited in support of that proposition, however, describes *Blockburger* as a test to determine the permissibility of cumulative punishments. None of the cases even suggests that *Blockburger* is the exclusive definition of

"same offense" in the context of successive prosecutions.

To further support its contention that *Blockburger* is the exclusive means of defining "same offence" within the meaning of the Double Jeopardy Clause, Justice Scalia's dissent relies on a lengthy historical discussion. We have not previously found, and we do not today find, history to be dispositive of double jeopardy claims.

firearm did not require proof of a death. Nevertheless, because the State admitted that " 'it was necessary for all the ingredients of the underlying felony of Robbery with Firearms to be proved' " in the felony-murder trial, the Court unanimously held that the subsequent prosecution was barred by the Double Jeopardy Clause. As we later described our reasoning, "we did not consider the crime generally described as felony murder as a separate offense distinct from its various elements. Rather, we treated a killing in the course of a robbery as itself a separate statutory offense, and the robbery as a species of lesser-included offense." *Vitale.*

These cases all recognized that a technical comparison of the elements of the two offenses as required by *Blockburger* does not protect defendants sufficiently from the burdens of multiple trials. This case similarly demonstrates the limitations of the *Blockburger* analysis. If *Blockburger* constituted the entire double jeopardy inquiry in the context of successive prosecutions, the State could try Corbin in four consecutive trials: for failure to keep right of the median, for driving while intoxicated, for assault, and for homicide. The State could improve its presentation of proof with each trial, assessing which witnesses gave the most persuasive testimony, which documents had the greatest impact, which opening and closing arguments most persuaded the jurors. Corbin would be forced either to contest each of these trials or to plead guilty to avoid the harassment and expense.

Thus, a subsequent prosecution must do more than merely survive the *Blockburger*

test. As we suggested in *Vitale,* the Double Jeopardy Clause bars any subsequent prosecution in which the government, to establish an essential element of an offense charged in that prosecution, will prove conduct that constitutes an offense for which the defendant has already been prosecuted.[11] This is not an "actual evidence" or "same evidence" test. The critical inquiry is what conduct the State will prove, not the evidence the State will use to prove that conduct. As we have held, the presentation of specific evidence in one trial does not forever prevent the government from introducing that same evidence in a subsequent proceeding. See *Dowling v. United States,* [Supp. p. 50]. On the other hand, a State cannot avoid the dictates of the Double Jeopardy Clause merely by altering in successive prosecutions the evidence offered to prove the same conduct. For example, if two bystanders had witnessed Corbin's accident, it would make no difference to our double jeopardy analysis if the State called one witness to testify in the first trial that Corbin's vehicle crossed the median (or if nobody testified in the first trial because Corbin, as he did, pleaded guilty) and called the other witness to testify to the same conduct in the second trial.

Applying this analysis to the facts of this case is straightforward. Respondent concedes that *Blockburger* does not bar prosecution of the reckless manslaughter, criminally negligent homicide, and third-degree reckless assault offenses.[13] The rest of our inquiry in this case is simplified by the bill of particulars filed by the State on January 25, 1988.[14] That statement of

---

11. Similarly, if in the course of securing a conviction for one offense the State necessarily has proved the conduct comprising all of the elements of another offense not yet prosecuted (a "component offense"), the Double Jeopardy Clause would bar subsequent prosecution of the component offense. See *Harris v. Oklahoma,* supra * * *.

13. Because the State does not contest the New York Court of Appeals' ruling that the driving while intoxicated and vehicular manslaughter charges are barred under state law and *Block-*

burger, respectively, we need decide only whether the Double Jeopardy Clause prohibits the State from prosecuting Corbin on the homicide and assault charges.

14. Application of the test we adopt today will not depend, as Justice Scalia's dissent argues, on whether the indictment "happens to show that the same evidence is at issue" or whether the jurisdiction "happen[s] to require the prosecution to submit a bill of particulars that cannot be exceeded." The Courts of Appeals, which long ago recognized that the Douthe prosecution's theory of proof is binding on the State until amended, and the State has not amended it to date. The bill of particulars states that the prosecution will prove the following:

"[T]he defendant [(1)] operated a motor vehicle on a public highway in an intoxicated condition having more than .10 percent of alcohol content in his blood, [(2)] failed to keep right and in fact crossed nine feet over the median of the highway [and (3) drove] at approximately forty-five to fifty miles an hour in heavy rain, which was a speed too fast for the weather and road conditions then pending. . . . By so operating his vehicle in the manner above described, the defendant was aware of and consciously disregarded a substantial and unjustifiable risk of the likelihood of the result which occurred. . . . By his failure to perceive this risk while operating a vehicle in a criminally negligent and reckless manner, he caused physical injury to Daniel Dirago and the death of his wife, Brenda Dirago."

By its own pleadings, the State has admitted that it will prove the entirety of the conduct for which Corbin was convicted—driving while intoxicated and failing to keep right of the median—to establish essential elements of the homicide and assault offenses. Therefore, the Double Jeopardy Clause bars this successive prosecution, and the New York Court of Appeals properly granted respondent's petition for a writ of prohibition. This holding would not bar a subse-

quent prosecution on the homicide and assault charges if the bill of particulars revealed that the State would not rely on proving the conduct for which Corbin had already been convicted (*i.e.*, if the State relied solely on Corbin's driving too fast in heavy rain to establish recklessness or negligence).15 * * *

The judgment of the New York Court of Appeals is

Affirmed.

JUSTICE O'CONNOR, dissenting.

I agree with much of what Justice Scalia says in his dissenting opinion. I write separately, however, to note that my dissent is premised primarily on my view that the inconsistency between the Court's opinion today and *Dowling v. United States,* decided earlier this Term, indicates that the Court has strayed from a proper interpretation of the scope of the Double Jeopardy Clause. * * *

JUSTICE SCALIA, with whom CHIEF JUSTICE REHNQUIST and JUSTICE KENNEDY join, dissenting. * * *

Subject to the *Harris* and *Ashe* exceptions, I would adhere to the *Blockburger* rule that successive prosecutions under two different statutes do not constitute double jeopardy if each statutory crime contains an element that the other does not, regardless of the overlap between the proof required for each prosecution in the particular case. That rule best gives effect to the language of the Clause, which protects individuals from being twice put in jeopardy "for the same *offence*," not for the same

---

ble Jeopardy Clause requires more than a technical comparison of statutory elements when a defendant is confronting successive prosecutions, have adopted an essential procedural mechanism for assessing double jeopardy claims prior to a second trial. All nine federal Circuits which have addressed the issue have held that "when a defendant puts double jeopardy in issue with a non-frivolous showing that an indictment charges him with an offense for which he was formerly placed in jeopardy, the burden shifts to the government to establish that there were in fact two separate offenses." *United States v. Ragins,* 840 F.2d 1184, 1192 (CA4 1988)

(collecting cases). This procedural mechanism will ensure that the test set forth today is in fact "implementable".

15. Adoption of a "same transaction" test would bar the homicide and assault prosecutions even if the State were able to establish the essential elements of those crimes without proving the conduct for which Corbin previously was convicted. The Court, however, has "steadfastly refused to adopt the 'single transaction' view of the Double Jeopardy Clause." *Garrett v. United States,* [7th ed., p. 1003].

conduct or *actions.* "Offence" was commonly understood in 1791 to mean "transgression," that is, "the Violation or Breaking of a Law." * * *

Another textual element also supports the *Blockburger* test. Since the Double Jeopardy Clause protects the defendant from being "twice put in jeopardy," *i.e.,* made to stand trial for the "same offence," it presupposes that sameness can be determined before the second trial. Otherwise, the Clause would have prohibited a second "conviction" or "sentence" for the same offense. A court can always determine, before trial, whether the second prosecution involves the "same offence" in the *Blockburger* sense, since the Constitution entitles the defendant "to be informed of the nature and cause of the accusation." But since the Constitution does not entitle the defendant to be informed of the *evidence* against him, the Court's "proof-of-same-conduct" test will be implementable before trial only if the indictment happens to show that the same evidence is at issue, or only if the jurisdiction's rules of criminal procedure happen to require the prosecution to submit a bill of particulars that cannot be exceeded. More often than not, in other words, the Court's test will not succeed in preventing the defendant from being tried twice.

Relying on text alone, therefore, one would conclude that the Double Jeopardy Clause meant what *Blockburger* said. But there is in addition a wealth of historical evidence to the same effect. The Clause was based on the English common-law pleas of *auterfoits acquit* and *auterfoits convict,* which pleas were valid only "upon a prosecution for the same identical act *and* crime." * * *

The English practice, as understood in 1791, did not recognize *auterfoits acquit* and *auterfoits convict* as good pleas against successive prosecutions for crimes whose elements were distinct, even though based on the same act.

The early American cases adhere to the same rule. * * *

Thus, the *Blockburger* definition of "same offence" was not invented in 1932 * * *.

[T]he argument that *Vitale* said to be "substantial" finds no support whatever in the two cases that *Vitale* thought gave it substance, *Brown v. Ohio* and *Harris v. Oklahoma.* The first, *Brown,* involved nothing more than a straightforward application of *Blockburger.* There a car thief was first convicted of "joyriding," an offense that consisted of "tak[ing], operat[ing], or keep[ing] any motor vehicle without the consent of its owner." He was then charged with auto theft, which required all the elements of joyriding plus an intent permanently to deprive the owner of his car. We held that *Blockburger* barred the second prosecution: because joyriding was simply a lesser included offense of auto theft, proof of the latter would "invariably" require proof of the former. We did not even hint that double jeopardy would also have barred the prosecution if the two statutes had *passed* the *Blockburger* test but the second prosecution could not be successful without proving the same facts. The second case, our brief *per curiam* disposition in *Harris,* involved a prosecution for armed robbery that followed a conviction for felony murder based on the same armed robbery. The felony murder statute by definition incorporated all of the elements of the underlying felony charged; thus the later prosecution (rather than, as in *Brown,* the earlier conviction) involved a lesser included offense. "When," we said, "conviction of a greater crime, murder, cannot be had without conviction of the lesser crime, robbery with firearms, the Double Jeopardy Clause bars prosecution for the lesser crime after conviction of the greater one." Again, we gave no indication that the second prosecution would have been barred if—not because of the statutory definition of the crimes but merely because of the circumstances of the particular case—guilt could not be established without proving the same conduct charged in the first prosecution. In short, to call the latter proposition "substantial" in *Vitale* took more than a little stretching of the cited cases.

I would have thought the result the Court reaches today foreclosed by our decision just a few months ago in *Dowling v. United States.* There the State, in a prosecution for robbery, introduced evidence of the defendant's perpetration of another robbery committed in similar fashion (both involved ski masks), of which he had previously been acquitted. Proof of the prior robbery tended to establish commission of the later one. The State, in other words, "to establish an essential element of an offense charged in [the second] prosecution, [had] prove[d] conduct that constitute[d] an offense for which the defendant ha[d] already been prosecuted." We held, however, that the Double Jeopardy Clause was not violated. The difference in our holding today cannot rationally be explained by the fact that in *Dowling,* unlike the present case, the two crimes were part of separate transactions; that in no way alters the central vice (according to today's holding) that the defendant was forced a second time to defend against proof that he had committed a robbery for which he had already been prosecuted. In *Dowling,* as here, conduct establishing a previously prosecuted offense was relied upon, not because that offense was a statutory element of the second offense, but only because the conduct would *prove the existence* of a statutory element. If that did not offend the Double Jeopardy Clause in *Dowling,* it should not do so here.

The principle the Court adopts today is not only radically out of line with our double jeopardy jurisprudence; its practical effect, whenever it applies, will come down to a requirement that where the charges arise from a " 'single criminal act, occurrence, episode, or transaction,' " they "must be tried in a single proceeding"—a requirement we have hitherto "steadfastly refused" to impose. Suppose, for exam-

ple, that the State prosecutes a group of individuals for a substantive offense, and then prosecutes them for conspiracy. In the conspiracy trial it *will prove* (if it can) that the defendants actually committed the substantive offense—even though there is evidence of other overt acts sufficient to sustain the conspiracy charge. For proof of the substantive offense, though not an *element* of the conspiracy charge, will assuredly be *persuasive* in establishing that a conspiracy existed. Or suppose an initial prosecution for burglary and a subsequent prosecution for murder that occurred in the course of the same burglary. In the second trial the State *will prove* (if it can) that the defendant was engaged in a burglary—not because that is itself an element of the murder charge, but because by providing a motive for intentional killing it will be *persuasive* that murder occurred. Under the analysis embraced by the Court today, I take it that the second prosecution in each of these cases would be barred, because the State, "to establish an essential element of an offense charged in that prosecution, will prove conduct that constitutes an offense for which the defendant has already been prosecuted." Just as, in today's case, proof of drunk driving or of crossing the median strip invalidates the second prosecution even though they are not elements of the homicide and assault offenses of which respondent is charged; so also, in the hypotheticals given, proof of the substantive offense will invalidate the conspiracy prosecution and proof of the burglary the murder prosecution.

The Court seeks to shrink the apparent application of its novel principle by saying that repetitive proof violates the Double Jeopardy Clause only if it is introduced "to establish an essential element of an offense charged in [the second] prosecution." That is a meaningless limitation, of course. *All* evidence pertaining to guilt seeks "to establish an essential element of [the] offense," and should be excluded if it does not have that tendency.

The other half of the Court's new test does seem to import some limitation, though I am not sure precisely what it means and cannot imagine what principle justifies it. I refer to the requirement that the evidence introduced in the second prosecution must "prove conduct that constitutes an offense for which the defendant has already been prosecuted." This means, presumably, that prosecutors who wish to use facts sufficient to prove one crime in order to establish guilt of another crime must bring both prosecutions simultaneously; but that those who wish to use only *some of* the facts establishing one crime—not enough facts to "prove conduct that constitutes an offense"—can bring successive prosecutions. But, one may reasonably ask, what justification is there *even in reason alone* (having abandoned text and precedent) for limiting the Court's new rule in this fashion? The Court defends the rule on the ground that a successive prosecution based on the same proof exposes the defendant to the burden and embarrassment of resisting proof of the same facts in multiple proceedings, and enables the State to "rehearse its presentation of proof, thus increasing the risk of an erroneous conviction for one or more of the offenses charged." But that vice does not exist only when the second prosecution seeks to prove *all* the facts necessary to support the first prosecution; it exists as well when the second prosecution seeks to prove some, rather than all of them—*i.e.,* whenever two prosecutions each require proof of facts (or even a single fact) common to both. If the Court were correct that the Double Jeopardy Clause protects individuals against the necessity of twice proving (or refuting) the same *evidence,* as opposed to the necessity of twice defending against the same *charge,* then the second prosecution should be equally bad whether it contains all or merely some of the proof necessary for the first.

Apart from the lack of rational basis for this latter limitation, I am greatly perplexed (as will be the unfortunate trial-court judges who must apply today's rootless decision) as to what precisely it means. It is not at all apparent how a court is to go about deciding whether the evidence that has been introduced (or that will be introduced) at the second trial "proves conduct" that constitutes an offense for which the defendant has already been prosecuted. Is the judge in the second trial supposed to pretend that he is the judge in the first one, and to let the second trial proceed *only if* the evidence would not be enough to go to the jury on the earlier charge? Or (as the language of the Court's test more readily suggests) is the judge in the second trial supposed to decide on his own whether the evidence before him really "proves" the earlier charge (perhaps beyond a reasonable doubt)? Consider application of the Court's new rule in the unusually simple circumstances of the present case: Suppose that, in the trial upon remand, the prosecution's evidence shows, among other things, that when the vehicles came to rest after the collision they were located on what was, for the defendant's vehicle, the wrong side of the road. The prosecution also produces a witness who testifies that prior to the collision the defendant's vehicle was "weaving back and forth"—*without* saying, however, that it was weaving back and forth over the center line. Is this enough to meet today's requirement of "proving" the offense of operating a vehicle on the wrong side of the road? If not, suppose in addition that defense counsel asks the witness on cross-examination, "When you said the defendant's vehicle was 'weaving back and forth,' did you mean weaving back and forth across the center line?"—to which the witness replies yes. Will this self-inflicted wound count for purposes of determining what the prosecution has "proved"? If so, can the prosecution then seek to impeach its own witness by showing that his recollection of the vehicle's crossing the center line was inaccurate? Or can it at least introduce another witness to establish that fact? There are many questions here, and the answers to all of them are ridiculous. Whatever line is selected as the criterion of "proving" the prior offense—enough evidence to go to the jury, more likely than not, or beyond a reasonable doubt—the prosecutor in the second trial will presumably seek to introduce as much evidence as he can without crossing that line; and the defense attorney will presumably seek to provoke the prosecutor into (or assist him in) proving the defendant guilty of the earlier crime. This delicious role-reversal, discovered to have been mandated by the Double Jeopardy Clause lo these 200 years, makes for high comedy but inferior justice. Often, the performance will even have an encore. If the judge initially decides that the previously prosecuted offense "will not be proved" (whatever that means) he will have to decide at the conclusion of the trial whether it "has been proved" (whatever that means). Indeed, he may presumably be asked to make the latter determination periodically during the course of the trial, since the Double Jeopardy Clause assuredly entitles the defendant to have the proceedings terminated as soon as its violation is evident. Even if we had no constitutional text and no prior case-law to rely upon, rejection of today's opinion is adequately supported by the modest desire to protect our criminal legal system from ridicule. * * * [P]rosecutors confronted with the inscrutability of today's opinion will be well advised to proceed on the assumption that the "same transaction" theory has already been adopted. It is hard to tell what else has. * * *

Notes and Questions

1. Assess these pre-*Corbin* cases: *People* [continue with Note 1, 7th ed., p. 1003].

7th ed., p. 1013, in lieu of last 7 lines in Note 3, add:

Dowling v. United States, ___ U.S. ___, 110 S.Ct. 668, 107 L.Ed.2d 708 (1990) (earlier acquittal, even if it established a reasonable doubt as to the existence of a matter to be proved as an evidentiary fact at a later trial, is no bar to proof of the evidentiary fact by a lesser standard).

SECTION 3. JOINDER AND SEVERANCE OF DEFENDANTS

7th ed., p. 1025; end of fn. b, add:

More recent contrary holdings rely on *Richardson.* See, e.g., *United States v. Vasquez,* 874 F.2d 1515 (11th Cir.1989) (upholding substitution of "individual" for defendant's name).

Part Four

THE ADVERSARY SYSTEM AND THE DETERMINATION OF GUILT OR INNOCENCE

Chapter 22

COERCED, INDUCED, AND NEGOTIATED GUILTY PLEAS; PROFESSIONAL RESPONSIBILITY

SECTION 2. REJECTED, KEPT AND BROKEN BARGAINS; UNREALIZED EXPECTATIONS

7th ed., p. 1225; end of first paragraph of Note 3, add:

What then of a plea conditioned upon the defendant not interviewing the victim? See *State v. Draper,* 784 P.2d 259 (Ariz.1989) (not per se improper, but requires close judicial scrutiny because it "may interfere with a defendant's due process rights to prepare a defense").

7th ed., p. 1228; end of Note 4, add:

Where, as in *Rosa,* there is no per se rule against judicial participation, the outcome of a later challenge to the plea will turn on the extent and character of the judge's involvement. Compare, e.g., *State v. Ditter,* 441 N.W.2d 622 (Neb.1989) (did not coerce plea, as defense initiated the discussion, judge talked only with defense counsel and defendant was not present, judge only indicated possible penalties depending on defendant's course of action, and judge made no comments on the weight of the evidence or that he thought defendant was guilty); with *State v. Svoboda,* 287 N.W.2d 41 (Neb.1980) (coerced the plea, as judge initiated discussion directly with defendant and told defendant the evidence was overwhelming and that defendant should not go to trial).

7th ed., p. 1230; end of Note 8, add:

Evans is a minority but constitutionally permissible alternative. As stated in *Carwile v. Smith,* 874 F.2d 382 (6th Cir.1989), the fact "that under federal law, as well as under the law of 40 out of 49 states, a criminal defendant who has pleaded guilty must be given an opportunity to withdraw his plea when an agreed sentencing recommendation is rejected by the sentencing court" does not mean it is a violation of due process for a state not to permit withdrawal absent a showing "that petitioner was 'misled' into thinking that the judge would be bound by the prosecutor's recommendation."

In a state which, unlike *Evans,* provides that a defendant must be allowed to withdraw his plea if the judge decides upon a sentence higher than contemplated in the

Mod. & Basic Crim.Proc., 7th Ed. (K., L. & I.) ACB—3
1990 Supp.

51

plea agreement, should the prosecution have a corresponding right to withdraw if the judge opts for a sentence lower than the parties earlier agreed to? See *State v. Warren,* 558 A.2d 1312 (N.J.1989) (no, as though "notions of fairness apply to each side, * * * the defendant's constitutional rights and interests weigh more heavily in the scale").

7th ed., p. 1233; before Note 5, add:

4a. The new federal sentencing guidelines have given rise to other types of plea bargain terms regarding the sentence to be imposed. For example, one possibility is that the prosecutor will stipulate to some fact (e.g., that defendant was a minor participant in the crime) which, if true, would permit reduction of defendant's offense level for sentencing purposes. The federal sentencing guidelines expressly state that the court is not bound by such a stipulation, and consequently there is no broken bargain if the court concludes the mitigating circumstance was not present and that therefore defendant should not receive the contemplated sentence reduction. *United States v. Howard,* 894 F.2d 1085 (9th Cir.1990). (The result would presumably be otherwise if, as is permitted under the federal guidelines, the defendant entered a guilty plea on the express condition that the judge find, e.g., that he was a minor participant.) Moreover, in the stipulation-only case, if the defendant then appeals from the trial judge's determination, the prosecution does not violate the plea bargain by arguing the lower court did not err. *United States v. Howard,* supra. In somewhat the reverse situation, where the plea bargain stipulation is that the sentence will not exceed a certain amount, and that amount would be appropriate if the court found an aggravating circumstance present which sufficed to take the case above the usual guideline range, the stipulation does not bar the defendant from questioning on appeal whether there was a sufficient finding of the necessary aggravating circumstance.

United States v. Newsome, 894 F.2d 852 (6th Cir.1990).

7th ed., p. 1235; end of Note 8, add:

Consider *Staten v. Neal,* 880 F.2d 962 (7th Cir.1989) (though "United States Attorneys arguably speak for the entire federal government, the same cannot be said of state's attorneys in Illinois," and thus plea agreement term that defendant would not be prosecuted in another county not entitled to specific performance).

SECTION 3. PROFESSIONAL RESPONSIBILITY; THE ROLE OF PROSECUTOR AND DEFENSE COUNSEL

7th ed., p. 1249; end of Note 2, add:

Query, what level of noninvestigation, under what circumstances, will entitle the guilty plea defendant to relief on Sixth Amendment grounds? Recall that *Strickland,* 7th ed., p. 1077, also requires proof of prejudice for the defendant to prevail on an ineffective assistance claim while *Chronic,* 7th ed., p. 1090, says prejudice is presumed upon complete lack of representation, including when counsel "fails to subject the prosecutor's case to meaningful adversarial testing." Consider *Woodard v. Collins,* 898 F.2d 1027 (5th Cir.1990) ("a decision to investigate some issues and not others or even a decision to conduct virtually no investigation is governed by *Strickland*").

SECTION 4. RECEIVING THE DEFENDANT'S PLEA; PLEA WITHDRAWAL

7th ed., p. 1271; after Note 4, add:

5. What then of somewhat the reverse situation? That is, if a court finds that the factual basis only establishes a lesser-included offense, may the court direct entry of a guilty plea to such an offense? See *State v. Barboza,* 558 A.2d 1303 (N.J.1989) (no, as this would be "tantamount to permitting a court to direct a verdict against a defendant in a criminal case").

Chapter 23
TRIAL BY JURY

SECTION 2. JURY SELECTION

7th ed., p. 1303; end of Note 1, add:

The Court continues to be divided as to just how many "distinctive groups" there might be. In *Holland v. Illinois,* discussed below, Scalia, J., for the Court, said that if the cross-section requirement applied to juries (rather than the panels from which juries are chosen) then "many commonly exercised bases for peremptory challenges would be rendered unavailable," while Marshall, J., dissenting, objected to the "majority's exaggerated claim that 'postmen, or lawyers, or clergymen' are distinctive groups within the meaning of our fair cross-section cases."

7th ed., p. 1304; end of first paragraph of Note 4, add:

In *Holland v. Illinois,* Supp. p. 54, dictum reflects "agreement of five Justices that a defendant's race is irrelevant to the Fourteenth Amendment standing inquiry," i.e., that a white defendant may raise an equal protection claim on behalf of excluded black prospective jurors.

7th ed., p. 1306; in Note 5 after *Zicarelli,* add:

Indeed, *Jones* was itself overruled in *Hernandez v. Municipal Court,* 781 P.2d 547 (Cal.1989), reasoning that in a state context "the boundaries of the vicinage are coterminous with the boundaries of the county" and that consequently it is sufficient that the jurors are selected from the county—they need not be from the particular judicial district therein where the crime occurred.

7th ed., p. 1329; in lieu of Note 5, add:

5. A *Batson*-type challenge to the prosecutor's use of peremptories, grounded instead in the Sixth Amendment's cross-section requirement, was rejected 5–4 in HOLLAND v. ILLINOIS, ___ U.S. ___, 110 S.Ct. 803, 107 L.Ed.2d 905 (1990). SCALIA, J., for the majority, reasoned:

"The Sixth Amendment requirement of a fair cross section on the venire is a means of assuring, not a *representative* jury (which the Constitution does not demand), but an *impartial* one (which it does). Without that requirement, the State could draw up jury lists in such manner as to produce a pool of prospective jurors disproportionately ill disposed towards one or all classes of defendants, and thus more likely to yield petit juries with similar disposition. The State would have, in effect, unlimited peremptory challenges to compose the pool in its favor. The fair-cross-section venire requirement assures, in other words, that in the process of selecting the petit jury the prosecution and defense will compete on an equal basis.

"But to say that the Sixth Amendment deprives the State of the ability to 'stack the deck' in its favor is not to say that each side may not, once a fair hand is dealt, use peremptory challenges to eliminate prospective jurors belonging to groups it believes would unduly favor the other side. Any theory of the Sixth Amendment leading to that result is implausible. The tradition of peremptory challenges for both the prosecution and the accused was already venerable at the time of Blackstone, was reflected in a federal statute enacted by the same Congress that proposed the Bill of Rights, was recognized in an opinion by Justice Story to be part of the common law of the United States, and has endured through two centuries in all the States. The constitutional phrase 'impartial jury' must surely take its content from this unbroken tradition. * * *

"The rule we announce today is not only the only plausible reading of the text of the Sixth Amendment, but we think it best furthers the Amendment's central purpose as well. Although the constitutional guarantee runs only to the individual and not to the State, the goal it expresses is jury impartiality with respect to both contestants: neither the defendant nor the State should be favored. This goal, it seems to us, would positively be obstructed by a petit jury cross section requirement which, as we have described, would cripple the device of peremptory challenge."

Marshall, J., dissenting, argued that "the purposes of the cross-section requirement [as stated in *Taylor,* 7th ed., p. 1300] cannot be served unless prosecutors are precluded from exercising racially motivated peremptory challenges of prospective jurors."

7th ed., p. 1330; in lieu of Note 7, add:

7. In HOLLAND v. ILLINOIS, Supp. p. 53, itself *not* a *Batson* equal protection case, five members of the Court (the four dissenters and Kennedy, J., concurring) expressed the view that a defendant's race is irrelevant to his standing to raise the equal protection claim. As KENNEDY, J., explained:

"Many of the concerns expressed in *Batson,* a case where a black defendant objected to the exclusion of black jurors, support as well an equal protection claim by a defendant whose race or ethnicity is different from the dismissed juror's. To bar the claim whenever the defendant's race is not the same as the juror's would be to concede that racial exclusion of citizens from

the duty, and honor, of jury service will be tolerated, or even condoned. We cannot permit even the inference that this principle will be accepted, for it is inconsistent with the equal participation in civic life that the Fourteenth Amendment guarantees. I see no obvious reason to conclude that a defendant's race should deprive him of standing in his own trial to vindicate his own jurors' right to sit. * * *

"Support can be drawn also from our established rules of standing, given the premise that a juror's right to equal protection is violated when he is excluded because of his race. Individual jurors subjected to peremptory racial exclusion have the legal right to bring suit on their own behalf, but as a practical matter this sort of challenge is most unlikely. The reality is that a juror dismissed because of his race will leave the courtroom with a lasting sense of exclusion from the experience of jury participation, but possessing little incentive or resources to set in motion the arduous process needed to vindicate his own rights. We have noted that a substantial relation may entitle one party to raise the rights of another. An important bond of this type links the accused and an excluded juror. In sum, the availability of a Fourteenth Amendment claim by a defendant not of the same race as the excluded juror is foreclosed neither by today's decision, nor by *Batson.*

"*Batson* did contain language indicating that the peremptory challenge of jurors of the same race as the defendant presents a different situation from the peremptory challenge of jurors of another race, but I consider the significance of the discussion to be procedural. An explicit part of the evidentiary scheme adopted in *Batson* was the defendant's showing that he was a member of a 'cognizable racial group,' and that the excluded juror was a member of the same group. The structure of this scheme rests upon grounds for suspicion where the prosecutor uses his strikes to exclude jurors whose only connection with the defendant is the irrelevant factor of race. It is reasonable in this context to suspect the presence of an illicit motivation, the 'belief that blacks could not fairly try a black defendant.' (White, J., concurring). Where this obvious ground for suspicion is absent, different methods of proof may be appropriate."

7th ed., p. 1331; before Note 11, add:

10(a). Can a racial reason for exclusion ever have a "neutral explanation"? Compare *Minniefield v. State,* 539 N.E.2d 464 (Ind.1989) (striking black veniremen because prosecution's evidence would of necessity reveal that victim enjoyed racist jokes not a neutral explanation, as "race-based use of peremptory challenges * * *, even if allegedly dictated by strategic considerations, is a *per se* violation of the equal protection clause"); with *People v. Hernandez,* 552 N.E.2d 621 (N.Y.1990) (striking Spanish-speaking prospective jurors who might not accept official translator's version of Spanish-speaking witnesses' testimony proper; dissent objects this "necessarily produces disparate impact on a single ethnic group").

Chapter 25

THE CRIMINAL TRIAL

SECTION 2. PRESENCE OF THE DEFENDANT

7th ed., p. 1371, end of fn. b, add:

In *Maryland v. Craig* ___ U.S. ___, 110 S.Ct. 3157, ___ L.Ed.2d ___ (1990), the Court responded to the issue left open in *Coy*, and in an opinion by Justice O'Connor, adopted the position suggested by her *Coy* concurrence. The *Craig* majority upheld a statutory procedure that allows the use of one-way closed circuit television to provide the testimony of a child witness who is alleged to be the victim of child abuse (in *Craig*, the testimony of a six-year-old alleged to have been sexually abused by defendant while attending her preschool center). Use of the televised testimony is conditioned on the trial court first determining, after a factfinding hearing, that requiring the child to give courtroom testimony would result, because of the presence of the defendant, in the child "suffering serious emotion distress, such that the child cannot reasonably communicate." The Court ruled that the state interest in protecting the child from trauma caused by defendant's physical presence, "at least where such trauma would impair the child's ability to communicate," as supported by a case-specific finding of necessity, justified dispensing with element of face-to-face confrontation. It stressed that all other elements of confrontation—oath, cross-examination by defense counsel present in the room in which the child testified (with defendant in electronic communication with counsel), and observation of demeanor by the judge and jury (who remained in the courtroom)—would be preserved. Justice Scalia, in a dissent joined by Justices Brennan, Marshall, and Stevens, characterized the Court's ruling as a "subordination of explicit constitutional text to currently favored public policy."

Part Five

APPEALS, POST–CONVICTION REVIEW

Chapter 28

HABEAS CORPUS AND RELATED COLLATERAL REMEDIES

SECTION 1. ISSUES COGNIZABLE

7th ed., p. 1555; end of Note 1, add:

In *Saffle v. Parks,* ___ U.S. ___, 110 S.Ct. 1257, 108 L.Ed.2d 415 (1990), the four Justices in the plurality in *Teague* were joined by Justice White in applying Teague to reject consideration of a habeas claim deemed to require creation of a "new rule." The majority noted that, under *Teague,* it could "neither announce nor apply the new rule sought by [habeas petitioner] Parks unless it would fall into one of two narrow exceptions." The majority also looked to Justice O'Connor's plurality opinion in *Teague* in defining those exceptions and in determining that the habeas petitioner's claim would rest on a new rule. [a] In both *Saffle* and *Butler v. McKellar* [Note 3 infra], Justices Marshall, Blackmun, and Stevens joined a dissent by Justice Brennan claiming that the majority had erred in characterizing the habeas petitioner's claim as resting on a "new rule."

a. In *Collins v. Youngblood,* ___ U.S. ___, 110 S.Ct. 1316, 108 L.Ed.2d 492 (1990), the Court noted: "Although the *Teague* rule is grounded on important considerations of federal-state relations, we think it is not 'jurisdictional' in the sense that this Court, despite a limited grant of certiorari *must* raise and decide the issue *sua*

7th ed., p. 1556; end of Note 3, add:

In BUTLER v. McKELLAR, ___ U.S. ___, 110 S.Ct. 1212, 108 L.Ed.2d 347 (1990), a 5–4 Court held that the ruling in *Arizona v. Roberson* (7th ed., p. 512) was a new ruling under the *Teague* standard. The majority reasoned (per REHNQUIST, C.J.):

"The 'new rule' principle * * * validates reasonable, good faith interpretations of existing precedents made by state courts even though they are shown to be contrary to later decisions. Cf. *United States v. Leon* [7th ed., p. 124]. * * * According to [petitioner's] counsel, the opinion in *Roberson* showed that the Court believed Roberson's case to be within the 'logical compass' of *Edwards.* But the fact that a court says that its decision is within the 'logical compass' of an earlier decision, or indeed that it is 'controlled' by a prior decision, is not conclusive for purposes of deciding whether the current decision is a 'new rule' under *Teague.* Courts frequently

sponte." Where certiorari was granted to consider the merits of the defendant's claim, and the state failed to raise a *Teague* issue in its brief and expressly disclaimed reliance on *Teague* in oral argument, the Court decided the claim on the merits without deciding whether its adoption would constitute a "new rule."

view their decisions as being 'controlled' or 'governed' by prior opinions even when aware of reasonable contrary conclusions reached by other courts. In *Roberson,* for instance, the Court found *Edwards* controlling but acknowledged a significant difference of opinion on the part of several lower courts that had considered the question previously. That the outcome in *Roberson* was susceptible to debate among reasonable minds is evidenced further by the differing positions taken by the judges of the Courts of Appeals for the Fourth and Seventh Circuits. * * * It would not have been an illogical or even a grudging application of *Edwards* to decide that it did not extend to the facts of *Roberson.* We hold, therefore, that *Roberson* announced a 'new rule.' "

Justice BRENNAN, speaking for the four dissenters in *Butler,* found "perplexing" the majority's reliance on the "fact that the court below and several state courts had incorrectly predicted the outcome of *Roberson.*" It would be an "odd criterion for 'reasonableness' " to "suggest that a particular result is reasonable so long as a certain number of courts reach the same result," yet the majority had not otherwise indicated why "the lower court decisions foreshadowing the dissent's position in *Roberson,* though ultimately erroneous, were nevertheless 'reasonable.' " The end result of the majority's position, Justice Brennan contended, was to "limit [the] federal courts' habeas corpus function to reviewing state courts' legal analysis under the equivalent of a 'clearly erroneous' standard of review." The Court thus was departing from a fundamental feature of the retroactivity jurisprudence of Justice Harlan that "undergirds *Teague*"—the recognition that the state courts' obligation of "adjudication according to prevailing law demands that a court exhibit 'conceptual faithfulness' to the principles underlying prior precedents, not just 'decisional obedience' to precise holdings based upon their unique factual patterns."

7th ed., p. 1557, end of Note 4, add:

Consider also SAWYER v. SMITH, ___ U.S. ___, 110 S.Ct. 2822, ___ L.Ed.2d ___ (1990), holding that the ruling in *Caldwell v. Mississippi,* 472 U.S. 320, 105 S.Ct. 2633, 86 L.Ed.2d 231 (1985)—prohibiting imposition of a death sentence by a jury that had been led to the false belief that the responsibility for determining the appropriateness of the defendant's capital sentence rested with the appellate court—constituted a new rule under *Teague.* Justice KENNEDY's opinion for the Court noted:

"The second *Teague* exception applies to new 'watershed rules of criminal procedure' that are necessary to the fundamental fairness of the criminal proceeding. Petitioner here challenges the Court of Appeals' conclusion that *Caldwell* does not come within this exception. Petitioner contends that the second *Teague* exception should be read to include new rules of capital sentencing that 'preserve the accuracy and fairness of capital sentencing judgments.' But this test looks only to half of our definition of the second exception. * * * [It is] not enough under *Teague* to say that a new rule is aimed at improving the accuracy of trial. More is required. A rule that qualifies under this exception must not only improve accuracy, but also 'alter our understanding of the *bedrock procedural elements*' essential to the fairness of a proceeding. * * *

"At the time of petitioner's trial and appeal, the rule of *Donnelly* [7th ed., p. 1393] was in place to protect any defendant who could show that a prosecutor's remarks had in fact made a proceeding fundamentally unfair. * * * Petitioner has not contested the Court of Appeals' finding that he has no claim for relief under the *Donnelly* standard. And as the Court of Appeals stated: '[T]he only defendants who need to rely on *Caldwell* rather than *Donnelly* are those who must concede that the prosecutorial argument in their case was not so harmful as to render their sentencing trial "fundamentally unfair." ' * * * Rather than focusing on the prejudice to the defendant that must be shown to establish a *Donnelly* violation, our concern in *Caldwell* was with the 'unacceptable risk' that misleading remarks could affect the reliability of the sentence. *Caldwell* must therefore be read as providing an additional measure of protection against error, beyond that afforded by *Donnelly,* in the special context of capital sentencing. See *Darden v. Wainwright,* n. 15 [7th ed., p. 1393]. The *Caldwell* rule was designed as an enhancement of the accuracy of capital sentencing, a protection of systemic value for state and federal courts charged with reviewing capital proceedings. But given that it was added to an existing guarantee of due process protection against fundamental unfairness, we cannot say this systemic rule enhancing reliability is an 'absolute prerequisite to fundamental fairness,' of the type that may come within *Teague*'s second exception."

A dissent by MARSHALL, J. (joined in this part by Justices Brennan, Blackmun and Stevens) contended that: (i) "*Caldwell* did not create a new rule," and (ii) "even if *Caldwell* established a new rule, that rule nonetheless is available on federal habeas corpus because it is a rule 'without which the likelihood of an accurate [verdict] is seriously diminished, *Teague.*' " The dissent reasoned: "The majority's contrary conclusion rests on a misunderstanding of the relationship between *Caldwell* and *Donnelly.* * * * *Caldwell* is not, as the majority argues, 'an additional measure of protection against error, beyond that afforded by *Donnelly,* in the special text of capital sentencing.' This analysis erroneously presumes precisely what *Caldwell* denies, that 'focused, unambiguous, and strong,' prosecutorial arguments that mislead a jury about its sentencing role in the capital context can ever be deemed harmless. *Caldwell* rests on the view that *any* strong, uncorrected, and unequivocal prosecutorial argument minimizing the jury's sense of responsibility for its capital sentencing decision 'presents an intolerable danger that the jury will in fact choose to minimize the importance of its role.' *Caldwell* thus tells us that a capital trial in which the jury has been misled about its sentencing role is fundamentally unfair and therefore violates *Donnelly* as well."

Appendix A

SELECTED PROVISIONS OF THE UNITED STATES CONSTITUTION

ARTICLE I

Section 9. ＊ ＊ ＊

[2] The privilege of the Writ of Habeas Corpus shall not be suspended, unless when in Cases of Rebellion or Invasion the public Safety may require it.

[3] No Bill of Attainder or ex post facto Law shall be passed.

ARTICLE III

Section 1. The judicial Power of the United States, shall be vested in one supreme Court, and in such inferior Courts as the Congress may from time to time ordain and establish. The Judges, both of the supreme and inferior Courts, shall hold their Offices during good Behaviour, and shall, at stated Times, receive for their Services a Compensation, which shall not be diminished during their Continuance in Office.

Section 2. [1] The judicial Power shall extend to all Cases, in Law and Equity, arising under this Constitution, the Laws of the United States, and Treaties made, or which shall be made, under their Authority;—to all Cases affecting Ambassadors, other public Ministers and Consuls;—to all Cases of admiralty and maritime Jurisdiction;—to Controversies to which the United States shall be a Party;—to Controversies between two or more States;—between a State and Citizens of another State;—between Citizens of different States;—between Citizens of the same State claiming Lands under the Grants of different States, and between a State, or the Citizens thereof, and foreign States, Citizens or Subjects.

[3] The trial of all Crimes, except in Cases of Impeachment, shall be by Jury; and such Trial shall be held in the State where the said Crimes shall have been committed; but when not committed within any State, the Trial shall be at such Place or Places as the Congress may by Law have directed.

Section 3. [1] Treason against the United States, shall consist only in levying War against them, or, in adhering to their Enemies, giving them Aid and Comfort. No Person shall be convicted of Treason unless on the Testimony of two Witnesses to the same overt Act, or on Confession in open Court.

[2] The Congress shall have Power to declare the Punishment of Treason, but no Attainder of Treason shall work Corruption of Blood, or Forfeiture except during the Life of the Person attainted.

ARTICLE IV

Section 2. [1] The Citizens of each State shall be entitled to all Privileges and Immunities of Citizens in the several States.

[2] A Person charged in any State with Treason, Felony, or other Crime, who shall flee from Justice, and be found in another State, shall on demand of the executive Authority of the State from which he fled, be delivered up, to be removed to the State having Jurisdiction of the Crime.

60

ARTICLE VI

[2] This Constitution, and the Laws of the United States which shall be made in Pursuance thereof; and all Treaties made, or which shall be made, under the Authority of the United States, shall be the supreme Law.

AMENDMENT I [1791]

Congress shall make no law respecting an establishment of religion, or prohibiting the free exercise thereof; or abridging the freedom of speech, or of the press; or the right of the people peaceably to assemble, and to petition the Government for a redress of grievances.

AMENDMENT II [1791]

A well regulated Militia, being necessary to the security of a free State, the right of the people to keep and bear Arms, shall not be infringed.

AMENDMENT III [1791]

No Soldier shall, in time of peace be quartered in any house, without the consent of the Owner, nor in time of war, but in a manner to be prescribed by law.

AMENDMENT IV [1791]

The right of the people to be secure in their persons, houses, papers, and effects, against unreasonable searches and seizures, shall not be violated, and no Warrants shall issue, but upon probable cause, supported by Oath or affirmation, and particularly describing the place to be searched, and the persons or things to be seized.

AMENDMENT V [1791]

No person shall be held to answer for a capital, or otherwise infamous crime, unless on a presentment or indictment of a Grand Jury, except in cases arising in the land or naval forces, or in the Militia, when in actual service in time of War or public danger; nor shall any person be subject for the same offence to be twice put in jeopardy of life or limb; nor shall be compelled in any criminal case to be a witness against himself, nor be deprived of life, liberty, or property, without due process of law; nor shall private property be taken for public use, without just compensation.

AMENDMENT VI [1791]

In all criminal prosecutions, the accused shall enjoy the right to a speedy and public trial, by an impartial jury of the State and district wherein the crime shall have been committed, which district shall have been previously ascertained by law, and to be informed of the nature and cause of the accusation; to be confronted with the witnesses against him; to have compulsory process for obtaining witnesses in his favor, and to have the Assistance of Counsel for his defence.

AMENDMENT VII [1791]

In Suits at common law, where the value in controversy shall exceed twenty dollars, the right of trial by jury shall be preserved, and no fact tried by jury, shall be otherwise re-examined in any Court of the United States, than according to the rules of the common law.

AMENDMENT VIII [1791]

Excessive bail shall not be required, nor excessive fines imposed, nor cruel and unusual punishments inflicted.

AMENDMENT IX [1791]

The enumeration in the Constitution, of certain rights, shall not be construed to deny or disparage others retained by the people.

AMENDMENT X [1791]

The powers not delegated to the United States by the Constitution, nor prohibited by it to the States, are reserved to the States respectively, or to the people.

AMENDMENT XIII [1865]

Section 1. Neither slavery nor involuntary servitude, except as a punishment for crime whereof the party shall have been duly convicted, shall exist within the United States, or any place subject to their jurisdiction.

Section 2. Congress shall have power to enforce this article by appropriate legislation.

AMENDMENT XIV [1868]

Section 1. All persons born or naturalized in the United States, and subject to the jurisdiction thereof, are citizens of the United States and of the State wherein they reside. No State shall make or enforce any law which shall abridge the privileges or immunities of citizens of the United States; nor shall any State deprive any person of life, liberty, or property, without due process of law; nor deny to any person within its jurisdiction the equal protection of the laws.

Section 5. The Congress shall have power to enforce, by appropriate legislation, the provisions of the article.

AMENDMENT XV [1870]

Section 1. The right of citizens of the United States to vote shall not be denied or abridged by the United States or by any State on account of race, color, or previous condition of servitude.

Section 2. The Congress shall have power to enforce this article by appropriate legislation.

Appendix B

SELECTED FEDERAL STATUTORY PROVISIONS

Analysis

WIRE AND ELECTRONIC COMMUNICATIONS INTERCEPTION AND INTERCEPTION OF ORAL COMMUNICATIONS

(18 U.S.C. §§ 2510–2511, 2515–2518, 2520–2521).

§ 2510. Definitions

As used in this chapter—

(1) "wire communication" means any aural transfer made in whole or in part through the use of facilities for the transmission of communications by the aid of wire, cable, or other like connection between the point of origin and the point of reception (including the use of such connection in a switching station) furnished or operated by any person engaged in providing or operating such facilities for the transmission of interstate or foreign communications or communications affecting interstate or foreign commerce and such term includes any electronic storage of such communication, but such term does not include the radio portion of a cordless telephone communication that is transmitted between the cordless telephone handset and the base unit;

(2) "oral communication" means any oral communication uttered by a person exhibiting an expectation that such communication is not subject to interception under circumstances justifying such expectation, but such term does not include any electronic communication;

(3) "State" means any State of the United States, the District of Columbia, the Commonwealth of Puerto Rico, and any territory or possession of the United States;

(4) "intercept" means the aural or other acquisition of the contents of any wire, electronic, or oral communication through the use of any electronic, mechanical, or other device;

(5) "electronic, mechanical, or other device" means any device or apparatus which can be used to intercept a wire, oral, or electronic communication other than—

(a) any telephone or telegraph instrument, equipment or facility, or any component thereof, (i) furnished to the subscriber or user by a provider of wire or electronic communication service in the ordinary course of its business and being used by the subscriber or user in the ordinary course of its business or furnished by such subscriber or user for connection to the facilities of such service and used in the ordinary course of its business; or (ii) being used by a provider of wire or electronic communication service in the ordinary course of its business, or by an investigative or law enforcement officer in the ordinary course of his duties;

(b) a hearing aid or similar device being used to correct subnormal hearing to not better than normal;

(6) "person" means any employee, or agent of the United States or any State or political subdivision thereof, and any individual, partnership, association, joint stock company, trust, or corporation;

(7) "Investigative or law enforcement officer" means any officer of the United States or of a State or political subdivision thereof, who is empowered by law to conduct investigations of or to make arrests for offenses enumerated in this chapter, and any attorney authorized by law to prosecute or participate in the prosecution of such offenses;

(8) "contents", when used with respect to any wire, oral, or electronic communication, includes any information concerning the substance, purport, or meaning of that communication;

(9) "Judge of competent jurisdiction" means—

(a) a judge of a United States district court or a United States court of appeals; and

(b) a judge of any court of general criminal jurisdiction of a State who is authorized by a statute of that State to enter orders authorizing interceptions of wire, oral, or electronic communications;

(10) "communication common carrier" shall have the same meaning which is given the term "common carrier" by section 153(h) of title 47 of the United States Code;

(11) "aggrieved person" means a person who was a party to any intercepted wire, oral, or electronic communication or a person against whom the interception was directed;

(12) "electronic communication" means any transfer of signs, signals, writing, images, sounds, data, or intelligence of any nature transmitted in whole or in part by a wire, radio, electromagnetic, photoelectronic or photooptical system that affects interstate or foreign commerce, but does not include—

(A) the radio portion of a cordless telephone communication that is transmitted between the cordless telephone handset and the base unit;

(B) any wire or oral communication;

(C) any communication made through a tone-only paging device; or

(D) any communication from a tracking device (as defined in section 3117 of this title);

(13) "user" means any person or entity who—

(A) uses an electronic communication service; and

(B) is duly authorized by the provider of such service to engage in such use;

(14) "electronic communications system" means any wire, radio, electromagnetic, photooptical or photoelectronic facilities for the transmission of electronic communications, and any computer facilities or related electronic equipment for the electronic storage of such communications;

(15) "electronic communication service" means any service which provides to users thereof the ability to send or receive wire or electronic communications;

(16) "readily accessible to the general public" means, with respect to a radio communication, that such communication is not—

(A) scrambled or encrypted;

(B) transmitted using modulation techniques whose essential parameters have been withheld from the public with the intention of preserving the privacy of such communication;

(C) carried on a subcarrier or other signal subsidiary to a radio transmission;

(D) transmitted over a communication system provided by a common carrier, unless the communication is a tone only paging system communication; or

(E) transmitted on frequencies allocated under part 25, subpart D, E, or F of part 74, or part 94 of the Rules of the Federal Communications Commission, unless, in the case of a communication transmitted on a frequency allocated under part 74 that is not exclusively allocated to broadcast auxiliary services, the communication is a two-way voice communication by radio;

(17) "electronic storage" means—

(A) any temporary, intermediate storage of a wire or electronic communication incidental to the electronic transmission thereof; and

(B) any storage of such communication by an electronic communication service for purposes of backup protection of such communication; and

(18) "aural transfer" means a transfer containing the human voice at any point between and including the point of origin and the point of reception.

§ 2511. Interception and disclosure of wire, oral, or electronic communications prohibited

(1) Except as otherwise specifically provided in this chapter any person who—

(a) intentionally intercepts, endeavors to intercept, or procures any other person to intercept or endeavor to intercept, any wire, oral, or electronic communication;

(b) intentionally uses, endeavors to use, or procures any other person to use or endeavor to use any electronic, mechanical, or other device to intercept any oral communication when—

(i) such device is affixed to, or otherwise transmits a signal through, a wire, cable, or other like connection used in wire communication; or

(ii) such device transmits communications by radio, or interferes with the transmission of such communication; or

(iii) such person knows, or has reason to know, that such device or any component thereof has been sent through the mail or transported in interstate or foreign commerce; or

(iv) such use or endeavor to use (A) takes place on the premises of any business or other commercial establishment the operations of which affect interstate or foreign commerce; or (B) obtains or is for the purpose of obtaining information relating to the operations of any business or other commercial establishment the operations of which affect interstate or foreign commerce; or

(v) such person acts in the District of Columbia, the Commonwealth of Puerto Rico, or any territory or possession of the United States;

(c) intentionally discloses, or endeavors to disclose, to any other person the contents of any wire, oral, or electronic communication, knowing or having reason to know that the information was obtained through the interception of a wire, oral, or electronic communication in violation of this subsection; or

(d) intentionally uses, or endeavors to use, the contents of any wire, oral, or electronic communication, knowing or having reason to know that the information was obtained through the interception of a wire, oral, or electronic communication in violation of this subsection;

shall be punished as provided in subsection (4) or shall be subject to suit as provided in subsection (5).

(2)(a)(i) It shall not be unlawful under this chapter for an operator of a switchboard, or an officer, employee, or agent of a provider of wire or electronic communication service, whose facilities are used in the transmission of a wire communication, to intercept, disclose, or use that communication in the normal course of his employment while engaged in any activity which is a necessary incident to the rendition of his service or to the protection of the rights or property of the provider of that service, except that a provider of wire communication service to the public shall not utilize service observing or random monitoring except for mechanical or service quality control checks.

(ii) Notwithstanding any other law, providers of wire or electronic communication service, their officers, employees, and agents, landlords, custodians, or other persons, are authorized to provide information, facilities, or technical assistance to persons authorized by law to intercept wire, oral, or electronic communications or to conduct electronic surveillance, as defined in section 101 of the Foreign Intelligence Surveillance Act of 1978, if such provider, its officers, employees, or agents, landlord, custodian, or other specified person, has been provided with—

(A) a court order directing such assistance signed by the authorizing judge, or

(B) a certification in writing by a person specified in section 2518(7) of this title or the Attorney General of the United States that no warrant or court order is required by law, that all statutory requirements have been met, and that the specified assistance is required,

setting forth the period of time during which the provision of the information, facilities, or technical assistance is authorized and specifying the information, facilities, or technical assistance required. No provider of wire or electronic communication service, officer, employee, or agent thereof, or landlord, custodian, or other specified person shall disclose the existence of any interception or surveillance or the device used to accomplish the interception or surveillance with respect to which the person has been furnished a court order or certification under this chapter except as may otherwise be required by legal process and then only after prior notification to the Attorney General or to the principal prosecuting attorney of a State or any political subdivision of a State, as may be appropriate. Any such disclosure, shall render such person liable for the civil damages provided for in section 2520. No cause of action shall lie in any court against any provider of wire or electronic communication service, its officers, employees, or agents, landlord, custodian, or other specified person for providing information, facilities, or assistance in accordance with the terms of an order or certification under this subpar.

(b) It shall not be unlawful under this chapter for an officer, employee, or agent of the Federal Communications Commission, in the normal course of his employment and in discharge of the monitoring responsibilities exercised by the Commission in the enforcement of chapter 5 of title 47 of the United States Code, to intercept a wire or electronic communication, or oral communication transmitted by radio, or to disclose or use the information thereby obtained.

(c) It shall not be unlawful under this chapter for a person acting under color of law to intercept a wire, oral, or electronic communication, where such person is a party to the communication or one of the parties to the communication has given prior consent to such interception.

(d) It shall not be unlawful under this chapter for a person not acting under color of law to intercept a wire, oral, or electronic communication where such person is a party to the communication or where one of the parties to the communication has given prior consent to such interception unless such communication is intercepted for the purpose of committing any criminal or tortious act in violation of the Constitution or laws of the United States or of any State.

(e) Notwithstanding any other provision of this title or section 705 or 706 of the Communications Act of 1934, it shall not be unlawful for an officer, employee, or agent of the United States in the normal course of his official duty to conduct electronic surveillance, as defined in section 101 of the Foreign Intelligence Surveillance Act of 1978, as authorized by that Act.

(f) Nothing contained in this chapter or chapter 121, or section 705 of the Communications Act of 1934, shall be deemed to affect the acquisition by the United States Government of foreign intelligence information from international or foreign communications, or foreign intelligence activities conducted in accordance with otherwise applicable Federal law involving a foreign electronic communications system, utilizing a means other than electronic surveillance as defined in section 101 of the Foreign Intelligence Surveillance Act of 1978, and procedures in this chapter and the Foreign Intelligence Surveillance Act of 1978 shall be the exclusive means by which electronic surveillance, as defined in section 101 of such Act, and the interception of domestic wire and oral communications may be conducted.

(g) It shall not be unlawful under this chapter or chapter 121 of this title for any person—

(i) to intercept or access an electronic communication made through an electronic communication system that is configured so that such electronic communication is readily accessible to the general public;

(ii) to intercept any radio communication which is transmitted—

(I) by any station for the use of the general public, or that relates to ships, aircraft, vehicles, or persons in distress;

(II) by any governmental, law enforcement, civil defense, private land mobile, or public safety communications system, including police and fire, readily accessible to the general public;

(III) by a station operating on an authorized frequency within the bands allocated to the amateur, citizens band, or general mobile radio services; or

(IV) by any marine or aeronautical communications system;

(iii) to engage in any conduct which—

(I) is prohibited by section 633 of the Communications Act of 1934; or

(II) is excepted from the application of section 705(a) of the Communications Act of 1934 by section 705(b) of that Act;

(iv) to intercept any wire or electronic communication the transmission of which is causing harmful interference to any lawfully operating station or consumer electronic equipment, to the extent necessary to identify the source of such interference; or

(v) for other users of the same frequency to intercept any radio communication made through a system that utilizes frequencies monitored by individuals engaged in the provision or the use of such system, if such communication is not scrambled or encrypted.

(h) It shall not be unlawful under this chapter—

(i) to use a pen register or a trap and trace device (as those terms are defined for the purposes of chapter 206 (relating to pen registers and trap and trace devices) of this title); or

(ii) for a provider of electronic communication service to record the fact that a wire or electronic communication was initiated or completed in order to protect such provider, another provider furnishing service toward the completion of the wire or electronic communication, or a user of that service, from fraudulent, unlawful or abusive use of such service.

(3)(a) Except as provided in paragraph (b) of this subsection, a person or entity providing an electronic communication service to the public shall not intentionally divulge the contents of any communication (other than one to such person or entity, or an agent thereof) while in transmission on that service to any person or entity other than an addressee or intended recipient of such communication or an agent of such addressee or intended recipient.

(b) A person or entity providing electronic communication service to the public may divulge the contents of any such communication—

(i) as otherwise authorized in section 2511(2)(a) or 2517 of this title;

(ii) with the lawful consent of the originator or any addressee or intended recipient of such communication;

(iii) to a person employed or authorized, or whose facilities are used, to forward such communication to its destination; or

(iv) which were inadvertently obtained by the service provider and which appear to pertain to the commission of a crime, if such divulgence is made to a law enforcement agency.

(4)(a) Except as provided in paragraph (b) of this subsection or in subsection (5), whoever violates subsection (1) of this section shall be fined under this title or imprisoned not more than five years, or both.

(b) If the offense is a first offense under paragraph (a) of this subsection and is not for a tortious or illegal purpose or for purposes of direct or indirect commercial advantage or private commercial gain, and the wire or electronic communication with respect to which the offense under paragraph (a) is a radio communication that is not scrambled or encrypted, then—

(i) if the communication is not the radio portion of a cellular telephone communication, a public land mobile radio service communication or a paging service communication, and the conduct is not that described in subsection (5), the offender shall be fined under this title or imprisoned not more than one year or both; and

(ii) if the communication is the radio portion of a cellular telephone communication, a public land mobile radio service communication or a paging service communication, the offender shall be fined not more than $500.

(c) Conduct otherwise an offense under this subsection that consists of or relates to the interception of a satellite transmission that is not encrypted or scrambled and that is transmitted—

(i) to a broadcasting station for purposes of retransmission to the general public; or

(ii) as an audio subcarrier intended for redistribution to facilities open to the public, but not including data transmissions or telephone calls,

is not an offense under this subsection unless the conduct is for the purposes of direct or indirect commercial advantage or private financial gain.

(5)(a)(i) If the communication is—

(A) a private satellite video communication that is not scrambled or encrypted and the conduct in violation of this chapter is the private viewing of that communication and is not for a tortious or illegal purpose or for purposes of direct or indirect commercial advantage or private commercial gain; or

(B) a radio communication that is transmitted on frequencies allocated under subpart D of part 74 of the rules of the Federal Communications Commission that is not scrambled or encrypted and the conduct in violation of this chapter is not for a tortious or illegal purpose or for purposes of direct or indirect commercial advantage or private commercial gain,

then the person who engages in such conduct shall be subject to suit by the Federal Government in a court of competent jurisdiction.

(ii) In an action under this subsection—

(A) if the violation of this chapter is a first offense for the person under paragraph (a) of subsection (4) and such person has not been found liable in a civil action under section 2520 of this title, the Federal Government shall be entitled to appropriate injunctive relief; and

(B) if the violation of this chapter is a second or subsequent offense under paragraph (a) of subsection (4) or such person has been found liable in any prior civil action under section 2520, the person shall be subject to a mandatory $500 civil fine.

(b) The court may use any means within its authority to enforce an injunction issued under paragraph (ii)(A), and shall impose a civil fine of not less than $500 for each violation of such an injunction.

§ 2515. Prohibition of use as evidence of intercepted wire or oral communications

Whenever any wire or oral communication has been intercepted, no part of the contents of such communication and no evidence derived therefrom may be received in evidence in any trial, hearing, or other proceeding in or before any court, grand jury, department, officer, agency, regulatory body, legislative committee, or other authority of the United States, a State, or a political subdivision thereof if the disclosure of that information would be in violation of this chapter.

§ 2516. Authorization for interception of wire, oral, or electronic communications

(1) The Attorney General, Deputy Attorney General, Associate Attorney General, any Assistant Attorney General, any acting Assistant Attorney General, or any Deputy Assistant Attorney General in the Criminal Division specially designated by the Attorney General, may authorize an application to a Federal judge of competent jurisdiction for, and such judge may grant in conformity with section 2518 of this chapter an order authorizing or approving the interception of wire or oral communications by the Federal Bureau of Investigation, or a Federal agency having responsibility for the investigation of the offense as to which the application is made, when such interception may provide or has provided evidence of—

(a) any offense punishable by death or by imprisonment for more than one year under sections 2274 through 2277 of title 42 of the United States Code (relating to the enforcement of the Atomic Energy Act of 1954), section 2284 of title 42 of the

United States Code (relating to sabotage of nuclear facilities or fuel), or under the following chapters of this title: chapter 37 (relating to espionage), chapter 105 (relating to sabotage), chapter 115 (relating to treason), chapter 102 (relating to riots); chapter 65 (relating to malicious mischief), chapter 111 (relating to destruction of vessels), or chapter 81 (relating to piracy);

(b) a violation of section 186 or section 501(c) of title 29, United States Code (dealing with restrictions on payments and loans to labor organizations), or any offense which involves murder, kidnapping, robbery, or extortion, and which is punishable under this title;

(c) any offense which is punishable under the following sections of this title: section 201 (bribery of public officials and witnesses), section 224 (bribery in sporting contests), subsection (d), (e), (f), (g), (h), or (i) of section 844 (unlawful use of explosives), section 1084 (transmission of wagering information), section 751 (relating to escape), sections 1503, 1512, and 1513 (influencing or injuring an officer, juror, or witness generally), section 1510 (obstruction of criminal investigations), section 1511 (obstruction of State or local law enforcement), section 1751 (Presidential and Presidential staff assassination, kidnaping, and assault), section 1951 (interference with commerce by threats or violence), section 1952 (interstate and foreign travel or transportation in aid of racketeering enterprises), section 1952A (relating to use of interstate commerce facilities in the commission of murder for hire), section 1952B (relating to violent crimes in aid of racketeering activity), section 1954 (offer, acceptance, or solicitation to influence operations of employee benefit plan), section 1955 (prohibition of business enterprises of gambling), section 1956 (laundering of monetary instruments), section 1957 (relating to engaging in monetary transactions in property derived from specified unlawful activity), section 659 (theft from interstate shipment), section 664 (embezzlement from pension and welfare funds), section 1343 (fraud by wire, radio, or television), sections 2251 and 2252 (sexual exploitation of children), sections 2312, 2313, 2314, and 2315 (interstate transportation of stolen property), the second section 2320 (relating to trafficking in certain motor vehicles or motor vehicle parts), section 1203 (relating to hostage taking), section 1029 (relating to fraud and related activity in connection with access devices), section 3146 (relating to penalty for failure to appear), section 3521(b)(3) (relating to witness relocation and assistance), section 32 (relating to destruction of aircraft or aircraft facilities), section 1963 (violations with respect to racketeer influenced and corrupt organizations), section 115 (relating to threatening or retaliating against a Federal official), the section in chapter 65 (relating to destruction of an energy facility), and section 1341 (relating to mail fraud), section 351 (violations with respect to congressional, Cabinet, or Supreme Court assassinations, kidnaping, and assault), section 831 (relating to prohibited transactions involving nuclear materials), section 33 (relating to destruction of motor vehicles or motor vehicle facilities), or section 1992 (relating to wrecking trains);

(d) any offense involving counterfeiting punishable under section 471, 472, or 473 of this title;

(e) any offense involving fraud connected with a case under title 11 or the manufacture, importation, receiving, concealment, buying, selling, or otherwise dealing in narcotic drugs, marihuana, or other dangerous drugs, punishable under any law of the United States;

(f) any offense including extortionate credit transactions under sections 892, 893, or 894 of this title;

(g) a violation of section 5322 of title 31, United States Code (dealing with the reporting of currency transactions);

(h) any felony violation of sections 2511 and 2512 (relating to interception and disclosure of certain communications and to certain intercepting devices) of this title;

(i) any felony violation of chapter 71 (relating to obscenity) of this title;

(j) any violation of section 1679a(c)(2) (relating to destruction of a natural gas pipeline) or subsection (i) or (n) of section 1472 (relating to aircraft piracy) of title 49, of the United States Code;

(k) any criminal violation of section 2778 of title 22 (relating to the Arms Export Control Act);

(*l*) the location of any fugitive from justice from an offense described in this section; or

(m) any conspiracy to commit any of the foregoing offenses.

(m) [1] any felony violation of sections 922 and 924 of title 18, United States Code (relating to firearms); and

(n) any violation of section 5861 of the Internal Revenue Code of 1986 (relating to firearms).

(2) The principal prosecuting attorney of any State, or the principal prosecuting attorney of any political subdivision thereof, if such attorney is authorized by a statute of that State to make application to a State court judge of competent jurisdiction for an order authorizing or approving the interception of wire, oral, or electronic communications, may apply to such judge for, and such judge may grant in conformity with section 2518 of this chapter and with the applicable State statute an order authorizing, or approving the interception of wire, oral, or electronic communications by investigative or law enforcement officers having responsibility for the investigation of the offense as to which the application is made, when such interception may provide or has provided evidence of the commission of the offense of murder, kidnapping, gambling, robbery, bribery, extortion, or dealing in narcotic drugs, marihuana or other dangerous drugs, or other crime dangerous to life, limb, or property, and punishable by imprisonment for more than one year, designated in any applicable State statute authorizing such interception, or any conspiracy to commit any of the foregoing offenses.

(3) Any attorney for the Government (as such term is defined for the purposes of the Federal Rules of Criminal Procedure) may authorize an application to a Federal judge of competent jurisdiction for, and such judge may grant, in conformity with section 2518 of this title, an order authorizing or approving the interception of electronic communications by an investigative or law enforcement officer having responsibility for the investigation of the offense as to which the application is made, when such interception may provide or has provided evidence of any Federal felony.

§ 2517. Authorization for disclosure and use of intercepted wire, oral, or electronic communications

(1) Any investigative or law enforcement officer who, by any means authorized by this chapter, has obtained knowledge of the contents of any wire, oral, or electronic communication, or evidence derived therefrom, may disclose such contents to another investigative or law enforcement officer to the extent that such disclosure is appropriate to the proper performance of the official duties of the officer making or receiving the disclosure.

(2) Any investigative or law enforcement officer who, by any means authorized by this chapter, has obtained knowledge of the contents of any wire, oral, or electronic

[1] So in original.

communication or evidence derived therefrom may use such contents to the extent such use is appropriate to the proper performance of his official duties.

(3) Any person who has received, by any means authorized by this chapter, any information concerning a wire, oral, or electronic communication, or evidence derived therefrom intercepted in accordance with the provisions of this chapter may disclose the contents of that communication or such derivative evidence while giving testimony under oath or affirmation in any proceeding held under the authority of the United States or of any State or political subdivision thereof.

(4) No otherwise privileged wire, oral, or electronic communication intercepted in accordance with, or in violation of, the provisions of this chapter shall lose its privileged character.

(5) When an investigative or law enforcement officer, while engaged in intercepting wire, oral, or electronic communications in the manner authorized herein, intercepts wire, oral, or electronic communications relating to offenses other than those specified in the order of authorization or approval, the contents thereof, and evidence derived therefrom, may be disclosed or used as provided in subsections (1) and (2) of this section. Such contents and any evidence derived therefrom may be used under subsection (3) of this section when authorized or approved by a judge of competent jurisdiction where such judge finds on subsequent application that the contents were otherwise intercepted in accordance with the provisions of this chapter. Such application shall be made as soon as practicable.

§ 2518. Procedure for interception of wire, oral, or electronic communications

(1) Each application for an order authorizing or approving the interception of a wire, oral, or electronic communication under this chapter shall be made in writing upon oath or affirmation to a judge of competent jurisdiction and shall state the applicant's authority to make such application. Each application shall include the following information:

(a) the identity of the investigative or law enforcement officer making the application, and the officer authorizing the application;

(b) a full and complete statement of the facts and circumstances relied upon by the applicant, to justify his belief that an order should be issued, including (i) details as to the particular offense that has been, is being, is about to be committed, (ii) except as provided in subsection (11), a particular description of the nature and location of the facilities from which or the place where the communication is to be intercepted, (iii) a particular description of the type of communications sought to be intercepted, (iv) the identity of the person, if known, committing the offense and whose communications are to be intercepted;

(c) a full and complete statement as to whether or not other investigative procedures have been tried and failed or why they reasonably appear to be unlikely to succeed if tried or to be too dangerous;

(d) a statement of the period of time for which the interception is required to be maintained. If the nature of the investigation is such that the authorization for interception should not automatically terminate when the described type of communication has been first obtained, a particular description of facts establishing probable cause to believe that additional communications of the same type will occur thereafter;

(e) a full and complete statement of the facts concerning all previous applications known to the individual authorizing and making the application, made to any judge for authorization to intercept, or for approval of interceptions of, wire, oral, or electronic communications involving any of the same persons, facilities or places specified in the application, and the action taken by the judge on each such application; and

(f) where the application is for the extension of an order, a statement setting forth the results thus far obtained from the interception, or a reasonable explanation of the failure to obtain such results.

(2) The judge may require the applicant to furnish additional testimony or documentary evidence in support of the application.

(3) Upon such application the judge may enter an ex parte order, as requested or as modified, authorizing or approving interception of wire, oral, or electronic communications within the territorial jurisdiction of the court in which the judge is sitting (and outside that jurisdiction but within the United States in the case of a mobile interception device authorized by a Federal court within such jurisdiction), if the judge determines on the basis of the facts submitted by the applicant that—

(a) there is probable cause for belief that an individual is committing, has committed, or is about to commit a particular offense enumerated in section 2516 of this chapter;

(b) there is probable cause for belief that particular communications concerning that offense will be obtained through such interception;

(c) normal investigative procedures have been tried and have failed or reasonably appear to be unlikely to succeed if tried or to be too dangerous;

(d) except as provided in subsection (11), there is probable cause for belief that the facilities from which, or the place where, the wire, oral, or electronic communications are to be intercepted are being used, or are about to be used, in connection with the commission of such offense, or are leased to, listed in the name of, or commonly used by such person.

(4) Each order authorizing or approving the interception of any wire, oral, or electronic communication under this chapter shall specify—

(a) the identity of the person, if known, whose communications are to be intercepted;

(b) the nature and location of the communications facilities as to which, or the place where, authority to intercept is granted;

(c) a particular description of the type of communication sought to be intercepted, and a statement of the particular offense to which it relates;

(d) the identity of the agency authorized to intercept the communications, and of the person authorizing the application; and

(e) the period of time during which such interception is authorized, including a statement as to whether or not the interception shall automatically terminate when the described communication has been first obtained.

An order authorizing the interception of a wire, oral, or electronic communication under this chapter shall, upon request of the applicant, direct that a provider of wire or electronic communication service, landlord, custodian or other person shall furnish the applicant forthwith all information, facilities, and technical assistance necessary to accomplish the interception unobtrusively and with a minimum of interference with the services that such service provider, landlord, custodian, or person is according the person whose communications are to be intercepted. Any provider of wire or electronic communication service, landlord, custodian or other person furnishing such facilities or technical assistance shall be compensated therefor by the applicant for reasonable expenses incurred in providing such facilities or assistance.

(5) No order entered under this section may authorize or approve the interception of any wire, oral, or electronic communication for any period longer than is necessary to achieve the objective of the authorization, nor in any event longer than thirty

days. Such thirty-day period begins on the earlier of the day on which the investigative or law enforcement officer first begins to conduct an interception under the order or ten days after the order is entered. Extensions of an order may be granted, but only upon application for an extension made in accordance with subsection (1) of this section and the court making the findings required by subsection (3) of this section. The period of extension shall be no longer than the authorizing judge deems necessary to achieve the purposes for which it was granted and in no event for longer than thirty days. Every order and extension thereof shall contain a provision that the authorization to intercept shall be executed as soon as practicable, shall be conducted in such a way as to minimize the interception of communications not otherwise subject to interception under this chapter, and must terminate upon attainment of the authorized objective, or in any event in thirty days. In the event the intercepted communication is in a code or foreign language, and an expert in that foreign language or code is not reasonably available during the interception period, minimization may be accomplished as soon as practicable after such interception. An interception under this chapter may be conducted in whole or in part by Government personnel, or by an individual operating under a contract with the Government, acting under the supervision of an investigative or law enforcement officer authorized to conduct the interception.

(6) Whenever an order authorizing interception is entered pursuant to this chapter,. the order may require reports to be made to the judge who issued the order showing what progress has been made toward achievement of the authorized objective and the need for continued interception. Such reports shall be made at such intervals as the judge may require.

(7) Notwithstanding any other provision of this chapter, any investigative or law enforcement officer, specially designated by the Attorney General, the Deputy Attorney General, the Associate Attorney General or by the principal prosecuting attorney of any State or subdivision thereof acting pursuant to a statute of that State, who reasonably determines that—

(a) an emergency situation exists that involves—

(i) immediate danger of death or serious physical injury to any person,

(ii) conspiratorial activities threatening the national security interest, or

(iii) conspiratorial activities characteristic of organized crime,

that requires a wire, oral, or electronic communication to be intercepted before an order authorizing such interception can, with due diligence, be obtained, and

(b) there are grounds upon which an order could be entered under this chapter to authorize such interception,

may intercept such wire, oral, or electronic communication if an application for an order approving the interception is made in accordance with this section within forty-eight hours after the interception has occurred, or begins to occur. In the absence of an order, such interception shall immediately terminate when the communication sought is obtained or when the application for the order is denied, whichever is earlier. In the event such application for approval is denied, or in any other case where the interception is terminated without an order having been issued, the contents of any wire, oral, or electronic communication intercepted shall be treated as having been obtained in violation of this chapter, and an inventory shall be served as provided for in subsection (d) of this section on the person named in the application.

(8)(a) The contents of any wire, oral, or electronic communication intercepted by any means authorized by this chapter shall, if possible, be recorded on tape or wire or other comparable device. The recording of the contents of any wire, oral or electronic communication under this subsection shall be done in such way as will protect the recording from editing or other alterations. Immediately upon the expiration of the period of the order, or extensions thereof, such recordings shall be made available to the judge issuing such order and sealed under his directions. Custody of the recordings shall be wherever the judge orders. They shall not be destroyed except upon an order of the issuing or denying judge and in any event shall be kept for ten years. Duplicate recordings may be made for use or disclosure pursuant to the provisions of subsections (1) and (2) of section 2517 of this chapter for investigations. The presence of the seal provided for by this subsection, or a satisfactory explanation for the absence thereof, shall be a prerequisite for the use or disclosure of the contents of any wire, oral, or electronic communication or evidence derived therefrom under subsection (3) of section 2517.

(b) Applications made and orders granted under this chapter shall be sealed by the judge. Custody of the applications and orders shall be wherever the judge directs. Such applications and orders shall be disclosed only upon a showing of good cause before a judge of competent jurisdiction and shall not be destroyed except on order of the issuing or denying judge, and in any event shall be kept for ten years.

(c) Any violation of the provisions of this subsection may be punished as contempt of the issuing or denying judge.

(d) Within a reasonable time but not later than ninety days after the filing of an application for an order of approval under section 2518(7)(b) which is denied or the termination of the period of an order or extensions thereof, the issuing or denying judge shall cause to be served, on the persons named in the order or the application, and such other parties to intercepted communications as the judge may determine in his discretion that is in the interest of justice, an inventory which shall include notice of—

(1) the fact of the entry of the order or the application;

(2) the date of the entry and the period of authorized, approved or disapproved interception, or the denial of the application; and

(3) the fact that during the period wire, oral or electronic communications were or were not intercepted.

The judge, upon the filing of a motion, may in his discretion make available to such person or his counsel for inspection such portions of the intercepted communications, applications and orders as the judge determines to be in the interest of justice. On an ex parte showing of good cause to a judge of competent jurisdiction the serving of the inventory required by this subsection may be postponed.

(9) The contents of any wire, oral, or electronic communication intercepted pursuant to this chapter or evidence derived therefrom shall not be received in evidence or otherwise disclosed in any trial, hearing, or other proceeding in a Federal or State court unless each party, not less than ten days before the trial, hearing, or proceeding, has been furnished with a copy of the court order, and accompanying application, under which the interception was authorized or approved. This ten-day period may be waived by the judge if he finds that it was not possible to furnish the party with the above information ten days before the trial, hearing, or proceeding and that the party will not be prejudiced by the delay in receiving such information.

(10)(a) Any aggrieved person in any trial, hearing, or proceeding in or before any court, department, officer, agency, regulatory body, or other authority of the United States, a State, or a political subdivision thereof, may move to suppress the contents of any wire or oral communication intercepted pursuant to this chapter, or evidence derived therefrom, on the grounds that—

(i) the communication was unlawfully intercepted;

(ii) the order of authorization or approval under which it was intercepted is insufficient on its face; or

(iii) the interception was not made in conformity with the order of authorization or approval.

Such motion shall be made before the trial, hearing, or proceeding unless there was no opportunity to make such motion or the person was not aware of the grounds of the motion. If the motion is granted, the contents of the intercepted wire or oral communication, or evidence derived therefrom, shall be treated as having been obtained in violation of this chapter. The judge, upon the filing of such motion by the aggrieved person, may in his discretion make available to the aggrieved person or his counsel for inspection such portions of the intercepted communication or evidence derived therefrom as the judge determines to be in the interests of justice.

(b) In addition to any other right to appeal, the United States shall have the right to appeal from an order granting a motion to suppress made under paragraph (a) of this subsection, or the denial of an application for an order of approval, if the United States attorney shall certify to the judge or other official granting such motion or denying such application that the appeal is not taken for purposes of delay. Such appeal shall be taken within thirty days after the date the order was entered and shall be diligently prosecuted.

(c) The remedies and sanctions described in this chapter with respect to the interception of electronic communications are the only judicial remedies and sanctions for nonconstitutional violations of this chapter involving such communications.

(11) The requirements of subsections (1)(b)(ii) and (3)(d) of this section relating to the specification of the facilities from which, or the place where, the communication is to be intercepted do not apply if—

(a) in the case of an application with respect to the interception of an oral communication—

(i) the application is by a Federal investigative or law enforcement officer and is approved by the Attorney General, the Deputy Attorney General, the Associate Attorney General, an Assistant Attorney General, or an acting Assistant Attorney General;

(ii) the application contains a full and complete statement as to why such specification is not practical and identifies the person committing the offense and whose communications are to be intercepted; and

(iii) the judge finds that such specification is not practical; and

(b) in the case of an application with respect to a wire or electronic communication—

(i) the application is by a Federal investigative or law enforcement officer and is approved by the Attorney General, the Deputy Attorney General, the Associate Attorney General, an Assistant Attorney General, or an acting Assistant Attorney General;

(ii) the application identifies the person believed to be committing the offense and whose communications are to be intercepted and the applicant makes a showing of a purpose, on the part of that person, to thwart interception by changing facilities; and

(iii) the judge finds that such purpose has been adequately shown.

(12) An interception of a communication under an order with respect to which the requirements of subsections (1)(b)(ii) and (3)(d) of this section do not apply by reason of subsection (11) shall not begin until the facilities from which, or the place where, the communication is to be intercepted is ascertained by the person implementing the interception order. A provider of wire or electronic communications service that has received an order as provided for in subsection (11)(b) may move the court to modify or quash the order on the ground that its assistance with respect to the

interception cannot be performed in a timely or reasonable fashion. The court, upon notice to the government, shall decide such a motion expeditiously.

§ 2520. Recovery of civil damages authorized

(a) **In general.**—Except as provided in section 2511(2)(a)(ii), any person whose wire, oral, or electronic communication is intercepted, disclosed, or intentionally used in violation of this chapter may in a civil action recover from the person or entity which engaged in that violation such relief as may be appropriate.

(b) **Relief.**—In an action under this section, appropriate relief includes—

(1) such preliminary and other equitable or declaratory relief as may be appropriate;

(2) damages under subsection (c) and punitive damages in appropriate cases; and

(3) a reasonable attorney's fee and other litigation costs reasonably incurred.

(c) **Computation of damages.**—(1) In an action under this section, if the conduct in violation of this chapter is the private viewing of a private satellite video communication that is not scrambled or encrypted or if the communication is a radio communication that is transmitted on frequencies allocated under subpart D of part 74 of the rules of the Federal Communications Commission that is not scrambled or encrypted and the conduct is not for a tortious or illegal purpose or for purposes of direct or indirect commercial advantage or private commercial gain, then the court shall assess damages as follows:

(A) If the person who engaged in that conduct has not previously been enjoined under section 2511(5) and has not been found liable in a prior civil action under this section, the court shall assess the greater of the sum of actual damages suffered by the plaintiff, or statutory damages of not less than $50 and not more than $500.

(B) If, on one prior occasion, the person who engaged in that conduct has been enjoined under section 2511(5) or has been found liable in a civil action under this section, the court shall assess the greater of the sum of actual damages suffered by the plaintiff, or statutory damages of not less than $100 and not more than $1000.

(2) In any other action under this section, the court may assess as damages whichever is the greater of—

(A) the sum of the actual damages suffered by the plaintiff and any profits made by the violator as a result of the violation; or

(B) statutory damages of whichever is the greater of $100 a day for each day of violation or $10,000.

(d) **Defense.**—A good faith reliance on—

(1) a court warrant or order, a grand jury subpoena, a legislative authorization, or a statutory authorization;

(2) a request of an investigative or law enforcement officer under section 2518(7) of this title; or

(3) a good faith determination that section 2511(3) of this title permitted the conduct complained of;

is a complete defense against any civil or criminal action brought under this chapter or any other law.

(e) **Limitation.**—A civil action under this section may not be commenced later than two years after the date upon which the claimant first has a reasonable opportunity to discover the violation.

§ 2521. Injunction against illegal interception

Whenever it shall appear that any person is engaged or is about to engage in any act which constitutes or will constitute a felony violation of this chapter, the Attorney General may initiate a civil action in a district court of the United States to enjoin such violation. The court shall proceed as soon as practicable to the hearing and determination of such an action, and may, at any time before final determination, enter such a restraining order or prohibition, or take such other action, as is warranted to prevent a continuing and substantial injury to the United States or to any person or class of persons for whose protection the action is brought. A proceeding under this section is governed by the Federal Rules of Civil Procedure, except that, if an indictment has been returned against the respondent, discovery is governed by the Federal Rules of Criminal Procedure.

CRIMINAL JUSTICE ACT

(18 U.S.C. § 3006A).

§ 3006A. Adequate representation of defendants

(a) **Choice of plan.**—Each United States district court, with the approval of the judicial council of the circuit, shall place in operation throughout the district a plan for furnishing representation for any person financially unable to obtain adequate representation in accordance with this section. Representation under each plan shall include counsel and investigative, expert, and other services necessary for adequate representation. Each plan shall provide the following:

(1) Representation shall be provided for any financially eligible person who—

(A) is charged with a felony or a Class A misdemeanor;

(B) is a juvenile alleged to have committed an act of juvenile delinquency as defined in section 5031 of this title;

(C) is charged with a violation of probation;

(D) is under arrest, when such representation is required by law;

(E) is charged with a violation of supervised release or faces modification, reduction, or enlargement of a condition, or extension or revocation of a term of supervised release;

(F) is subject to a mental condition hearing under chapter 313 of this title;

(G) is in custody as a material witness;

(H) is entitled to appointment of counsel under the sixth amendment to the Constitution; or

(I) faces loss of liberty in a case, and Federal law requires the appointment of counsel; or

(J) is entitled to the appointment of counsel under section 4019 of this title.

(2) Whenever the United States magistrate or the court determines that the interests of justice so require, representation may be provided for any financially eligible person who—

(A) is charged with a Class B or C misdemeanor, or an infraction for which a sentence to confinement is authorized; or

(B) is seeking relief under section 2241, 2254, or 2255 of title 28.

(3) Private attorneys shall be appointed in a substantial proportion of the cases. Each plan may include, in addition to the provisions for private attorneys, either of the following or both:

(A) Attorneys furnished by a bar association or a legal aid agency.

(B) Attorneys furnished by a defender organization established in accordance with the provisions of subsection (g).

Prior to approving the plan for a district, the judicial council of the circuit shall supplement the plan with provisions for representation on appeal. The district court may modify the plan at any time with the approval of the judicial council of the circuit. It shall modify the plan when directed by the judicial council of the circuit. The district court shall notify the Administrative Office of the United States Courts of any modification of its plan.

(b) Appointment of counsel.—Counsel furnishing representation under the plan shall be selected from a panel of attorneys designated or approved by the court, or from a bar association, legal aid agency, or defender organization furnishing representation pursuant to the plan. In every case in which a person entitled to representation under a plan approved under subsection (a) appears without counsel, the United States magistrate or the court shall advise the person that he has the right to be represented by counsel and that counsel will be appointed to represent him if he is financially unable to obtain counsel. Unless the person waives representation by counsel, the United States magistrate or the court, if satisfied after appropriate inquiry that the person is financially unable to obtain counsel, shall appoint counsel to represent him. Such appointment may be made retroactive to include any representation furnished pursuant to the plan prior to appointment. The United States magistrate or the court shall appoint separate counsel for persons having interests that cannot properly be represented by the same counsel, or when other good cause is shown.

(c) Duration and substitution of appointments.—A person for whom counsel is appointed shall be represented at every stage of the proceedings from his initial appearance before the United States magistrate or the court through appeal, including ancillary matters appropriate to the proceedings. If at any time after the appointment of counsel the United States magistrate or the court finds that the person is financially able to obtain counsel or to make partial payment for the representation, it may terminate the appointment of counsel or authorize payment as provided in subsection (f), as the interests of justice may dictate. If at any stage of the proceedings, including an appeal, the United States magistrate or the court finds that the person is financially unable to pay counsel whom he had retained, it may appoint counsel as provided in subsection (b) and authorize payment as provided in subsection (d), as the interests of justice may dictate. The United States magistrate or the court may, in the interests of justice, substitute one appointed counsel for another at any stage of the proceedings.

(d) Payment for representation.—

(1) Hourly rate.—Any attorney appointed pursuant to this section or a bar association or legal aid agency or community defender organization which has provided the appointed attorney shall, at the conclusion of the representation or any segment thereof, be compensated at a rate not exceeding $60 per hour for time expended in court or before a United States magistrate and $40 per hour for time reasonably expended out of court, unless the Judicial Conference determines that a higher rate of not in excess of $75 per hour is justified for a circuit or for particular districts within a circuit, for time expended in court or before a United States magistrate and for time expended out of court. The Judicial Conference shall develop guidelines for determining the maximum hourly rates for each circuit in accordance with the preceding sentence, with variations by district, where appropriate, taking into account such factors as the minimum range of the prevailing hourly rates for qualified attorneys in the district in which the representation is provided and the recommendations of the judicial councils of the circuits. Not less than 3 years after the effective date of the Criminal Justice Act Revision of 1986, the

Judicial Conference is authorized to raise the maximum hourly rates specified in this paragraph up to the aggregate of the overall average percentages of the adjustments in the rates of pay under the General Schedule made pursuant to section 5305 of title 5 on or after such effective date. After the rates are raised under the preceding sentence, such maximum hourly rates may be raised at intervals of not less than 1 year each, up to the aggregate of the overall average percentages of such adjustments made since the last raise was made under this paragraph. Attorneys shall be reimbursed for expenses reasonably incurred, including the costs of transcripts authorized by the United States magistrate or the court.

(2) **Maximum amounts.**—For representation of a defendant before the United States magistrate or the district court, or both, the compensation to be paid to an attorney or to a bar association or legal aid agency or community defender organization shall not exceed $3,500 for each attorney in a case in which one or more felonies are charged, and $1,000 for each attorney in a case in which only misdemeanors are charged. For representation of a defendant in an appellate court, the compensation to be paid to an attorney or to a bar association or legal aid agency or community defender organization shall not exceed $2,500 for each attorney in each court. For representation of an offender before the United States Parole Commission in a proceeding under section 4106A of this title, the compensation shall not exceed $750 for each attorney in each proceeding; for representation of an offender in an appeal from a determination of such Commission under such section, the compensation shall not exceed 2,500 for each attorney in each court. For any other representation required or authorized by this section, the compensation shall not exceed $750 for each attorney in each proceeding.

(3) **Waiving maximum amounts.**—Payment in excess of any maximum amount provided in paragraph (2) of this subsection may be made for extended or complex representation whenever the court in which the representation was rendered, or the United States magistrate if the representation was furnished exclusively before him, certifies that the amount of the excess payment is necessary to provide fair compensation and the payment is approved by the chief judge of the circuit. The chief judge of the circuit may delegate such approval authority to an active circuit judge.

(4) **Filing claims.**—A separate claim for compensation and reimbursement shall be made to the district court for representation before the United States magistrate and the court, and to each appellate court before which the attorney provided representation to the person involved. Each claim shall be supported by a sworn written statement specifying the time expended, services rendered, and expenses incurred while the case was pending before the United States magistrate and the court, and the compensation and reimbursement applied for or received in the same case from any other source. The court shall fix the compensation and reimbursement to be paid to the attorney or to the bar association or legal aid agency or community defender organization which provided the appointed attorney. In cases where representation is furnished exclusively before a United States magistrate, the claim shall be submitted to him and he shall fix the compensation and reimbursement to be paid. In cases where representation is furnished other than before the United States magistrate, the district court, or an appellate court, claims shall be submitted to the district court which shall fix the compensation and reimbursement to be paid.

(5) **New trials.**—For purposes of compensation and other payments authorized by this section, an order by a court granting a new trial shall be deemed to initiate a new case.

(6) **Proceedings before appellate courts.**—If a person for whom counsel is appointed under this section appeals to an appellate court or petitions for a writ of

certiorari, he may do so without prepayment of fees and costs or security therefor and without filing the affidavit required by section 1915(a) of title 28.

(e) Services other than counsel.—

(1) Upon request.—Counsel for a person who is financially unable to obtain investigative, expert, or other services necessary for an adequate representation may request them in an ex parte application. Upon finding, after appropriate inquiry in an ex parte proceeding, that the services are necessary and that the person is financially unable to obtain them, the court, or the United States magistrate if the services are required in connection with a matter over which he has jurisdiction, shall authorize counsel to obtain the services.

(2) Without prior request.—(A) Counsel appointed under this section may obtain, subject to later review, investigative, expert, and other services without prior authorization if necessary for adequate representation. Except as provided in subparagraph (B) of this paragraph, the total cost of services obtained without prior authorization may not exceed $300 and expenses reasonably incurred.

(B) The court, or the United States magistrate (if the services were rendered in a case disposed of entirely before the United States magistrate), may, in the interest of justice, and upon the finding that timely procurement of necessary services could not await prior authorization, approve payment for such services after they have been obtained, even if the cost of such services exceeds $300.

(3) Maximum amounts.—Compensation to be paid to a person for services rendered by him to a person under this subsection, or to be paid to an organization for services rendered by an employee thereof, shall not exceed $1,000, exclusive of reimbursement for expenses reasonably incurred, unless payment in excess of that limit is certified by the court, or by the United States magistrate if the services were rendered in connection with a case disposed of entirely before him, as necessary to provide fair compensation for services of an unusual character or duration, and the amount of the excess payment is approved by the chief judge of the circuit. The chief judge of the circuit may delegate such approval authority to an active circuit judge.

(f) Receipt of other payments.—Whenever the United States magistrate or the court finds that funds are available for payment from or on behalf of a person furnished representation, it may authorize or direct that such funds be paid to the appointed attorney, to the bar association or legal aid agency or community defender organization which provided the appointed attorney, to any person or organization authorized pursuant to subsection (e) to render investigative, expert, or other services, or to the court for deposit in the Treasury as a reimbursement to the appropriation, current at the time of payment, to carry out the provisions of this section. Except as so authorized or directed, no such person or organization may request or accept any payment or promise of payment for representing a defendant.

(g) Defender organization.—

(1) Qualifications.—A district or a part of a district in which at least two hundred persons annually require the appointment of counsel may establish a defender organization as provided for either under subparagraphs (A) or (B) of paragraph (2) of this subsection or both. Two adjacent districts or parts of districts may aggregate the number of persons required to be represented to establish eligibility for a defender organization to serve both areas. In the event that adjacent districts or parts of districts are located in different circuits, the plan for furnishing representation shall be approved by the judicial council of each circuit.

(2) Types of defender organizations.—

(A) Federal Public Defender Organization.—A Federal Public Defender Organization shall consist of one or more full-time salaried attorneys. An organization for a district or part of a district or two adjacent districts or parts of districts shall be supervised by a Federal Public Defender appointed by the court of appeals of the circuit, without regard to the provisions of title 5 governing appointments in the competitive service, after considering recommendations from the district court or courts to be served. Nothing contained herein shall be deemed to authorize more than one Federal Public Defender within a single judicial district. The Federal Public Defender shall be appointed for a term of four years, unless sooner removed by the court of appeals of the circuit for incompetency, misconduct in office, or neglect of duty. Upon the expiration of his term, a Federal Public Defender may, by a majority vote of the judges of the court of appeals, continue to perform the duties of his office until his successor is appointed, or until one year after the expiration of such Defender's term, whichever is earlier. The compensation of the Federal Public Defender shall be fixed by the court of appeals of the circuit at a rate not to exceed the compensation received by the United States attorney for the district where representation is furnished or, if two districts or parts of districts are involved, the compensation of the higher paid United States attorney of the districts. The Federal Public Defender may appoint, without regard to the provisions of title 5 governing appointments in the competitive service, full-time attorneys in such number as may be approved by the court of appeals of the circuit and other personnel in such number as may be approved by the Director of the Administrative Office of the United States Courts. Compensation paid to such attorneys and other personnel of the organization shall be fixed by the Federal Public Defender at a rate not to exceed that paid to attorneys and other personnel of similar qualifications and experience in the Office of the United States attorney in the district where representation is furnished or, if two districts or parts of districts are involved, the higher compensation paid to persons of similar qualifications and experience in the districts. Neither the Federal Public Defender nor any attorney so appointed by him may engage in the private practice of law. Each organization shall submit to the Director of the Administrative Office of the United States Courts, at the time and in the form prescribed by him, reports of its activities and financial position and its proposed budget. The Director of the Administrative Office shall submit, in accordance with section 605 of title 28, a budget for each organization for each fiscal year and shall out of the appropriations therefor make payments to and on behalf of each organization. Payments under this subparagraph to an organization shall be in lieu of payments under subsection (d) or (e).

(B) Community Defender Organization.—A Community Defender Organization shall be a nonprofit defense counsel service established and administered by any group authorized by the plan to provide representation. The organization shall be eligible to furnish attorneys and receive payments under this section if its bylaws are set forth in the plan of the district or districts in which it will serve. Each organization shall submit to the Judicial Conference of the United States an annual report setting forth its activities and financial position and the anticipated caseload and expenses for the next fiscal year. Upon application an organization may, to the extent approved by the Judicial Conference of the United States:

(i) receive an initial grant for expenses necessary to establish the organization; and

(ii) in lieu of payments under subsection (d) or (e), receive periodic sustaining grants to provide representation and other expenses pursuant to this section.

* * *

BAIL REFORM ACT OF 1984

(18 U.S.C. §§ 3141–3150).

§ 3141. Release and detention authority generally

(a) Pending Trial.—A judicial officer authorized to order the arrest of a person under section 3041 of this title before whom an arrested person is brought shall order that such person be released or detained, pending judicial proceedings, under this chapter.

(b) Pending sentence or appeal.—A judicial officer of a court of original jurisdiction over an offense, or a judicial officer of a Federal appellate court, shall order that, pending imposition or execution of sentence, or pending appeal of conviction or sentence, a person be released or detained under this chapter.

§ 3142. Release or detention of a defendant pending trial

(a) In general.—Upon the appearance before a judicial officer of a person charged with an offense, the judicial officer shall issue an order that, pending trial, the person be—

(1) released on his personal recognizance or upon execution of an unsecured appearance bond, under subsection (b) of this section;

(2) released on a condition or combination of conditions under subsection (c) of this section;

(3) temporarily detained to permit revocation of conditional release, deportation, or exclusion under subsection (d) of this section; or

(4) detained under subsection (e) of this section.

(b) Release on personal recognizance or unsecured appearance bond.—The judicial officer shall order the pretrial release of the person on personal recognizance, or upon execution of an unsecured appearance bond in an amount specified by the court, subject to the condition that the person not commit a Federal, State, or local crime during the period of release, unless the judicial officer determines that such release will not reasonably assure the appearance of the person as required or will endanger the safety of any other person or the community.

(c) Release on conditions.—(1) If the judicial officer determines that the release described in subsection (b) of this section will not reasonably assure the appearance of the person as required or will endanger the safety of any other person or the community, such judicial officer shall order the pretrial release of the person—

(A) subject to the condition that the person not commit a Federal, State, or local crime during the period of release; and

(B) subject to the least restrictive further condition, or combination of conditions, that such judicial officer determines will reasonably assure the appearance of the person as required and the safety of any other person and the community, which may include the condition that the person—

    (i) remain in the custody of a designated person, who agrees to assume supervision and to report any violation of a release condition to the court, if the designated person is able reasonably to assure the judicial officer that the person will appear as required and will not pose a danger to the safety of any other person or the community;

    (ii) maintain employment, or, if unemployed, actively seek employment;

    (iii) maintain or commence an educational program;

(iv) abide by specified restrictions on personal associations, place of abode, or travel;

(v) avoid all contact with an alleged victim of the crime and with a potential witness who may testify concerning the offense;

(vi) report on a regular basis to a designated law enforcement agency, pretrial services agency, or other agency;

(vii) comply with a specified curfew;

(viii) refrain from possessing a firearm, destructive device, or other dangerous weapon;

(ix) refrain from excessive use of alcohol, or any use of a narcotic drug or other controlled substance, as defined in section 102 of the Controlled Substances Act (21 U.S.C. 802), without a prescription by a licensed medical practitioner;

(x) undergo available medical or psychiatric treatment, including treatment for drug or alcohol dependency, and remain in a specified institution if required for that purpose;

(xi) execute an agreement to forfeit upon failing to appear as required, such designated property, including money, as is reasonably necessary to assure the appearance of the person as required, and post with the court such indicia of ownership of the property or such percentage of the money as the judicial officer may specify;

(xii) execute a bail bond with solvent sureties in such amount as is reasonably necessary to assure the appearance of the person as required;

(xiii) return to custody for specified hours following release for employment, schooling, or other limited purposes; and

(xiv) satisfy any other condition that is reasonably necessary to assure the appearance of the person as required and to assure the safety of any other person and the community.

(2) The judicial officer may not impose a financial condition that results in the pretrial detention of the person.

(3) The judicial officer may at any time amend the order to impose additional or different conditions of release.

(d) Temporary detention to permit revocation of conditional release, deportation, or exclusion.—If the judicial officer determines that—

(1) the person—

(A) is, and was at the time the offense was committed, on—

(i) release pending trial for a felony under Federal, State, or local law;

(ii) release pending imposition or execution of sentence, appeal of sentence or conviction, or completion of sentence, for any offense under Federal, State, or local law; or

(iii) probation or parole for any offense under Federal, State, or local law; or

(B) is not a citizen of the United States or lawfully admitted for permanent residence, as defined in section 101(a)(20) of the Immigration and Nationality Act (8 U.S.C. 1101(a)(20)); and

(2) the person may flee or pose a danger to any other person or the community; such judicial officer shall order the detention of the person, for a period of not more than ten days, excluding Saturdays, Sundays, and holidays, and direct the attorney for the Government to notify the appropriate court, probation or parole official, or State or local law enforcement official, or the appropriate official of the Immigration and Naturalization Service. If the official fails or declines to take the person into

custody during that period, the person shall be treated in accordance with the other provisions of this section, notwithstanding the applicability of other provisions of law governing release pending trial or deportation or exclusion proceedings. If temporary detention is sought under paragraph (1)(B) of this subsection, the person has the burden of proving to the court such person's United States citizenship or lawful admission for permanent residence.

(e) Detention.—If, after a hearing pursuant to the provisions of subsection (f) of this section, the judicial officer finds that no condition or combination of conditions will reasonably assure the appearance of the person as required and the safety of any other person and the community, such judicial officer shall order the detention of the person before trial. In a case described in (f)(1) of this section, a rebuttable presumption arises that no condition or combination of conditions will reasonably assure the safety of any other person and the community if such judicial officer finds that—

(1) the person has been convicted of a Federal offense that is described in subsection (f)(1) of this section, or of a State or local offense that would have been an offense described in subsection (f)(1) of this section if a circumstance giving rise to Federal jurisdiction had existed;

(2) the offense described in paragraph (1) of this subsection was committed while the person was on release pending trial for a Federal, State, or local offense; and

(3) a period of not more than five years has elapsed since the date of conviction, or the release of the person from imprisonment, for the offense described in paragraph (1) of this subsection, whichever is later.

Subject to rebuttal by the person, it shall be presumed that no condition or combination of conditions will reasonably assure the appearance of the person as required and the safety of the community if the judicial officer finds that there is probable cause to believe that the person committed an offense for which a maximum term of imprisonment of ten years or more is prescribed in the Controlled Substances Act (21 U.S.C. 801 et seq.), the Controlled Substances Import and Export Act (21 U.S.C. 951 et seq.), section 1 of the Act of September 15, 1980 (21 U.S.C. 955a), or an offense under section 924(c) of title 18 of the United States Code.

(f) Detention hearing.—The judicial officer shall hold a hearing to determine whether any condition or combination of conditions set forth in subsection (c) of this section will reasonably assure the appearance of the person as required and the safety of any other person and the community in a case—

(1) upon motion of the attorney for the Government, that involves—

(A) a crime of violence;*

(B) an offense for which the maximum sentence is life imprisonment or death;

(C) an offense for which a maximum term of imprisonment of ten years or more is prescribed in the Controlled Substances Act (21 U.S.C. 801 et seq.), the Controlled Substances Import and Export Act (21 U.S.C. 951 et seq.), or section 1 of the Act of September 15, 1980 (21 U.S.C. 955a); or

(D) any felony if the person had been convicted of two or more prior offenses described in subparagraphs (A) through (C) of this paragraph, or two or more State or local offenses that would have been offenses described in subparagraphs (A) through (C) of this paragraph if a circumstance giving rise to Federal jurisdiction had existed or a combination of such offenses; or

* The phrase "crime of violence" is defined in 18 U.S.C. § 3156(a)(4) as meaning: "(A) an offense that has an element of the offense the use, attempted use, or threatened use of physical force against the person or property of another, or (B) any other offense that is a felony and that, by its nature, involves a substantial risk that physical force against the person or property of another may be used in the course of committing the offense."

(2) upon motion of the attorney for the Government or upon the judicial officer's own motion in a case, that involves—

(A) a serious risk that such person will flee;

(B) a serious risk that the person will obstruct or attempt to obstruct justice, or threaten, injure, or intimidate, or attempt to threaten, injure, or intimidate, a prospective witness or juror.

The hearing shall be held immediately upon the person's first appearance before the judicial officer unless that person, or the attorney for the Government, seeks a continuance. Except for good cause, a continuance on motion of the person may not exceed five days, and a continuance on motion of the attorney for the Government may not exceed three days. During a continuance, the person shall be detained, and the judicial officer, on motion of the attorney for the Government or sua sponte, may order that, while in custody, a person who appears to be a narcotics addict receive a medical examination to determine whether such person is an addict. At the hearing, the person has the right to be represented by counsel, and, if financially unable to obtain adequate representation, to have counsel appointed. The person shall be afforded an opportunity to testify, to present witnesses, to cross-examine witnesses who appear at the hearing, and to present information by proffer or otherwise. The rules concerning admissibility of evidence in criminal trials do not apply to the presentation and consideration of information at the hearing. The facts the judicial officer uses to support a finding pursuant to subsection (e) that no condition or combination of conditions will reasonably assure the safety of any other person and the community shall be supported by clear and convincing evidence. The person may be detained pending completion of the hearing. The hearing may be reopened before or after a determination by the judicial officer, at any time before trial if the judicial officer finds that information exists that was not known to the movant at the time of the hearing and that has a material bearing on the issue of whether there are conditions of release that will reasonably assure the appearance of the person as required and the safety of any other person and the community.

(g) Factors to be considered.—The judicial officer shall, in determining whether there are conditions of release that will reasonably assure the appearance of the person as required and the safety of any other person and the community, take into account the available information concerning—

(1) the nature and circumstances of the offense charged, including whether the offense is a crime of violence or involves a narcotic drug;

(2) the weight of the evidence against the person;

(3) the history and characteristics of the person, including—

(A) the person's character, physical and mental condition, family ties, employment, financial resources, length of residence in the community, community ties, past conduct, history relating to drug or alcohol abuse, criminal history, and record concerning appearance at court proceedings; and

(B) whether, at the time of the current offense or arrest, the person was on probation, on parole, or on other release pending trial, sentencing, appeal, or completion of sentence for an offense under Federal, State, or local law; and

(4) the nature and seriousness of the danger to any person or the community that would be posed by the person's release. In considering the conditions of release described in subsection (c)(2)(K) or (c)(2)(L) [eds. note: intended references are to what is now subsection (c)(1)(B)(xi) or (c)(1)(B)(xii)], the judicial officer may upon his own motion, or shall upon the motion of the Government, conduct an inquiry into the source of the property to be designated for potential forfeiture or offered as collateral to secure a bond, and shall decline to accept the designation, or

the use as collateral, of property that, because of its source, will not reasonably assure the appearance of the person as required.

(h) Contents of release order.—In a release order issued under subsection (b) or (c) of this section, the judicial officer shall—

(1) include a written statement that sets forth all the conditions to which the release is subject, in a manner sufficiently clear and specific to serve as a guide for the person's conduct; and

(2) advise the person of—

(A) the penalties for violating a condition of release, including the penalties for committing an offense while on pretrial release;

(B) the consequences of violating a condition of release, including the immediate issuance of a warrant for the person's arrest; and

(C) the provisions of sections 1503 of this title (relating to intimidation of witnesses, jurors, and officers of the court), 1510 (relating to obstruction of criminal investigations), 1512 (tampering with a witness, victim, or an informant), and 1513 (retaliating against a witness, victim, or an informant).

(i) Contents of detention order.—In a detention order issued under subsection (e) of this section, the judicial officer shall—

(1) include written findings of fact and a written statement of the reasons for the detention;

(2) direct that the person be committed to the custody of the Attorney General for confinement in a corrections facility separate, to the extent practicable, from persons awaiting or serving sentences or being held in custody pending appeal;

(3) direct that the person be afforded reasonable opportunity for private consultation with counsel; and

(4) direct that, on order of a court of the United States or on request of an attorney for the Government, the person in charge of the corrections facility in which the person is confined deliver the person to a United States marshal for the purpose of an appearance in connection with a court proceeding.

The judicial officer may, by subsequent order, permit the temporary release of the person, in the custody of a United States marshal or another appropriate person, to the extent that the judicial officer determines such release to be necessary for preparation of the person's defense or for another compelling reason.

(j) Presumption of innocence.—Nothing in this section shall be construed as modifying or limiting the presumption of innocence.

§ 3143. Release or detention of a defendant pending sentence or appeal

(a) Release or detention pending sentence.—The judicial officer shall order that a person who has been found guilty of an offense and who is waiting imposition or execution of sentence, be detained, unless the judicial officer finds by clear and convincing evidence that the person is not likely to flee or pose a danger to the safety of any other person or the community if release pursuant to section 3142(b) or (c). If the judicial officer makes such a finding, such judicial officer shall order the release of the person in accordance with the provisions of section 3142(b) or (c).

(b) Release of detention pending appeal by the defendant.—The judicial officer shall order that a person who has been found guilty of an offense and sentenced to a term of imprisonment, and who has filed an appeal or a petition for a writ of certiorari, be detained, unless the judicial officer finds—

(1) by clear and convincing evidence that the person is not likely to flee or pose a danger to the safety of any other person or the community if released under section 3142(b) or (c) of this title; and

(2) that the appeal is not for the purpose of delay and raises a substantial question of law or fact likely to result in—

(A) reversal,

(B) an order for a new trial,

(C) a sentence that does not include a term of imprisonment, or

(D) a reduced sentence to a term of imprisonment less than the total of the time already served plus the expected duration of the appeal process.

If the judicial officer makes such findings, such judicial officer shall order the release of the person in accordance with the provisions of section 3142(b) or (c) of this title, except that in the circumstance described in paragraph (b)(2)(D), the judicial officer shall order the detention terminated at the expiration of the likely reduced sentence.

(c) **Release or detention pending appeal by the government.**—The judicial officer shall treat a defendant in a case in which an appeal has been taken by the United States under section 3731 of this title, in accordance with the provisions of section 3142 of this title, unless the defendant is otherwise subject to a release or detention order.

§ 3144. Release or detention of a material witness

If it appears from an affidavit filed by a party that the testimony of a person is material in a criminal proceeding, and if it is shown that it may become impracticable to secure the presence of the person by subpena, a judicial officer may order the arrest of the person and treat the person in accordance with the provisions of section 3142 of this title. No material witness may be detained because of inability to comply with any condition of release if the testimony of such witness can adequately be secured by deposition, and if further detention is not necessary to prevent a failure of justice. Release of a material witness may be delayed for a reasonable period of time until the deposition of the witness can be taken pursuant to the Federal Rules of Criminal Procedure.

§ 3145. Review and appeal of a release or detention order

(a) **Review of a release order.**—If a person is ordered released by a magistrate, or by a person other than a judge of a court having original jurisdiction over the offense and other than a Federal appellate court—

(1) the attorney for the Government may file, with the court having original jurisdiction over the offense, a motion for revocation of the order or amendment of the conditions of release; and

(2) the person may file, with the court having original jurisdiction over the offense, a motion for amendment of the conditions of release.

The motion shall be determined promptly.

(b) **Review of a detention order.**—If a person is ordered detained by a magistrate, or by a person other than a judge of a court having original jurisdiction over the offense and other than a Federal appellate court, the person may file, with the court having original jurisdiction over the offense, a motion for revocation or amendment of the order. The motion shall be determined promptly.

(c) **Appeal from a release or detention order.**—An appeal from a release or detention order, or from a decision denying revocation or amendment of such an order, is governed by the provisions of section 1291 of title 28 and section 3731 of this title. The appeal shall be determined promptly.

§ 3146. Penalty for failure to appear

(a) Offense.—Whoever, having been released under this chapter knowingly—

(1) fails to appear before a court as required by the conditions of his release; or

(2) fails to surrender for service of sentence pursuant to a court order; shall be punished as provided in subsection (b) of this section.

(b) Punishment.—(1) The punishment for an offense under this section is—

(A) if the person was released in connection with a charge of, or while awaiting sentence, surrender for service of sentence, or appeal or certiorari after conviction, for—

(i) an offense punishable by death, life imprisonment, or imprisonment for a term of 15 years or more, a fine under this title or imprisonment for not more than ten years, or both;

(ii) an offense punishable by imprisonment for a term of five years or more, a fine under this title or imprisonment for not more than five years, or both;

(iii) any other felony, a fine under this title or imprisonment for not more than two years, or both; or

(iv) a misdemeanor, a fine under this chapter or imprisonment for not more than one year, or both; and

(B) if the person was released for appearance as a material witness, a fine under this chapter or imprisonment for not more than one year, or both.

(2) A term of imprisonment imposed under this section shall be consecutive to the sentence of imprisonment for any other offense.

(c) Affirmative defense.—It is an affirmative defense to a prosecution under this section that uncontrollable circumstances prevented the person from appearing or surrendering, and that the person did not contribute to the creation of such circumstances in reckless disregard of the requirement that he appear or surrender, and that the person appeared or surrendered as soon as such circumstances ceased to exist.

(d) Declaration of forfeiture.—If a person fails to appear before a court as required, and the person executed an appearance bond pursuant to section 3142(b) of this title or is subject to the release condition set forth in clause (xi) or (xii) of section 3142(c)(1)(B) of this title, the judicial officer may, regardless of whether the person has been charged with an offense under this section, declare any property designated pursuant to that section to be forfeited to the United States.

§ 3147. Penalty for an offense committed while on release

A person convicted of an offense committed while released under this chapter shall be sentenced, in addition to the sentence prescribed for the offense to—

(1) a term of imprisonment of not less than two years and not more than ten years if the offense is a felony; or

(2) a term of imprisonment of not less than ninety days and not more than one year if the offense is a misdemeanor.

A term of imprisonment imposed under this section shall be consecutive to any other sentence of imprisonment.

§ 3148. Sanctions for violation of a release condition

(a) Available sanctions.—A person who has been released under section 3142 of this title, and who has violated a condition of his release, is subject to a revocation of release, an order of detention, and a prosecution for contempt of court.

(b) **Revocation of release.**—The attorney for the Government may initiate a proceeding for revocation of an order of release by filing a motion with the district court. A judicial officer may issue a warrant for the arrest of a person charged with violating a condition of release, and the person shall be brought before a judicial officer in the district in which such person's arrest was ordered for a proceeding in accordance with this section. To the extent practicable, a person charged with violating the condition of release that such person not commit a Federal, State, or local crime during the period of release shall be brought before the judicial officer who ordered the release and whose order is alleged to have been violated. The judicial officer shall enter an order of revocation and detention if, after a hearing, the judicial officer—

(1) finds that there is—

(A) probable cause to believe that the person has committed a Federal, State, or local crime while on release; or

(B) clear and convincing evidence that the person has violated any other condition of his release; and

(2) finds that—

(A) based on the factors set forth in section 3142(g) of this title, there is no condition or combination of conditions of release that will assure that the person will not flee or pose a danger to the safety of any other person or the community; or

(B) the person is unlikely to abide by any condition or combination of conditions of release.

If there is probable cause to believe that, while on release, the person committed a Federal, State, or local felony, a rebuttable presumption arises that no condition or combination of conditions will assure that the person will not pose a danger to the safety of any other person or the community. If the judicial officer finds that there are conditions of release that will assure that the person will not flee or pose a danger to the safety of any other person or the community, and that the person will abide by such conditions, the judicial officer shall treat the person in accordance with the provisions of section 3142 of this title and may amend the conditions of release accordingly.

(c) **Prosecution for contempt.**—The judge may commence a prosecution for contempt, pursuant to the provisions of section 401 of this title, if the person has violated a condition of release.

§ 3149. Surrender of an offender by a surety

A person charged with an offense, who is released upon the execution of an appearance bond with a surety, may be arrested by the surety, and if so arrested, shall be delivered promptly to a United States marshal and brought before a judicial officer. The judicial officer shall determine in accordance with the provisions of section 3148(b) whether to revoke the release of the person, and may absolve the surety of responsibility to pay all or part of the bond in accordance with the provisions of Rule 46 of the Federal Rules of Criminal Procedure. The person so committed shall be held in official detention until released pursuant to this chapter or another provision of law.

§ 3150. Applicability to a case removed from a State court

The provisions of this chapter apply to a criminal case removed to a Federal court from a State court.

SPEEDY TRIAL ACT OF 1974 (AS AMENDED)

(18 U.S.C. §§ 3161–3162, 3164).

§ 3161. Time limits and exclusions

(a) In any case involving a defendant charged with an offense, the appropriate judicial officer, at the earliest practicable time, shall, after consultation with the counsel for the defendant and the attorney for the Government, set the case for trial on a day certain, or list it for trial on a weekly or other short-term trial calendar at a place within the judicial district, so as to assure a speedy trial.

(b) Any information or indictment charging an individual with the commission of an offense shall be filed within thirty days from the date on which such individual was arrested or served with a summons in connection with such charges. If an individual has been charged with a felony in a district in which no grand jury has been in session during such thirty-day period, the period of time for filing of the indictment shall be extended an additional thirty days.

(c) (1) In any case in which a plea of not guilty is entered, the trial of a defendant charged in an information or indictment with the commission of an offense shall commence within seventy days from the filing date (and making public) of the information or indictment, or from the date the defendant has appeared before a judicial officer of the court in which such charge is pending, whichever date last occurs. If a defendant consents in writing to be tried before a magistrate on a complaint, the trial shall commence within seventy days from the date of such consent.

(2) Unless the defendant consents in writing to the contrary, the trial shall not commence less than thirty days from the date on which the defendant first appears through counsel or expressly waives counsel and elects to proceed pro se.

(d) (1) If any indictment or information is dismissed upon motion of the defendant, or any charge contained in a complaint filed against an individual is dismissed or otherwise dropped, and thereafter a complaint is filed against such defendant or individual charging him with the same offense or an offense based on the same conduct or arising from the same criminal episode, or an information or indictment is filed charging such defendant with the same offense or an offense based on the same conduct or arising from the same criminal episode, the provisions of subsections (b) and (c) of this section shall be applicable with respect to such subsequent complaint, indictment, or information, as the case may be.

(2) If the defendant is to be tried upon an indictment or information dismissed by a trial court and reinstated following an appeal, the trial shall commence within seventy days from the date the action occasioning the trial becomes final, except that the court retrying the case may extend the period for trial not to exceed one hundred and eighty days from the date the action occasioning the trial becomes final if the unavailability of witnesses or other factors resulting from the passage of time shall make trial within seventy days impractical. The periods of delay enumerated in section 3161(h) are excluded in computing the time limitations specified in this section. The sanctions of section 3162 apply to this subsection.

(e) If the defendant is to be tried again following a declaration by the trial judge of a mistrial or following an order of such judge for a new trial, the trial shall commence within seventy days from the date the action occasioning the retrial becomes final. If the defendant is to be tried again following an appeal or a collateral attack, the trial shall commence within seventy days from the date the action occasioning the retrial becomes final, except that the court retrying the case may extend the period for retrial not to exceed one hundred and eighty days from the date the action occasioning the retrial becomes final if unavailability of witnesses or other factors resulting from passage of time shall make trial within seventy days impractical. The periods of delay enumerated in section 3161(h) are excluded in computing the time limitations specified in this section. The sanctions of section 3162 apply to this subsection. * *. *

(h) The following periods of delay shall be excluded in computing the time within which an information or an indictment must be filed, or in computing the time within which the trial of any such offense must commence:

(1) Any period of delay resulting from other proceedings concerning the defendant, including but not limited to—

(A) delay resulting from any proceeding, including any examinations, to determine the mental competency or physical capacity of the defendant;

(B) delay resulting from any proceeding, including any examination of the defendant, pursuant to section 2902 of title 28, United States Code;

(C) delay resulting from deferral of prosecution pursuant to section 2902 of title 28, United States Code;

(D) delay resulting from trial with respect to other charges against the defendant;

(E) delay resulting from any interlocutory appeal;

(F) delay resulting from any pretrial motion, from the filing of the motion through the conclusion of the hearing on, or other prompt disposition of, such motion;

(G) delay resulting from any proceeding relating to the transfer of a case or the removal of any defendant from another district under the Federal Rules of Criminal Procedure;

(H) delay resulting from transportation of any defendant from another district, or to and from places of examination or hospitalization, except that any time consumed in excess of ten days from the date an order of removal or an order directing such transportation, and the defendant's arrival at the destination shall be presumed to be unreasonable;

(I) delay resulting from consideration by the court of a proposed plea agreement to be entered into by the defendant and the attorney for the Government; and

(J) delay reasonably attributable to any period, not to exceed thirty days, during which any proceeding concerning the defendant is actually under advisement by the court.

(2) Any period of delay during which prosecution is deferred by the attorney for the Government pursuant to written agreement with the defendant, with the approval of the court, for the purpose of allowing the defendant to demonstrate his good conduct.

(3) (A) Any period of delay resulting from the absence or unavailability of the defendant or an essential witness.

(B) For purposes of subparagraph (A) of this paragraph, a defendant or an essential witness shall be considered absent when his whereabouts are unknown and, in addition, he is attempting to avoid apprehension or prosecution or his whereabouts cannot be determined by due diligence. For purposes of such subparagraph, a defendant or an essential witness shall be considered unavailable whenever his whereabouts are known but his presence for trial cannot be obtained by due diligence or he resists appearing at or being returned for trial.

(4) Any period of delay resulting from the fact that the defendant is mentally incompetent or physically unable to stand trial.

(5) Any period of delay resulting from the treatment of the defendant pursuant to section 2902 of title 28, United States Code.

(6) If the information or indictment is dismissed upon motion of the attorney for the Government and thereafter a charge is filed against the defendant for the same offense, or any offense required to be joined with that offense, any period of delay from the date the charge was dismissed to the date the time limitation would commence to run as to the subsequent charge had there been no previous charge.

(7) A reasonable period of delay when the defendant is joined for trial with a codefendant as to whom the time for trial has not run and no motion for severance has been granted.

(8) (A) Any period of delay resulting from a continuance granted by any judge on his own motion or at the request of the defendant or his counsel or at the request of the attorney for the Government, if the judge granted such continuance on the basis of his findings that the ends of justice served by taking such action outweigh the best interest of the public and the defendant in a speedy trial. No such period of delay resulting from a continuance granted by the court in accordance with this paragraph shall be excludable under this subsection unless the court sets forth, in the record of the case, either orally or in writing, its reasons for finding that the ends of justice served by the granting of such continuance outweigh the best interests of the public and the defendant in a speedy trial.

(B) The factors, among others, which a judge shall consider in determining whether to grant a continuance under subparagraph (A) of this paragraph in any case are as follows:

(i) Whether the failure to grant such a continuance in the proceeding would be likely to make a continuation of such proceeding impossible, or result in a miscarriage of justice.

(ii) Whether the case is so unusual or so complex, due to the number of defendants, the nature of the prosecution, or the existence of novel questions of fact or law, that it is unreasonable to expect adequate preparation for pretrial proceedings or for the trial itself within the time limits established by this section.

(iii) Whether, in a case in which arrest precedes indictment, delay in the filing of the indictment is caused because the arrest occurs at a time such that it is unreasonable to expect return and filing of the indictment within the period specified in section 3161(b), or because the facts upon which the grand jury must base its determination are unusual or complex.

(iv) Whether the failure to grant such a continuance in a case which, taken as a whole, is not so unusual or so complex as to fall within clause (ii), would deny the defendant reasonable time to obtain counsel, would unreasonably deny the defendant or the Government continuity of counsel, or would deny counsel for the defendant or the attorney for the Government the reasonable time necessary for effective preparation, taking into account the exercise of due diligence.

(C) No continuance under subparagraph (A) of this paragraph shall be granted because of general congestion of the court's calendar, or lack of diligent preparation or failure to obtain available witnesses on the part of the attorney for the Government.

(9) Any period of delay, not to exceed one year, ordered by a district court upon an application of a party and a finding by a preponderance of the evidence that an official request, as defined in section 3292 of this title, has been made for evidence

of any such offense and that it reasonably appears, or reasonably appeared at the time the request was made, that such evidence is, or was, in such foreign country.

(i) If trial did not commence within the time limitation specified in section 3161 because the defendant had entered a plea of guilty or nolo contendere subsequently withdrawn to any or all charges in an indictment or information, the defendant shall be deemed indicted with respect to all charges therein contained within the meaning of section 3161, on the day the order permitting withdrawal of the plea becomes final.

(j) (1) If the attorney for the Government knows that a person charged with an offense is serving a term of imprisonment in any penal institution, he shall promptly—

(A) undertake to obtain the presence of the prisoner for trial; or

(B) cause a detainer to be filed with the person having custody of the prisoner and request him to so advise the prisoner and to advise the prisoner of his right to demand trial.

(2) If the person having custody of such prisoner receives a detainer, he shall promptly advise the prisoner of the charge and of the prisoner's right to demand trial. If at any time thereafter the prisoner informs the person having custody that he does demand trial, such person shall cause notice to that effect to be sent promptly to the attorney for the Government who caused the detainer to be filed.

(3) Upon receipt of such notice, the attorney for the Government shall promptly seek to obtain the presence of the prisoner for trial.

(4) When the person having custody of the prisoner receives from the attorney for the Government a properly supported request for temporary custody of such prisoner for trial, the prisoner shall be made available to that attorney for the Government (subject, in cases of interjurisdictional transfer, to any right of the prisoner to contest the legality of his delivery).

(k) (1) If the defendant is absent (as defined by subsection (h)(3)) on the day set for trial, and the defendant's subsequent appearance before the court on a bench warrant or other process or surrender to the court occurs more than 21 days after the day set for trial, the defendant shall be deemed to have first appeared before a judicial officer of the court in which the information or indictment is pending within the meaning of subsection (c) on the date of the defendant's subsequent appearance before the court.

(2) If the defendant is absent (as defined by subsection (h)(3)) on the day set for trial, and the defendant's subsequent appearance before the court on a bench warrant or other process or surrender to the court occurs not more than 21 days after the day set for trial, the time limit required by subsection (c), as extended by subsection (h), shall be further extended by 21 days.

§ 3162. Sanctions

(a) (1) If, in the case of any individual against whom a complaint is filed charging such individual with an offense, no indictment or information is filed within the time limit required by section 3161(b) as extended by section 3161(h) of this chapter, such charge against that individual contained in such complaint shall be dismissed or otherwise dropped. In determining whether to dismiss the case with or without prejudice, the court shall consider, among others, each of the following factors: the seriousness of the offense; the facts and circumstances of the case which led to the dismissal; and the impact of a reprosecution on the administration of this chapter and on the administration of justice.

(2) If a defendant is not brought to trial within the time limit required by section 3161(c) as extended by section 3161(h), the information or indictment shall be dismissed on motion of the defendant. The defendant shall have the burden of proof

of supporting such motion but the Government shall have the burden of going forward with the evidence in connection with any exclusion of time under subparagraph 3161(h)(3). In determining whether to dismiss the case with or without prejudice, the court shall consider, among others, each of the following factors: the seriousness of the offense; the facts and circumstances of the case which led to the dismissal; and the impact of a reprosecution on the administration of this chapter and on the administration of justice. Failure of the defendant to move for dismissal prior to trial or entry of a plea of guilty or nolo contendere shall constitute a waiver of the right to dismissal under this section.

(b) In any case in which counsel for the defendant or the attorney for the Government (1) knowingly allows the case to be set for trial without disclosing the fact that a necessary witness would be unavailable for trial; (2) files a motion solely for the purpose of delay which he knows is totally frivolous and without merit; (3) makes a statement for the purpose of obtaining a continuance which he knows to be false and which is material to the granting of a continuance; or (4) otherwise willfully fails to proceed to trial without justification consistent with section 3161 of this chapter, the court may punish any such counsel or attorney, as follows:

(A) in the case of an appointed defense counsel, by reducing the amount of compensation that otherwise would have been paid to such counsel pursuant to section 3006A of this title in an amount not to exceed 25 per centum thereof;

(B) in the case of a counsel retained in connection with the defense of a defendant, by imposing on such counsel a fine of not to exceed 25 per centum of the compensation to which he is entitled in connection with his defense of such defendant;

(C) by imposing on any attorney for the Government a fine of not to exceed $250;

(D) by denying any such counsel or attorney for the Government the right to practice before the court considering such case for a period of not to exceed ninety days; or

(E) by filing a report with an appropriate disciplinary committee.

The authority to punish provided for by this subsection shall be in addition to any other authority or power available to such court.

(c) The court shall follow procedures established in the Federal Rules of Criminal Procedure in punishing any counsel or attorney for the Government pursuant to this section.

§ 3164. Persons detained or designated as being of high risk

(a) The trial or other disposition of cases involving—

(1) a detained person who is being held in detention solely because he is awaiting trial, and

(2) a released person who is awaiting trial and has been designated by the attorney for the Government as being of high risk,

shall be accorded priority.

(b) The trial of any person described in subsection (a)(1) or (a)(2) of this section shall commence not later than ninety days following the beginning of such continuous detention or designation of high risk by the attorney for the Government. The periods of delay enumerated in section 3161(h) are excluded in computing the time limitation specified in this section.

(c) Failure to commence trial of a detainee as specified in subsection (b), through no fault of the accused or his counsel, or failure to commence trial of a designated releasee as specified in subsection (b), through no fault of the attorney for the Government, shall result in the automatic review by the court of the conditions of release. No detainee, as defined in subsection (a), shall be held in custody pending trial after the expiration of such ninety-day period required for the commencement of his trial. A designated releasee, as defined in subsection (a), who is found by the court to have intentionally delayed the trial of his case shall be subject to an order of the court modifying his nonfinancial conditions of release under this title to insure that he shall appear at trial as required.

LITIGATION CONCERNING SOURCES OF EVIDENCE

(18 U.S.C. § 3504).

§ 3504. Litigation concerning sources of evidence

(a) In any trial, hearing, or other proceeding in or before any court, grand jury, department, officer, agency, regulatory body, or other authority of the United States—

(1) upon a claim by a party aggrieved that evidence is inadmissible because it is the primary product of an unlawful act or because it was obtained by the exploitation of an unlawful act, the opponent of the claim shall affirm or deny the occurrence of the alleged unlawful act;

(2) disclosure of information for a determination if evidence is inadmissible because it is the primary product of an unlawful act occurring prior to June 19, 1968, or because it was obtained by the exploitation of an unlawful act occurring prior to June 19, 1968, shall not be required unless such information may be relevant to a pending claim of such inadmissibility; and

(3) no claim shall be considered that evidence of an event is inadmissible on the ground that such evidence was obtained by the exploitation of an unlawful act occurring prior to June 19, 1968, if such event occurred more than five years after such allegedly unlawful act.

(b) As used in this section "unlawful act" means any act the use of any electronic, mechanical, or other device (as defined in section 2510(5) of this title) in violation of the Constitution or laws of the United States or any regulation or standard promulgated pursuant thereto.

CRIMINAL APPEALS ACT OF 1970 (AS AMENDED)

(18 U.S.C. § 3731).

§ 3731. Appeal by United States

In a criminal case an appeal by the United States shall lie to a court of appeals from a decision, judgment, or order of a district court dismissing an indictment or information or granting a new trial after verdict or judgment, as to any one or more counts, except that no appeal shall lie where the double jeopardy clause of the United States Constitution prohibits further prosecution.

An appeal by the United States shall lie to a court of appeals from a decision or order of a district court suppressing or excluding evidence or requiring the return of seized property in a criminal proceeding, not made after the defendant has been put in jeopardy and before the verdict or finding on an indictment or information, if the United States attorney certifies to the district court that the appeal is not taken for purpose of delay and that the evidence is a substantial proof of a fact material in the proceeding.

An appeal by the United States shall lie to a court of appeals from a decision or order, entered by a district court of the United States, granting the release of a person charged with or convicted of an offense, or denying a motion for revocation of, or modification of the conditions of, a decision or order granting release.

The appeal in all such cases shall be taken within thirty days after the decision, judgment or order has been rendered and shall be diligently prosecuted.

The provisions of this section shall be liberally construed to effectuate its purposes.

JURY SELECTION AND SERVICE ACT OF 1968
(AS AMENDED)

(28 U.S.C. §§ 1861–1863, 1865–1867).

§ 1861. Declaration of policy

It is the policy of the United States that all litigants in Federal courts entitled to trial by jury shall have the right to grand and petit juries selected at random from a fair cross section of the community in the district or division wherein the court convenes. It is further the policy of the United States that all citizens shall have the opportunity to be considered for service on grand and petit juries in the district courts of the United States, and shall have an obligation to serve as jurors when summoned for that purpose.

§ 1862. Discrimination prohibited

No citizen shall be excluded from service as a grand or petit juror in the district courts of the United States or in the Court of International Trade on account of race, color, religion, sex, national origin, or economic status.

§ 1863. Plan for random jury selection

(a) Each United States district court shall devise and place into operation a written plan for random selection of grand and petit jurors that shall be designed to achieve the objectives of sections 1861 and 1862 of this title, and that shall otherwise comply with the provisions of this title. The plan shall be placed into operation after approval by a reviewing panel consisting of the members of the judicial council of the circuit and either the chief judge of the district whose plan is being reviewed or such other active district judge of that district as the chief judge of the district may designate. The panel shall examine the plan to ascertain that it complies with the provisions of this title. * * * The district court may modify a plan at any time and it shall modify the plan when so directed by the reviewing panel. * * *

(b) Among other things, such plan shall—

(1) either establish a jury commission, or authorize the clerk of the court, to manage the jury selection process. If the plan establishes a jury commission, the district court shall appoint one citizen to serve with the clerk of the court as the jury commission. * * * The citizen jury commissioner shall not belong to the same political party as the clerk serving with him. The clerk or the jury commission, as the case may be, shall act under the supervision and control of the chief judge of the district court or such other judge of the district court as the plan may provide. * * *

(2) specify whether the names of prospective jurors shall be selected from the voter registration lists or the lists of actual voters of the political subdivisions within the district or division. The plan shall prescribe some other source or sources of names in addition to voter lists where necessary to foster the policy and protect the rights secured by sections 1861 and 1862 of this title. * * *

(3) specify detailed procedures to be followed by the jury commission or clerk in selecting names from the sources specified in paragraph (2) of this subsection. These procedures shall be designed to ensure the random selection of a fair cross section of the persons residing in the community in the district or division wherein the court convenes. They shall ensure that names of persons residing in each of the counties, parishes, or similar political subdivisions within the judicial district or division are placed in a master jury wheel; and shall ensure that each county, parish, or similar political subdivision within the district or division is substantially proportionally represented in the master jury wheel for that judicial district, division, or combination of divisions. For the purposes of determining proportional representation in the master jury wheel, either the number of actual voters at the last general election in each county, parish, or similar political subdivision, or the number of registered voters if registration of voters is uniformly required throughout the district or division, may be used.

(4) provide for a master jury wheel (or a device similar in purpose and function) into which the names of those randomly selected shall be placed. The plan shall fix a minimum number of names to be placed initially in the master jury wheel, which shall be at least one-half of 1 per centum of the total number of persons on the lists used as a source of names for the district or division; but if this number of names is believed to be cumbersome and unnecessary, the plan may fix a smaller number of names to be placed in the master wheel, but in no event less than one thousand. The chief judge of the district court, or such other district court judge as the plan may provide, may order additional names to be placed in the master jury wheel from time to time as necessary. The plan shall provide for periodic emptying and refilling of the master jury wheel at specified times, the interval for which shall not exceed four years.

(5) (A) except as provided in subparagraph (B), specify those groups of persons or occupational classes whose members shall, on individual request therefor, be excused from jury service. Such groups or classes shall be excused only if the district court finds, and the plan states, that jury service by such class or group would entail undue hardship or extreme inconvenience to the members thereof, and excuse of members thereof would not be inconsistent with sections 1861 and 1862 of this title.

(B) specify that volunteer safety personnel, upon individual request, shall be excused from jury service. For purposes of this subparagraph, the term "volunteer safety personnel" means individuals serving a public agency (as defined in section 1203(6) of title I of the Omnibus Crime Control and Safe Streets Act of 1968) in an official capacity, without compensation, as firefighters or members of a rescue squad or ambulance crew.

(6) specify that the following persons are barred from jury service on the ground that they are exempt: (A) members in active service in the Armed Forces of the United States; (B) members of the fire or police departments of any State, the District of Columbia, any territory or possession of the United States, or any subdivision of a State, the District of Columbia, or such territory or possession; (C) public officers in the executive, legislative, or judicial branches of the Government of the United States, or of any State, the District of Columbia, any territory or possession of the United States, or any subdivision of a State, the District of Columbia, or such territory or possession, who are actively engaged in the performance of official duties.

(7) fix the time when the names drawn from the qualified jury wheel shall be disclosed to parties and to the public. If the plan permits these names to be made public, it may nevertheless permit the chief judge of the district court, or such

other district court judge as the plan may provide, to keep these names confidential in any case where the interests of justice so require.

(8) specify the procedures to be followed by the clerk or jury commission in assigning persons whose names have been drawn from the qualified jury wheel to grand and petit jury panels. * * *

§ 1865. Qualifications for jury service

(a) The chief judge of the district court, or such other district court judge as the plan may provide, on his initiative or upon recommendation of the clerk or jury commission, shall determine solely on the basis of information provided on the juror qualification form and other competent evidence whether a person is unqualified for, or exempt, or to be excused from jury service. The clerk shall enter such determination in the space provided on the juror qualification form and the alphabetical list of names drawn from the master jury wheel. If a person did not appear in response to a summons, such fact shall be noted on said list.

(b) In making such determination the chief judge of the district court, or such other district court judge as the plan may provide, shall deem any person qualified to serve on grand and petit juries in the district court unless he—

(1) is not a citizen of the United States eighteen years old who has resided for a period of one year within the judicial district;

(2) is unable to read, write, and understand the English language with a degree of proficiency sufficient to fill out satisfactorily the juror qualification form;

(3) is unable to speak the English language;

(4) is incapable, by reason of mental or physical infirmity, to render satisfactory jury service; or

(5) has a charge pending against him for the commission of, or has been convicted in a State or Federal court of record of, a crime punishable by imprisonment for more than one year and his civil rights have not been restored.

§ 1866. Selection and summoning of jury panels

* * *

(c) Except as provided in section 1865 of this title or in any jury selection plan provision adopted pursuant to paragraph (5) or (6) of section 1863(b) of this title, no person or class of persons shall be disqualified, excluded, excused, or exempt from service as jurors: *Provided*, That any person summoned for jury service may be (1) excused by the court, or by the clerk under supervision of the court if the court's jury selection plan so authorizes, upon a showing of undue hardship or extreme inconvenience, for such period as the court deems necessary, at the conclusion of which such person either shall be summoned again for jury service under subsections (b) and (c) of this section or, if the court's jury selection plan so provides, the name of such person shall be reinserted into the qualified jury wheel for selection pursuant to subsection (a) of this section, or (2) excluded by the court on the ground that such person may be unable to render impartial jury service or that his service as a juror would be likely to disrupt the proceedings, or (3) excluded upon peremptory challenge as provided by law, or (4) excluded pursuant to the procedure specified by law upon a challenge by any party for good cause shown, or (5) excluded upon determination by the court that his service as a juror would be likely to threaten the secrecy of the proceedings, or otherwise adversely affect the integrity of jury deliberations. No person shall be excluded under clause (5) of this subsection unless the judge, in open court, determines that such is warranted and that exclusion of the person will not be inconsistent with sections 1861 and 1862 of this title. The number of persons excluded under clause (5) of this subsection shall not exceed one per centum of the number of persons who return executed jury qualification forms during the period, specified in the plan, between two consecutive fillings of the master jury wheel. The names of persons excluded under clause (5) of this subsection, together with detailed explanations for the exclusions, shall be forwarded immediately to the judicial council of the circuit, which shall have the power to make any appropriate order, prospective or retroactive, to redress any misapplication of clause (5) of this subsection, but otherwise exclusions effectuated under such clause shall not be subject to challenge under the provisions of this title. Any person excluded from a particular jury under clause (2), (3), or (4) of this subsection shall be eligible to sit on another jury if the basis for his initial exclusion would not be relevant to his ability to serve on such other jury. * * *

§ 1867. Challenging compliance with selection procedures

(a) In criminal cases, before the voir dire examination begins, or within seven days after the defendant discovered or could have discovered, by the exercise of diligence, the grounds therefor, whichever is earlier, the defendant may move to dismiss the indictment or stay the proceedings against him on the ground of substantial failure to comply with the provisions of this title in selecting the grand or petit jury.

(b) In criminal cases, before the voir dire examination begins, or within seven days after the Attorney General of the United States discovered or could have discovered, by the exercise of diligence, the grounds therefor, whichever is earlier, the Attorney General may move to dismiss the indictment or stay the proceedings on the ground of substantial failure to comply with the provisions of this title in selecting the grand or petit jury. * * *

(d) Upon motion filed under subsection (a), (b), or (c) of this section, containing a sworn statement of facts which, if true, would constitute a substantial failure to comply with the provisions of this title, the moving party shall be entitled to present in support of such motion the testimony of the jury commission or clerk, if available, any relevant records and papers not public or otherwise available used by the jury commissioner or clerk, and any other relevant evidence. If the court determines that there has been a substantial failure to comply with the provisions of this title in selecting a grand jury, the court shall stay the proceedings pending the selection of a grand jury in conformity with this title or dismiss the indictment, whichever is appropriate. If the court determines that there has been a substantial failure to comply with the provisions of this title in selecting the petit jury, the court shall stay the proceedings pending the selection of a petit jury in conformity with this title.

(e) The procedures prescribed by this section shall be the exclusive means by which a person accused of a Federal crime, the Attorney General of the United States or a party in a civil case may challenge any jury on the ground that such jury was not selected in conformity with the provisions of this title. Nothing in this section shall preclude any person or the United States from pursuing any other remedy, civil or criminal, which may be available for the vindication or enforcement of any law prohibiting discrimination on account of race, color, religion, sex, national origin or economic status in the selection of persons for service on grand or petit juries.
* * *

HABEAS CORPUS

(28 U.S.C. §§ 2241–2244, 2254–2255).

§ 2241. Power to grant writ

(a) Writs of habeas corpus may be granted by the Supreme Court, any justice thereof, the district courts and any circuit judge within their respective jurisdictions. The order of a circuit judge shall be entered in the records of the district court of the district wherein the restraint complained of is had.

(b) The Supreme Court, any justice thereof, and any circuit judge may decline to entertain an application for a writ of habeas corpus and may transfer the application for hearing and determination to the district court having jurisdiction to entertain it.

(c) The writ of habeas corpus shall not extend to a prisoner unless—

(1) He is in custody under or by color of the authority of the United States or is committed for trial before some court there of; or

(2) He is in custody for an act done or omitted in pursuance of an Act of Congress, or an order, process, judgment or decree of a court or judge of the United States; or

(3) He is in custody in violation of the Constitution or laws or treaties of the United States; or

(4) He, being a citizen of a foreign state and domiciled therein is in custody for an act done or omitted under any alleged right, title, authority, privilege, protection, or exemption claimed under the commission, order or sanction of any foreign state, or under color thereof, the validity and effect of which depend upon the law of nations; or

(5) It is necessary to bring him into court to testify or for trial.

(d) Where an application for a writ of habeas corpus is made by a person in custody under the judgment and sentence of a State court of a State which contains two or more Federal judicial districts, the application may be filed in the district court for the district wherein such person is in custody or in the district court for the district within which the State court was held which convicted and sentenced him and each of such district courts shall have concurrent jurisdiction to entertain the application. The district court for the district wherein such an application is filed in the exercise of its discretion and in furtherance of justice may transfer the application to the other district court for hearing and determination.

§ 2242. Application

Application for a writ of habeas corpus shall be in writing signed and verified by the person for whose relief it is intended or by someone acting in his behalf.

It shall allege the facts concerning the applicant's commitment or detention, the name of the person who has custody over him and by virtue of what claim or authority, if known.

It may be amended or supplemented as provided in the rules of procedure applicable to civil actions.

If addressed to the Supreme Court, a justice thereof or a circuit judge it shall state the reasons for not making application to the district court of the district in which the applicant is held.

§ 2243. Issuance of writ; return; hearing; decision

A court, justice or judge entertaining an application for a writ of habeas corpus shall forthwith award the writ or issue an order directing the respondent to show cause why the writ should not be granted, unless it appears from the application that the applicant or person detained is not entitled thereto.

The writ, or order to show cause shall be directed to the person having custody of the person detained. It shall be returned within three days unless for good cause additional time, not exceeding twenty days, is allowed.

The person to whom the writ or order is directed shall make a return certifying the true cause of the detention.

When the writ or order is returned a day shall be set for hearing, not more than five days after the return unless for good cause additional time is allowed.

Unless the application for the writ and the return present only issues of law the person to whom the writ is directed shall be required to produce at the hearing the body of the person detained.

The applicant or the person detained may, under oath, deny any of the facts set forth in the return or allege any other material facts.

The return and all suggestions made against it may be amended, by leave of court, before or after being filed.

The court shall summarily hear and determine the facts, and dispose of the matter as law and justice require.

§ 2244. Finality of determination

(a) No circuit or district judge shall be required to entertain an application for a writ of habeas corpus to inquire into the detention of a person pursuant to a judgment of a court of the United States if it appears that the legality of such detention has been determined by a judge or court of the United States on a prior application for a writ of habeas corpus and the petition presents no new ground not theretofore presented and determined, and the judge of court is satisfied that the ends of justice will not be served by such inquiry.

(b) When after an evidentiary hearing on the merits of a material factual issue, or after a hearing on the merits of an issue of law, a person in custody pursuant to the judgment of a State court has been denied by a court of the United States or a justice or judge of the United States release from custody or other remedy on an application for a writ of habeas corpus, a subsequent application for a writ of habeas corpus in behalf of such person need not be entertained by a court of the United States or a justice or judge of the United States unless the application alleges and is predicated on a factual or other ground not adjudicated on the hearing of the earlier application for the writ, and unless the court, justice, or judge is satisfied that the applicant has not on the earlier application deliberately withheld the newly asserted ground or otherwise abused the writ.

(c) In a habeas corpus proceeding brought in behalf of a person in custody pursuant to the judgment of a State court, a prior judgment of the Supreme Court of the United States on an appeal or review by a writ of certiorari at the instance of the prisoner of the decision of such State court, shall be conclusive as to all issues of fact or law with respect to an asserted denial of a Federal right which constitutes ground for discharge in a habeas corpus proceeding, actually adjudicated by the Supreme Court therein, unless the applicant for the writ of habeas corpus shall plead and the court shall find the existence of a material and controlling fact which did not appear in the record of the proceeding in the Supreme Court and the court shall further find that the applicant for the writ of habeas corpus could not have caused such fact to appear in such record by the exercise of reasonable diligence.

§ 2254. State custody; remedies in State courts

(a) The Supreme Court, a Justice thereof, a circuit judge, or a district court shall entertain an application for a writ of habeas corpus in behalf of a person in custody pursuant to the judgment of a State court only on the ground that he is in custody in violation of the Constitution or laws or treaties of the United States.

(b) An application for a writ of habeas corpus in behalf of a person in custody pursuant to the judgment of a State court shall not be granted unless it appears that the applicant has exhausted the remedies available in the courts of the State, or that there is either an absence of available State corrective process or the existence of circumstances rendering such process ineffective to protect the rights of the prisoner.

(c) An applicant shall not be deemed to have exhausted the remedies available in the courts of the State, within the meaning of this section, if he has the right under the law of the State to raise, by any available procedure, the question presented.

(d) In any proceeding instituted in a Federal court by an application for a writ of habeas corpus by a person in custody pursuant to the judgment of a State court, a determination after a hearing on the merits of a factual issue, made by a State court of competent jurisdiction in a proceeding to which the applicant for the writ and the State or an officer or agent thereof were parties, evidenced by a written finding, written opinion, or other reliable and adequate written indicia, shall be presumed to be correct, unless the applicant shall establish or it shall otherwise appear, or the respondent shall admit—

(1) that the merits of the factual dispute were not resolved in the State court hearing;

(2) that the factfinding procedure employed by the State court was not adequate to afford a full and fair hearing;

(3) that the material facts were not adequately developed at the State court hearing;

(4) that the State court lacked jurisdiction of the subject matter or over the person of the applicant in the State court proceeding;

(5) that the applicant was an indigent and the State court, in deprivation of his constitutional right, failed to appoint counsel to represent him in the State court proceeding;

(6) that the applicant did not receive a full, fair, and adequate hearing in the State court proceeding; or

(7) that the applicant was otherwise denied due process of law in the State court proceeding;

(8) or unless that part of the record of the State court proceeding in which the determination of such factual issue was made, pertinent to a determination of the sufficiency of the evidence to support such factual determination, is produced as provided for hereinafter, and the Federal court on a consideration of such part of the record as a whole concludes that such factual determination is not fairly supported by the record:

And in an evidentiary hearing in the proceeding in the Federal court, when due proof of such factual determination has been made, unless the existence of one or more of the circumstances respectively set forth in paragraphs numbered (1) to (7), inclusive, is shown by the applicant, otherwise appears, or is admitted by the respondent, or unless the court concludes pursuant to the provisions of paragraph numbered (8) that the record in the State court proceeding, considered as a whole, does not fairly support such factual determination, the burden shall rest upon the applicant to establish by convincing evidence that the factual determination by the State court was erroneous.

(e) If the applicant challenges the sufficiency of the evidence adduced in such State court proceeding to support the State court's determination of a factual issue made therein, the applicant, if able, shall produce that part of the record pertinent to a determination of the sufficiency of the evidence to support such determination. If the applicant, because of indigency or other reason is unable to produce such part of the record, then the State shall produce such part of the record and the Federal court shall direct the State to do so by order directed to an appropriate State official. If the State cannot provide such pertinent part of the record, then the court shall determine under the existing facts and circumstances what weight shall be given to the State court's factual determination.

(f) A copy of the official records of the State court, duly certified by the clerk of such court to be a true and correct copy of a finding, judicial opinion, or other reliable written indicia showing such a factual determination by the State court shall be admissible in the Federal court proceeding.

§ 2255. Federal custody; remedies on motion attacking sentence

A prisoner in custody under sentence of a court established by Act of Congress claiming the right to be released upon the ground that the sentence was imposed in violation of the Constitution or laws of the United States, or that the court was without jurisdiction to impose such sentence, or that the sentence was in excess of the maximum authorized by law, or is otherwise subject to collateral attack, may move the court which imposed the sentence to vacate, set aside or correct the sentence.

A motion for such relief may be made at any time.

Unless the motion and the files and records of the case conclusively show that the prisoner is entitled to no relief, the court shall cause notice thereof to be served upon the United States attorney, grant a prompt hearing thereon, determine the issues and make findings of fact and conclusions of law with respect thereto. If the court finds that the judgment was rendered without jurisdiction, or that the sentence imposed was not authorized by law or otherwise open to collateral attack, or that there has been such a denial or infringement of the constitutional rights of the prisoner as to render the judgment vulnerable to collateral attack, the court shall vacate and set the judgment aside and shall discharge the prisoner or resentence him or grant a new trial or correct the sentence as may appear appropriate.

A court may entertain and determine such motion without requiring the production of the prisoner at the hearing.

The sentencing court shall not be required to entertain a second or successive motion for similar relief on behalf of the same prisoner.

An appeal may be taken to the court of appeals from the order entered on the motion as from a final judgment on application for a writ of habeas corpus.

An application for a writ of habeas corpus in behalf of a prisoner who is authorized to apply for relief by motion pursuant to this section, shall not be entertained if it appears that the applicant has failed to apply for relief, by motion, to the court which sentenced him, or that such court has denied him relief, unless it also appears that the remedy by motion is inadequate or ineffective to test the legality of his detention.

PRIVACY PROTECTION ACT OF 1980

(42 U.S.C. §§ 2000aa–2000aa–12).

§ 2000aa. Searches and seizures by government officers and employees in connection with investigation or prosecution of criminal offenses

(a) Notwithstanding any other law, it shall be unlawful for a government officer or employee, in connection with the investigation or prosecution of a criminal offense, to search for or seize any work product materials possessed by a person reasonably believed to have a purpose to disseminate to the public a newspaper, book, broadcast, or other similar form of public communication, in or affecting interstate or foreign commerce; but this provision shall not impair or affect the ability of any government officer or employee, pursuant to otherwise applicable law, to search for or seize such materials, if—

(1) there is probable cause to believe that the person possessing such materials has committed or is committing the criminal offense to which the materials relate: *Provided, however,* That a government officer or employee may not search for or

seize such materials under the provisions of this paragraph if the offense to which the materials relate consists of the receipt, possession, communication, or withholding of such materials or the information contained therein (but such a search or seizure may be conducted under the provisions of this paragraph if the offense consists of the receipt, possession, or communication of information relating to the national defense, classified information, or restricted data under the provisions of section 793, 794, 797, or 798 of Title 18, or section 2274, 2275 or 2277 of this title, or section 783 of Title 50); or

(2) there is reason to believe that the immediate seizure of such materials is necessary to prevent the death of, or serious bodily injury to, a human being.

(b) Notwithstanding any other law, it shall be unlawful for a government officer or employee, in connection with the investigation or prosecution of a criminal offense, to search for or seize documentary materials, other than work product materials, possessed by a person in connection with a purpose to disseminate to the public a newspaper, book, broadcast, or other similar form of public communication, in or affecting interstate or foreign commerce; but this provision shall not impair or affect the ability of any government officer or employee, pursuant to otherwise applicable law, to search for or seize such materials, if—

(1) there is probable cause to believe that the person possessing such materials has committed or is committing the criminal offense to which the materials relate: *Provided, however,* That a government officer or employee may not search for or seize such materials under the provisions of this paragraph if the offense to which the materials relate consists of the receipt, possession, communication, or withholding of such materials or the information contained therein (but such a search or seizure may be conducted under the provisions of this paragraph if the offense consists of the receipt, possession, or communication of information relating to the national defense, classified information, or restricted data under the provisions of section 793, 794, 797, or 798 of Title 18, or section 2274, 2275 or 2277 of this title, or section 783 of Title 50);

(2) there is reason to believe that the immediate seizure of such materials is necessary to prevent the death of, or serious bodily injury to, a human being;

(3) there is reason to believe that the giving of notice pursuant to a subpena duces tecum would result in the destruction, alteration, or concealment of such materials; or

(4) such materials have not been produced in response to a court order directing compliance with a subpena duces tecum, and—

(A) all appellate remedies have been exhausted; or

(B) there is reason to believe that the delay in an investigation or trial occasioned by further proceedings relating to the subpena would threaten the interests of justice.

(c) In the event a search warrant is sought pursuant to paragraph (4)(B) of subsection (b) of this section, the person possessing the materials shall be afforded adequate opportunity to submit an affidavit setting forth the basis for any contention that the materials sought are not subject to seizure.

§ 2000aa–5. Border and customs searches

This chapter shall not impair or affect the ability of a government officer or employee, pursuant to otherwise applicable law, to conduct searches and seizures at the borders of, or at international points of, entry into the United States in order to enforce the customs laws of the United States.

§ 2000aa–6. Civil actions by aggrieved persons

(a) A person aggrieved by a search for or seizure of materials in violation of this chapter shall have a civil cause of action for damages for such search or seizure—

(1) against the United States, against a State which has waived its sovereign immunity under the Constitution to a claim for damages resulting from a violation of this chapter, or against any other governmental unit, all of which shall be liable for violations of this chapter by their officers or employees while acting within the scope or under color of their office or employment; and

(2) against an officer or employee of a State who has violated this chapter while acting within the scope or under color of his office or employment, if such State has not waived its sovereign immunity as provided in paragraph (1).

(b) It shall be a complete defense to a civil action brought under paragraph (2) of subsection (a) of this section that the officer or employee had a reasonable good faith belief in the lawfulness of his conduct.

(c) The United States, a State, or any other governmental unit liable for violations of this chapter under subsection (a)(1) of this section, may not assert as a defense to a claim arising under this chapter the immunity of the officer or employee whose violation is complained of or his reasonable good faith belief in the lawfulness of his conduct, except that such a defense may be asserted if the violation complained of is that of a judicial officer.

(d) The remedy provided by subsection (a)(1) of this section against the United States, a State, or any other governmental unit is exclusive of any other civil action or proceeding for conduct constituting a violation of this chapter, against the officer or employee whose violation gave rise to the claim, or against the estate of such officer or employee.

(e) Evidence otherwise admissible in a proceeding shall not be excluded on the basis of a violation of this chapter.

(f) A person having a cause of action under this section shall be entitled to recover actual damages but not less than liquidated damages of $1,000, and such reasonable attorneys' fees and other litigation costs reasonably incurred as the court, in its discretion, may award: *Provided, however*, That the United States, a State, or any other governmental unit shall not be liable for interest prior to judgment.

(g) The Attorney General may settle a claim for damages brought against the United States under this section, and shall promulgate regulations to provide for the commencement of an administrative inquiry following a determination of a violation of this chapter by an officer or employee of the United States and for the imposition of administrative sanctions against such officer or employee, if warranted.

(h) The district courts shall have original jurisdiction of all civil actions arising under this section.

§ 2000aa–7. Definitions

(a) "Documentary materials", as used in this chapter, means materials upon which information is recorded, and includes, but is not limited to, written or printed materials, photographs, motion picture films, negatives, video tapes, audio tapes, and other mechanically, magnetically or electronically recorded cards, tapes, or discs, but does not include contraband or the fruits of a crime or things otherwise criminally possessed, or property designed or intended for use, or which is or has been used as, the means of committing a criminal offense.

(b) "Work product materials", as used in this chapter, means materials, other than contraband or the fruits of a crime or things otherwise criminally possessed, or property designed or intended for use, or which is or has been used, as the means of committing a criminal offense, and—

(1) in anticipation of communicating such materials to the public, are prepared, produced, authored, or created, whether by the person in possession of the materials or by any other person;

(2) are possessed for the purposes of communicating such materials to the public; and

(3) include mental impressions, conclusions, opinions, or theories of the person who prepared, produced, authored, or created such material.

(c) "Any other governmental unit", as used in this chapter, includes the District of Columbia, the Commonwealth of Puerto Rico, any territory or possession of the United States, and any local government, unit of local government, or any unit of State government.

§ 2000aa–11. Guidelines for federal officers and employees

(a) The Attorney General shall * * * issue guidelines for the procedures to be employed by any Federal officer or employee, in connection with the investigation or prosecution of an offense, to obtain documentary materials in the private possession of a person when the person is not reasonably believed to be a suspect in such offense or related by blood or marriage to such a suspect, and when the materials sought are not contraband or the fruits or instrumentalities of an offense. * * *

§ 2000aa–12. Binding nature of guidelines; disciplinary actions for violations; legal proceedings for non-compliance prohibited

Guidelines issued by the Attorney General under this subchapter shall have the full force and effect of Department of Justice regulations and any violation of these guidelines shall make the employee or officer involved subject to appropriate administrative disciplinary action. However, an issue relating to the compliance, or the failure to comply, with guidelines issued pursuant to this subchapter may not be litigated, and a court may not entertain such an issue as the basis for the suppression or exclusion of evidence.

[EDITOR'S NOTE: These guidelines appear in 28 C.F.R. Pt. 59. The procedural provisions are set out below.]

§ 59.4 Procedures

(a) *Provisions governing the use of search warrants generally.*

(1) A search warrant should not be used to obtain documentary materials believed to be in the private possession of a disinterested third party unless it appears that the use of a subpoena, summons, request, or other less intrusive alternative means of obtaining the materials would substantially jeopardize the availability or usefulness of the materials sought, and the application for the warrant has been authorized as provided in paragraph (a)(2) of this section.

(2) No federal officer or employee shall apply for a warrant to search for and seize documentary materials believed to be in the private possession of a disinterested third party unless the application for the warrant has been authorized by an attorney for the government. Provided, however, that in an emergency situation in which the immediacy of the need to seize the materials does not permit an opportunity to secure the authorization of an attorney for the government, the application may be authorized by a supervisory law enforcement officer in the applicant's department or agency, if the appropriate United States Attorney (or where the case is not being handled by a United States Attorney's Office, the appropriate supervisory official of

the Department of Justice) is notified of the authorization and the basis for justifying such authorization under this part within 24 hours of the authorization.

(b) *Provisions governing the use of search warrants which may intrude upon professional, confidential relationships.*

(1) A search warrant should not be used to obtain documentary materials believed to be in the private possession of a disinterested third party physician, lawyer, or clergyman, under circumstances in which the materials sought, or other materials likely to be reviewed during the execution of the warrant, contain confidential information on patients, clients, or parishioners which was furnished or developed for the purposes of professional counseling or treatment, unless—

(i) It appears that the use of a subpoena, summons, request or other less intrusive alternative means of obtaining the materials would substantially jeopardize the availability or usefulness of the materials sought;

(ii) Access to the documentary materials appears to be of substantial importance to the investigation or prosecution for which they are sought; and

(iii) The application for the warrant has been approved as provided in paragraph (b)(2) of this section.

(2) No federal officer or employee shall apply for a warrant to search for and seize documentary materials believed to be in the private possession of a disinterested third party physician, lawyer, or clergyman under the circumstances described in paragraph (b)(1) of this section, unless, upon the recommendation of the United States Attorney (or where a case is not being handled by a United States Attorney's Office, upon the recommendation of the appropriate supervisory official of the Department of Justice), an appropriate Deputy Assistant Attorney General has authorized the application for the warrant. Provided, however, that in an emergency situation in which the immediacy of the need to seize the materials does not permit an opportunity to secure the authorization of a Deputy Assistant Attorney General, the application may be authorized by the United States Attorney (or where the case is not being handled by a United States Attorney's Office, by the appropriate supervisory official of the Department of Justice) if an appropriate Deputy Assistant Attorney General is notified of the authorization and the basis for justifying such authorization under this part within 72 hours of the authorization.

(3) Whenever possible, a request for authorization by an appropriate Deputy Assistant Attorney General of a search warrant application pursuant to paragraph (b)(2) of this section shall be made in writing and shall include:

(i) The application for the warrant; and

(ii) A brief description of the facts and circumstances advanced as the basis for recommending authorization of the application under this part.

If a request for authorization of the application is made orally or if, in an emergency situation, the application is authorized by the United States Attorney or a supervisory official of the Department of Justice as provided in paragraph (b)(2) of this section, a written record of the request including the materials specified in paragraphs (b)(3) (i) and (ii) of this section shall be transmitted to an appropriate Deputy Assistant Attorney General within 7 days. The Deputy Assistant Attorneys General shall keep a record of the disposition of all requests for authorizations of search warrant applications made under paragraph (b) of this section.

(4) A search warrant authorized under paragraph (b)(2) of this section shall be executed in such a manner as to minimize, to the greatest extent practicable, scrutiny of confidential materials.

(5) Although it is impossible to define the full range of additional doctor-like therapeutic relationships which involve the furnishing or development of private

information, the United States Attorney (or where a case is not being handled by a United States Attorney's Office, the appropriate supervisory official of the Department of Justice) should determine whether a search for documentary materials held by other disinterested third party professionals involved in such relationships (e.g. psychologists or psychiatric social workers or nurses) would implicate the special privacy concerns which are addressed in paragraph (b) of this section. If the United States Attorney (or other supervisory official of the Department of Justice) determines that such a search would require review of extremely confidential information furnished or developed for the purposes of professional counseling or treatment, the provisions of this subsection should be applied. Otherwise, at a minimum, the requirements of paragraph (a) of this section must be met.

(c) *Considerations bearing on choice of methods.*

In determining whether, as an alternative to the use of a search warrant, the use of a subpoena or other less intrusive means of obtaining documentary materials would substantially jeopardize the availability or usefulness of the materials sought, the following factors, among others, should be considered:

(1) Whether it appears that the use of a subpoena or other alternative which gives advance notice of the government's interest in obtaining the materials would be likely to result in the destruction, alteration, concealment, or transfer of the materials sought; considerations, among others, bearing on this issue may include:

(i) Whether a suspect has access to the materials sought;

(ii) Whether there is a close relationship of friendship, loyalty, or sympathy between the possessor of the materials and a suspect;

(iii) Whether the possessor of the materials is under the domination or control of a suspect;

(iv) Whether the possessor of the materials has an interest in preventing the disclosure of the materials to the government;

(v) Whether the possessor's willingness to comply with a subpoena or request by the government would be likely to subject him to intimidation or threats of reprisal;

(vi) Whether the possessor of the materials has previously acted to obstruct a criminal investigation or judicial proceeding or refused to comply with or acted in defiance of court orders; or

(vii) Whether the possessor has expressed an intent to destroy, conceal, alter, or transfer the materials;

(2) The immediacy of the government's need to obtain the materials; considerations, among others, bearing on this issue may include:

(i) Whether the immediate seizure of the materials is necessary to prevent injury to persons or property;

(ii) Whether the prompt seizure of the materials is necessary to preserve their evidentiary value;

(iii) Whether delay in obtaining the materials would significantly jeopardize an ongoing investigation or prosecution; or

(iv) Whether a legally enforceable form of process, other than a search warrant, is reasonably available as a means of obtaining the materials.

The fact that the disinterested third party possessing the materials may have grounds to challenge a subpoena or other legal process is not in itself a legitimate basis for the use of a search warrant.

Appendix C

FEDERAL RULES OF CRIMINAL PROCEDURE FOR THE UNITED STATES DISTRICT COURTS

I. SCOPE, PURPOSE, AND CONSTRUCTION

Rule 1. Scope

These rules govern the procedure in all criminal proceedings in the courts of the United States, as provided in Rule 54(a); and, whenever specifically provided in one of the rules, to preliminary, supplementary, and special proceedings before United States magistrates and at proceedings before state and local judicial officers.

Rule 2. Purpose and Construction

These rules are intended to provide for the just determination of every criminal proceeding. They shall be construed to secure simplicity in procedure, fairness in administration and the elimination of unjustifiable expense and delay.

II. PRELIMINARY PROCEEDINGS

Rule 3. The Complaint

The complaint is a written statement of the essential facts constituting the offense charged. It shall be made upon oath before a magistrate.

Rule 4. Arrest Warrant or Summons upon Complaint

(a) Issuance. If it appears from the complaint, or from an affidavit or affidavits filed with the complaint, that there is probable cause to believe that an offense has been committed and that the defendant has committed it, a warrant for the arrest of the defendant shall issue to any officer authorized by law to execute it. Upon the request of the attorney for the government a summons instead of a warrant shall issue. More than one warrant or summons may issue on the same complaint. If a defendant fails to appear in response to the summons, a warrant shall issue.

(b) Probable Cause. The finding of probable cause may be based upon hearsay evidence in whole or in part.

(c) Form.

(1) Warrant. The warrant shall be signed by the magistrate and shall contain the name of the defendant or, if the defendant's name is unknown, any name or description by which the defendant can be identified with reasonable certainty. It shall describe the offense charged in the complaint. It shall command that the defendant be arrested and brought before the nearest available magistrate.

(2) Summons. The summons shall be in the same form as the warrant except that it shall summon the defendant to appear before a magistrate at a stated time and place.

(d) Execution or Service; and Return.

(1) By Whom. The warrant shall be executed by a marshal or by some other officer authorized by law. The summons may be served by any person authorized to serve a summons in a civil action.

(2) Territorial Limits. The warrant may be executed or the summons may be served at any place within the jurisdiction of the United States.

(3) Manner. The warrant shall be executed by the arrest of the defendant. The officer need not have the warrant at the time of the arrest but upon request shall show the warrant to the defendant as soon as possible. If the officer does not have the warrant at the time of the arrest, the officer shall then inform the defendant of the offense charged and of the fact that a warrant has been issued. The summons shall be served upon a defendant by delivering a copy to the defendant personally, or by leaving it at the defendant's dwelling house or usual place of abode with some person of suitable age and discretion then residing therein and by mailing a copy of the summons to the defendant's last known address.

(4) Return. The officer executing a warrant shall make return thereof to the magistrate or other officer before whom the defendant is brought pursuant to Rule 5. At the request of the attorney for the government any unexecuted warrant shall be returned to and canceled by the magistrate by whom it was issued. On or before the return day the person to whom a summons was delivered for service shall make return thereof to the magistrate before whom the summons is returnable. At the request of the attorney for the government made at any time while the complaint is pending, a warrant returned unexecuted and not canceled or a summons returned unserved or a duplicate thereof may be delivered by the magistrate to the marshal or other authorized person for execution or service.

Rule 5. Initial Appearance Before the Magistrate

(a) In General. An officer making an arrest under a warrant issued upon a complaint or any person making an arrest without a warrant shall take the arrested person without unnecessary delay before the nearest available federal magistrate or, in the event that a federal magistrate is not reasonably available, before a state or local judicial officer authorized by 18 U.S.C. § 3041. If a person arrested without a warrant is brought before a magistrate, a complaint shall be filed forthwith which shall comply with the requirements of Rule 4(a) with respect to the showing of probable cause. When a person, arrested with or without a warrant or given a summons, appears initially before the magistrate, the magistrate shall proceed in accordance with the applicable subdivisions of this rule.

(b) Misdemeanors. If the charge against the defendant is a misdemeanor triable by a United States magistrate under 18 U.S.C. § 3401, the United States magistrate shall proceed in accordance with the Rules of Procedure for the Trial of Misdemeanors Before United States Magistrates.

(c) Offenses Not Triable by the United States Magistrate. If the charge against the defendant is not triable by the United States magistrate, the defendant shall not be called upon to plead. The magistrate shall inform the defendant of the complaint against the defendant and of any affidavit filed therewith, of the defendant's right to retain counsel or to request the assignment of counsel if the defendant is unable to obtain counsel, and of the general circumstances under which the defendant may secure pretrial release. The magistrate shall inform the defendant that the defendant is not required to make a statement and that any statement made by the defendant may be used against the defendant. The magistrate shall also inform the defendant of the right to a preliminary examination. The magistrate shall allow the defendant reasonable time and opportunity to consult counsel and shall detain or conditionally release the defendant as provided by statute or in these rules.

A defendant is entitled to a preliminary examination, unless waived, when charged with any offense, other than a petty offense, which is to be tried by a judge of the district court. If the defendant waives preliminary examination, the magistrate shall forthwith hold the defendant to answer in the district court. If the defendant does not waive the preliminary examination, the magistrate shall schedule a preliminary examination. Such examination shall be held within a reasonable time but in any event not later than 10 days following the initial appearance if the defendant is in custody and no later than 20 days if the defendant is not in custody, provided, however, that the preliminary examination shall not be held if the defendant is indicted or if an information against the defendant is filed in district court before the date set for the preliminary examination. With the consent of the defendant and upon a showing of good cause, taking into account the public interest in the prompt disposition of criminal cases, time limits specified in this subdivision may be extended one or more times by a federal magistrate. In the absence of such consent by the defendant, time limits may be extended by a judge of the United States only upon a showing that extraordinary circumstances exist and that delay is indispensable to the interests of justice.

Rule 5.1. Preliminary Examination

(a) **Probable Cause Finding.** If from the evidence it appears that there is probable cause to believe that an offense has been committed and that the defendant committed it, the federal magistrate shall forthwith hold the defendant to answer in district court. The finding of probable cause may be based upon hearsay evidence in whole or in part. The defendant may cross-examine adverse witnesses and may introduce evidence. Objections to evidence on the ground that it was acquired by unlawful means are not properly made at the preliminary examination. Motions to suppress must be made to the trial court as provided in Rule 12.

(b) **Discharge of Defendant.** If from the evidence it appears that there is no probable cause to believe that an offense has been committed or that the defendant committed it, the federal magistrate shall dismiss the complaint and discharge the defendant. The discharge of the defendant shall not preclude the government from instituting a subsequent prosecution for the same offense.

(c) **Records.** After concluding the proceeding the federal magistrate shall transmit forthwith to the clerk of the district court all papers in the proceeding. The magistrate shall promptly make or cause to be made a record or summary of such proceeding.

(1) On timely application to a federal magistrate, the attorney for a defendant in a criminal case may be given the opportunity to have the recording of the hearing on preliminary examination made available to that attorney in connection with any further hearing or preparation for trial. The court may, by local rule, appoint the place for and define the conditions under which such opportunity may be afforded counsel.

(2) On application of a defendant addressed to the court or any judge thereof, an order may issue that the federal magistrate make available a copy of the transcript, or of a portion thereof, to defense counsel. Such order shall provide for prepayment of costs of such transcript by the defendant unless the defendant makes a sufficient affidavit that the defendant is unable to pay or to give security therefor, in which case the expense shall be paid by the Director of the Administrative Office of the United States Courts from available appropriated funds. Counsel for the government may move also that a copy of the transcript, in whole or in part, be made available to it, for good cause shown, and an order may be entered

granting such motion in whole or in part, on appropriate terms, except that the government need not prepay costs nor furnish security therefor.

III. INDICTMENT AND INFORMATION

Rule 6. The Grand Jury

(a) Summoning Grand Juries.

(1) Generally. The court shall order one or more grand juries to be summoned at such time as the public interest requires. The grand jury shall consist of not less than 16 nor more than 23 members. The court shall direct that a sufficient number of legally qualified persons be summoned to meet this requirement.

(2) Alternate Jurors. The court may direct that alternate jurors may be designated at the time a grand jury is selected. Alternate jurors in the order in which they were designated may thereafter be impanelled as provided in subdivision (g) of this rule. Alternate jurors shall be drawn in the same manner and shall have the same qualifications as the regular jurors, and if impanelled shall be subject to the same challenges, shall take the same oath and shall have the same functions, powers, facilities and privileges as the regular jurors.

(b) Objections to Grand Jury and to Grand Jurors.

(1) Challenges. The attorney for the government or a defendant who has been held to answer in the district court may challenge the array of jurors on the ground that the grand jury was not selected, drawn or summoned in accordance with law, and may challenge an individual juror on the ground that the juror is not legally qualified. Challenges shall be made before the administration of the oath to the jurors and shall be tried by the court.

(2) Motion to Dismiss. A motion to dismiss the indictment may be based on objections to the array or on the lack of legal qualification of an individual juror, if not previously determined upon challenge. It shall be made in the manner prescribed in 28 U.S.C. § 1867(e) and shall be granted under the conditions prescribed in that statute. An indictment shall not be dismissed on the ground that one or more members of the grand jury were not legally qualified if it appears from the record kept pursuant to subdivision (c) of this rule that 12 or more jurors, after deducting the number not legally qualified, concurred in finding the indictment.

(c) Foreperson and Deputy Foreperson. The court shall appoint one of the jurors to be foreperson and another to be deputy foreperson. The foreperson shall have power to administer oaths and affirmations and shall sign all indictments. The foreperson or another juror designated by the foreperson shall keep record of the number of jurors concurring in the finding of every indictment and shall file the record with the clerk of the court, but the record shall not be made public except on order of the court. During the absence of the foreperson, the deputy foreperson shall act as foreperson.

(d) Who May Be Present. Attorneys for the government, the witness under examination, interpreters when needed and, for the purpose of taking the evidence, a stenographer or operator of a recording device may be present while the grand jury is in session, but no person other than the jurors may be present while the grand jury is deliberating or voting.

(e) Recording and Disclosure of Proceedings.

(1) Recording of Proceedings. All proceedings, except when the grand jury is deliberating or voting, shall be recorded stenographically or by an electronic recording device. An unintentional failure of any recording to reproduce all or any portion of a proceeding shall not affect the validity of the prosecution. The recording or reporter's notes or any transcript prepared therefrom shall remain in the custody or control of the attorney for the government unless otherwise ordered by the court in a particular case.

(2) **General Rule of Secrecy.** A grand juror, an interpreter, a stenographer, an operator of a recording device, a typist who transcribes recorded testimony, an attorney for the government, or any person to whom disclosure is made under paragraph (3)(A)(ii) of this subdivision shall not disclose matters occurring before the grand jury, except as otherwise provided for in these rules. No obligation of secrecy may be imposed on any person except in accordance with this rule. A knowing violation of Rule 6 may be punished as a contempt of court.

(3) **Exceptions.**

(A) Disclosure otherwise prohibited by this rule of matters occurring before the grand jury, other than its deliberations and the vote of any grand juror, may be made to—

(i) an attorney for the government for use in the performance of such attorney's duty; and

(ii) such government personnel (including personnel of a state or subdivision of a state) as are deemed necessary by an attorney for the government to assist an attorney for the government in the performance of such attorney's duty to enforce federal criminal law.

(B) Any person to whom matters are disclosed under subparagraph (A)(ii) of this paragraph shall not utilize that grand jury material for any purpose other than assisting the attorney for the government in the performance of such attorney's duty to enforce federal criminal law. An attorney for the government shall promptly provide the district court, before which was impaneled the grand jury whose material has been so disclosed, with the names of the persons to whom such disclosure has been made, and shall certify that the attorney has advised such persons of their obligation of secrecy under this rule.

(C) Disclosure otherwise prohibited by this rule of matters occurring before the grand jury may also be made—

(i) when so directed by a court preliminarily to or in connection with a judicial proceeding;

(ii) when permitted by a court at the request of the defendant, upon a showing that grounds may exist for a motion to dismiss the indictment because of matters occurring before the grand jury;

(iii) when the disclosure is made by an attorney for the government to another federal grand jury; or

(iv) when permitted by a court at the request of an attorney for the government, upon a showing that such matters may disclose a violation of state criminal law, to an appropriate official of a state or subdivision of a state for the purpose of enforcing such law.

If the court orders disclosure of matters occurring before the grand jury, the disclosure shall be made in such manner, at such time, and under such conditions as the court may direct.

(D) A petition for disclosure pursuant to subdivision (e)(3)(C)(i) shall be filed in the district where the grand jury convened. Unless the hearing is ex parte, which it may be when the petitioner is the government, the petitioner shall serve written notice of the petition upon (i) the attorney for the government, (ii) the parties to the judicial proceeding if disclosure is sought in connection with such a proceeding, and (iii) such other persons as the court may direct. The court shall afford those persons a reasonable opportunity to appear and be heard.

(E) If the judicial proceeding giving rise to the petition is in a federal district court in another district, the court shall transfer the matter to that court unless it can reasonably obtain sufficient knowledge of the proceeding to determine whether disclosure is proper. The court shall order transmitted to the court to which the matter is transferred the material sought to be disclosed, if feasible, and a written evaluation of the need for continued grand jury secrecy. The court to which the matter is transferred shall afford the aforementioned persons a reasonable opportunity to appear and be heard.

(4) Sealed Indictments. The federal magistrate to whom an indictment is returned may direct that the indictment be kept secret until the defendant is in custody or has been released pending trial. Thereupon the clerk shall seal the indictment and no person shall disclose the return of the indictment except when necessary for the issuance and execution of a warrant or summons.

(5) Closed Hearing. Subject to any right to an open hearing in contempt proceedings, the court shall order a hearing on matters affecting a grand jury proceeding to be closed to the extent necessary to prevent disclosure of matters occurring before a grand jury.

(6) Sealed Records. Records, orders and subpoenas relating to grand jury proceedings shall be kept under seal to the extent and for such time as is necessary to prevent disclosure of matters occurring before a grand jury.

(f) Finding and Return of Indictment. An indictment may be found only upon the concurrence of 12 or more jurors. The indictment shall be returned by the grand jury to a federal magistrate in open court. If a complaint or information is pending against the defendant and 12 jurors do not concur in finding an indictment, the foreperson shall so report to a federal magistrate in writing forthwith.

(g) Discharge and Excuse. A grand jury shall serve until discharged by the court, but no grand jury may serve more than 18 months unless the court extends the service of the grand jury for a period of six months or less upon a determination that such extension is in the public interest. At any time for cause shown the court may excuse a juror either temporarily or permanently, and in the latter event the court may impanel another person in place of the juror excused.

Rule 7. The Indictment and the Information

(a) Use of Indictment or Information. An offense which may be punished by death shall be prosecuted by indictment. An offense which may be punished by imprisonment for a term exceeding one year or at hard labor shall be prosecuted by indictment or, if indictment is waived, it may be prosecuted by information. Any other offense may be prosecuted by indictment or by information. An information may be filed without leave of court.

(b) Waiver of Indictment. An offense which may be punished by imprisonment for a term exceeding one year or at hard labor may be prosecuted by information if the defendant, after having been advised of the nature of the charge and of the rights of the defendant, waives in open court prosecution by indictment.

(c) Nature and Contents.

(1) In General. The indictment or the information shall be a plain, concise and definite written statement of the essential facts constituting the offense charged. It shall be signed by the attorney for the government. It need not contain a formal commencement, a formal conclusion or any other matter not necessary to such statement. Allegations made in one count may be incorporated by reference in another count. It may be alleged in a single count that the means by which the defendant committed the offense are unknown or that the defendant committed it by one or more specified means. The indictment or information shall state for each count the official or customary citation of the statute, rule, regulation or other provision of law which the defendant is alleged therein to have violated.

(2) Criminal Forfeiture. No judgment of forfeiture may be entered in a criminal proceeding unless the indictment or the information shall allege the extent of the interest or property subject to forfeiture.

(3) Harmless Error. Error in the citation or its omission shall not be ground for dismissal of the indictment or information or for reversal of a conviction if the error or omission did not mislead the defendant to the defendant's prejudice.

(d) Surplusage. The court on motion of the defendant may strike surplusage from the indictment or information.

(e) Amendment of Information. The court may permit an information to be amended at any time before verdict or finding if no additional or different offense is charged and if substantial rights of the defendant are not prejudiced.

(f) Bill of Particulars. The court may direct the filing of a bill of particulars. A motion for a bill of particulars may be made before arraignment or within ten days after arraignment or at such later time as the court may permit. A bill of particulars may be amended at any time subject to such conditions as justice requires.

Rule 8. Joinder of Offenses and of Defendants

(a) Joinder of Offenses. Two or more offenses may be charged in the same indictment or information in a separate count for each offense if the offenses charged, whether felonies or misdemeanors or both, are of the same or similar character or are based on the same act or transaction or on two or more acts or transactions connected together or constituting parts of a common scheme or plan.

(b) Joinder of Defendants. Two or more defendants may be charged in the same indictment or information if they are alleged to have participated in the same act or transaction or in the same series of acts or transactions constituting an offense or offenses. Such defendants may be charged in one or more counts together or separately and all of the defendants need not be charged in each count.

Rule 9. Warrant or Summons Upon Indictment or Information

(a) Issuance. Upon the request of the attorney for the government the court shall issue a warrant for each defendant named in an information supported by a showing of probable cause under oath as is required by Rule 4(a), or in an indictment. Upon the request of the attorney for the government a summons instead of a warrant shall issue. If no request is made, the court may issue either a warrant or a summons in its discretion. More than one warrant or summons may issue for the same defendant. The clerk shall deliver the warrant or summons to the marshal or other person authorized by law to execute or serve it. If a defendant fails to appear in response to the summons, a warrant shall issue. When a defendant arrested with a warrant or given a summons appears initially before a magistrate, the magistrate shall proceed in accordance with the applicable subdivisions of Rule 5.

(b) Form.

(1) Warrant. The form of the warrant shall be as provided in Rule 4(c)(1) except that it shall be signed by the clerk, it shall describe the offense charged in the indictment or information and it shall command that the defendant be arrested and brought before the nearest available magistrate. The amount of bail may be fixed by the court and endorsed on the warrant.

(2) Summons. The summons shall be in the same form as the warrant except that it shall summon the defendant to appear before a magistrate at a stated time and place.

(c) Execution or Service; and Return.

(1) Execution or Service. The warrant shall be executed or the summons served as provided in Rule 4(d)(1), (2) and (3). A summons to a corporation shall be served by delivering a copy to an officer or to a managing or general agent or to any other agent authorized by appointment or by law to receive service of process and, if the agent is one authorized by statute to receive service and the statute so requires, by also mailing a copy to the corporation's last known address within the district or at its principal place of business elsewhere in the United States. The officer executing the warrant shall bring the arrested person without unnecessary delay before the nearest available federal magistrate or, in the event that a federal magistrate is not reasonably available, before a state or local judicial officer authorized by 18 U.S.C. § 3041.

(2) Return. The officer executing a warrant shall make return thereof to the magistrate or other officer before whom the defendant is brought. At the request of the attorney for the government any unexecuted warrant shall be returned and cancelled. On or before the return day the person to whom a summons was delivered for service shall make return thereof. At the request of the attorney for the government made at any time while the indictment or information is pending, a warrant returned unexecuted and not cancelled or a summons returned unserved or a duplicate thereof may be delivered by the clerk to the marshal or other authorized person for execution or service.

[(d) Remand to United States Magistrate for Trial of Minor Offenses] (Abrogated Apr. 28, 1982, eff. Aug. 1, 1982).

IV. ARRAIGNMENT AND PREPARATION FOR TRIAL

Rule 10. Arraignment

Arraignment shall be conducted in open court and shall consist of reading the indictment or information to the defendant or stating to the defendant the substance of the charge and calling on the defendant to plead thereto. The defendant shall be given a copy of the indictment or information before being called upon to plead.

Rule 11. Pleas

(a) Alternatives.

(1) In General. A defendant may plead not guilty, guilty, or nolo contendere. If a defendant refuses to plead or if a defendant corporation fails to appear, the court shall enter a plea of not guilty.

(2) Conditional Pleas. With the approval of the court and the consent of the government, a defendant may enter a conditional plea of guilty or nolo contendere, reserving in writing the right, on appeal from the judgment, to review of the adverse determination of any specified pretrial motion. A defendant who prevails on appeal shall be allowed to withdraw the plea.

(b) Nolo Contendere. A defendant may plead nolo contendere only with the consent of the court. Such a plea shall be accepted by the court only after due consideration of the views of the parties and the interest of the public in the effective administration of justice.

(c) Advice to Defendant. Before accepting a plea of guilty or nolo contendere, the court must address the defendant personally in open court and inform the defendant of, and determine that the defendant understands, the following:

(1) the nature of the charge to which the plea is offered, the mandatory minimum penalty provided by law, if any, and the maximum possible penalty provided by law, including the effect of any special parole or supervised release term, the fact that the court is required to consider any applicable sentencing guidelines but many depart from those guidelines under some circumstances, and, when applicable, that the court may also order the defendant to make restitution to any victim of the offense; and

(2) if the defendant is not represented by an attorney, that the defendant has the right to be represented by an attorney at every stage of the proceeding and, if necessary, one will be appointed to represent the defendant; and

(3) that the defendant has the right to plead not guilty or to persist in that plea if it has already been made, the right to be tried by a jury and at that trial the right to the assistance of counsel, the right to confront and cross-examine adverse witnesses, and the right against compelled self-incrimination; and

(4) that if a plea of guilty or nolo contendere is accepted by the court there will not be a further trial of any kind, so that by pleading guilty or nolo contendere the defendant waives the right to a trial; and

(5) if the court intends to question the defendant under oath, on the record, and in the presence of counsel about the offense to which the defendant has pleaded, that the defendant's answers may later be used against the defendant in a prosecution for perjury or false statement.

(d) Insuring That the Plea is Voluntary. The court shall not accept a plea of guilty or nolo contendere without first, by addressing the defendant personally in open court, determining that the plea is voluntary and not the result of force or threats or of promises apart from a plea agreement. The court shall also inquire as to whether the defendant's willingness to plead guilty or nolo contendere results from prior discussions between the attorney for the government and the defendant or the defendant's attorney.

(e) Plea Agreement Procedure.

(1) In General. The attorney for the government and the attorney for the defendant or the defendant when acting pro se may engage in discussions with a view toward reaching an agreement that, upon the entering of a plea of guilty or nolo contendere to a charged offense or to a lesser or related offense, the attorney for the government will do any of the following:

(A) move for dismissal of other charges; or

(B) make a recommendation, or agree not to oppose the defendant's request, for a particular sentence, with the understanding that such recommendation or request shall not be binding upon the court; or

(C) agree that a specific sentence is the appropriate disposition of the case.

The court shall not participate in any such discussions.

(2) Notice of Such Agreement. If a plea agreement has been reached by the parties, the court shall, on the record, require the disclosure of the agreement in open court or, on a showing of good cause, in camera, at the time the plea is offered. If the agreement is of the type specified in subdivision (e)(1)(A) or (C), the court may accept or reject the agreement, or may defer its decision as to the acceptance or rejection until there has been an opportunity to consider the presentence report. If the agreement is of the type specified in subdivision (e)(1) (B), the court shall advise the defendant that if the court does not accept the recommendation or request the defendant nevertheless has no right to withdraw the plea.

(3) Acceptance of a Plea Agreement. If the court accepts the plea agreement, the court shall inform the defendant that it will embody in the judgment and sentence the disposition provided for in the plea agreement.

(4) Rejection of a Plea Agreement. If the court rejects the plea agreement, the court shall, on the record, inform the parties of this fact, advise the defendant personally in open court or, on a showing of good cause, in camera, that the court is not bound by the plea agreement, afford the defendant the opportunity to then withdraw the plea, and advise the defendant that if the defendant persists in a guilty plea or plea of nolo contendere the disposition of the case may be less favorable to the defendant than that contemplated by the plea agreement.

(5) Time of Plea Agreement Procedure. Except for good cause shown, notification to the court of the existence of a plea agreement shall be given at the arraignment or at such other time, prior to trial, as may be fixed by the court.

(6) Inadmissibility of Pleas, Plea Discussions, and Related Statements. Except as otherwise provided in this paragraph, evidence of the following is not, in any civil or criminal proceeding, admissible against the defendant who made the plea or was a participant in the plea discussions:

(A) a plea of guilty which was later withdrawn;

(B) a plea of nolo contendere;

(C) any statement made in the course of any proceedings under this rule regarding either of the foregoing pleas; or

(D) any statement made in the course of plea discussions with an attorney for the government which do not result in a plea of guilty or which result in a plea of guilty later withdrawn.

However, such a statement is admissible (i) in any proceeding wherein another statement made in the course of the same plea or plea discussions has been introduced and the statement ought in fairness be considered contemporaneously with it, or (ii) in a criminal proceeding for perjury or false statement if the statement was made by the defendant under oath, on the record, and in the presence of counsel.

(f) Determining Accuracy of Plea. Notwithstanding the acceptance of a plea of guilty, the court should not enter a judgment upon such plea without making such inquiry as shall satisfy it that there is a factual basis for the plea.

(g) Record of Proceedings. A verbatim record of the proceedings at which the defendant enters a plea shall be made and, if there is a plea of guilty or nolo contendere, the record shall include, without limitation, the court's advice to the defendant, the inquiry into the voluntariness of the plea including any plea agreement, and the inquiry into the accuracy of a guilty plea.

(h) Harmless Error. Any variance from the procedures required by this rule which does not affect substantial rights shall be disregarded.

Rule 12. Pleadings and Motions Before Trial; Defenses and Objections

(a) Pleadings and Motions. Pleadings in criminal proceedings shall be the indictment and the information, and the pleas of not guilty, guilty and nolo contendere. All other pleas, and demurrers and motions to quash are abolished, and defenses and objections raised before trial which heretofore could have been raised by one or more of them shall be raised only by motion to dismiss or to grant appropriate relief, as provided in these rules.

(b) Pretrial Motions. Any defense, objection, or request which is capable of determination without the trial of the general issue may be raised before trial by motion. Motions may be written or oral at the discretion of the judge. The following must be raised prior to trial:

(1) Defenses and objections based on defects in the institution of the prosecution; or

(2) Defenses and objections based on defects in the indictment or information (other than that it fails to show jurisdiction in the court or to charge an offense which objections shall be noticed by the court at any time during the pendency of the proceedings); or

(3) Motions to suppress evidence; or

(4) Requests for discovery under Rule 16; or

(5) Requests for a severance of charges or defendants under Rule 14.

(c) Motion Date. Unless otherwise provided by local rule, the court may, at the time of the arraignment or as soon thereafter as practicable, set a time for the making of pretrial motions or requests and, if required, a later date of hearing.

(d) Notice by the Government of the Intention to Use Evidence.

(1) At the Discretion of the Government. At the arraignment or as soon thereafter as is practicable, the government may give notice to the defendant of its intention to use specified evidence at trial in order to afford the defendant an opportunity to raise objections to such evidence prior to trial under subdivision (b)(3) of this rule.

(2) At the Request of the Defendant. At the arraignment or as soon thereafter as is practicable the defendant may, in order to afford an opportunity to move to suppress evidence under subdivision (b)(3) of this rule, request notice of the government's intention to use (in its evidence in chief at trial) any evidence which the defendant may be entitled to discover under Rule 16 subject to any relevant limitations prescribed in Rule 16.

(e) Ruling on Motion. A motion made before trial shall be determined before trial unless the court, for good cause, orders that it be deferred for determination at the trial of the general issue or until after verdict, but no such determination shall be deferred if a party's right to appeal is adversely affected. Where factual issues are involved in determining a motion, the court shall state its essential findings on the record.

(f) Effect of Failure To Raise Defenses or Objections. Failure by a party to raise defenses or objections or to make requests which must be made prior to trial, at the time set by the court pursuant to subdivision (c), or prior to any extension thereof made by the court, shall constitute waiver thereof, but the court for cause shown may grant relief from the waiver.

(g) Records. A verbatim record shall be made of all proceedings at the hearing, including such findings of fact and conclusions of law as are made orally.

(h) Effect of Determination. If the court grants a motion based on a defect in the institution of the prosecution or in the indictment or information, it may also order that the defendant be continued in custody or that bail be continued for a specified time pending the filing of a new indictment or information. Nothing in this rule shall be deemed to affect the provisions of any Act of Congress relating to periods of limitations.

(i) Production of Statements at Suppression Hearing. Except as herein provided, rule 26.2 shall apply at a hearing on a motion to suppress evidence under subdivision (b)(3) of this rule. For purposes of this subdivision, a law enforcement officer shall be deemed a witness called by the government, and upon a claim of privilege the court shall excise the portions of the statement containing privileged matter.

Rule 12.1. Notice of Alibi

(a) **Notice by Defendant.** Upon written demand of the attorney for the government stating the time, date, and place at which the alleged offense was committed, the defendant shall serve within ten days, or at such different time as the court may direct, upon the attorney for the government a written notice of the defendant's intention to offer a defense of alibi. Such notice by the defendant shall state the specific place or places at which the defendant claims to have been at the time of the alleged offense and the names and addresses of the witnesses upon whom the defendant intends to rely to establish such alibi.

(b) **Disclosure of Information and Witness.** Within ten days thereafter, but in no event less than ten days before trial, unless the court otherwise directs, the attorney for the government shall serve upon the defendant or the defendant's attorney a written notice stating the names and addresses of the witnesses upon whom the government intends to rely to establish the defendant's presence at the scene of the alleged offense and any other witnesses to be relied on to rebut testimony of any of the defendant's alibi witnesses.

(c) **Continuing Duty to Disclose.** If prior to or during trial, a party learns of an additional witness whose identity, if known, should have been included in the information furnished under subdivision (a) or (b), the party shall promptly notify the other party or the other party's attorney of the existence and identity of such additional witness.

(d) **Failure to Comply.** Upon the failure of either party to comply with the requirements of this rule, the court may exclude the testimony of any undisclosed witness offered by such party as to the defendant's absence from or presence at, the scene of the alleged offense. This rule shall not limit the right of the defendant to testify.

(e) **Exceptions.** For good cause shown, the court may grant an exception to any of the requirements of subdivisions (a) through (d) of this rule.

(f) **Inadmissibility of Withdrawn Alibi.** Evidence of an intention to rely upon an alibi defense, later withdrawn, or of statements made in connection with such intention, is not, in any civil or criminal proceeding, admissible against the person who gave notice of the intention.

Rule 12.2. Notice of Insanity Defense or Expert Testimony of Defendant's Mental Condition

(a) **Defense of Insanity.** If a defendant intends to rely upon the defense of insanity at the time of the alleged offense, the defendant shall, within the time provided for the filing of pretrial motions or at such later time as the court may direct, notify the attorney for the government in writing of such intention and file a copy of such notice with the clerk. If there is a failure to comply with the requirements of this subdivision, insanity may not be raised as a defense. The court may for cause shown allow late filing of the notice or grant additional time to the parties to prepare for trial or make such other order as may be appropriate.

(b) **Expert Testimony of Defendant's Mental Condition.** If a defendant intends to introduce expert testimony relating to a mental disease or defect or any other mental condition of the defendant bearing upon the issue of guilt, the defendant shall, within the time provided for the filing of pretrial motions or at such later time as the court may direct, notify the attorney for the government in writing of such intention and file a copy of such notice with the clerk. The court may for cause shown allow late filing of the notice or grant additional time to the parties to prepare for trial or make such other order as may be appropriate.

(c) **Mental Examination of Defendant.** In an appropriate case the court may, upon motion of the attorney for the government, order the defendant to submit to an examination pursuant to 18 U.S.C. 4241 or 4242. No statement made by the defendant in the course of any examination provided for by this rule, whether the examination be with or without the consent of the defendant, no testimony by the expert based upon such statement, and no other fruits of the statement shall be admitted in evidence against the defendant in any criminal proceeding except on an issue respecting mental condition on which the defendant has introduced testimony.

(d) **Failure To Comply.** If there is a failure to give notice when required by subdivision (b) of this rule or to submit to an examination when ordered under subdivision (c) of this rule, the court may exclude the testimony of any expert witness offered by the defendant on the issue of the defendant's guilt.

(e) **Inadmissibility of Withdrawn Intention.** Evidence of an intention as to which notice was given under subdivision (a) or (b), later withdrawn, is not, in any civil or criminal proceeding, admissible against the person who gave notice of the intention.

Rule 12.3. Notice of Defense Based Upon Public Authority

(a) **Notice by Defendant; Government Response; Disclosure of Witnesses.**

(1) **Defendant's Notice and Government's Response.** A defendant intending to claim a defense of actual or believed exercise of public authority on behalf of a law enforcement or Federal intelligence agency at the time of the alleged offense shall, within the time provided for the filing of pretrial motions or at such later time as the court may direct, serve upon the attorney for the Government a written notice of such intention and file a copy of such notice with the clerk. Such notice shall identify the law enforcement or Federal intelligence agency and any member of such agency on behalf of which and the period of time in which the defendant claims the actual or believed exercise of public authority occurred. If the notice identifies a Federal intelligence agency, the copy filed with the clerk shall be under seal. Within ten days after receiving the defendant's notice, but in no event less than twenty days before the trial, the attorney for the Government shall serve upon the defendant or the defendant's attorney a written response which shall admit or deny that the defendant exercised the public authority identified in the defendant's notice.

(2) **Disclosure of Witnesses.** At the time that the Government serves its response to the notice or thereafter, but in no event less than twenty days before the trial, the attorney for the Government may serve upon the defendant or the defendant's attorney a written demand for the names and addresses of the witnesses, if any, upon whom the defendant intends to rely in establishing the defense identified in the notice. Within seven days after receiving the Government's demand, the defendant shall serve upon the attorney for the Government a written statement of the names and addresses of any such witnesses. Within seven days after receiving the defendant's written statement, the attorney for the Government shall serve upon the defendant or the defendant's attorney a written statement of the names and addresses of the witnesses, if any, upon whom the Government intends to rely in opposing the defense identified in the notice.

(3) **Additional Time.** If good cause is shown, the court may allow a party additional time to comply with any obligation imposed by this rule.

(b) **Continuing Duty to Disclose.** If, prior to or during trial, a party learns of any additional witness whose identity, if known, should have been included in the written statement furnished under subdivision (a)(2) of this rule, that party shall promptly notify in writing the other party or the other party's attorney of the name and address of any such witness.

(c) Failure to Comply. If a party fails to comply with the requirements of this rule, the court may exclude the testimony of any undisclosed witness offered in support of or in opposition to the defense, or enter such other order as it deems just under the circumstances. This rule shall not limit the right of the defendant to testify.

(d) Protective Procedures Unaffected. This rule shall be in addition to and shall not supersede the authority of the court to issue appropriate protective orders, or the authority of the court to order that any pleading be filed under seal.

(e) Inadmissibility of Withdrawn Defense Based Upon Public Authority. Evidence of an intention as to which notice was given under subdivision (a), later withdrawn, is not, in any civil or criminal proceeding, admissible against the person who gave notice of the intention.

Rule 13.   Trial Together of Indictments or Informations

The court may order two or more indictments or informations or both to be tried together if the offenses, and the defendants if there is more than one, could have been joined in a single indictment or information. The procedure shall be the same as if the prosecution were under such single indictment or information.

Rule 14.   Relief from Prejudicial Joinder

If it appears that a defendant or the government is prejudiced by a joinder of offenses or of defendants in an indictment or information or by such joinder for trial together, the court may order an election or separate trials of counts, grant a severance of defendants or provide whatever other relief justice requires. In ruling on a motion by a defendant for severance the court may order the attorney for the government to deliver to the court for inspection *in camera* any statements or confessions made by the defendants which the government intends to introduce in evidence at the trial.

Rule 15.   Depositions

(a) When Taken. Whenever due to exceptional circumstances of the case it is in the interest of justice that the testimony of a prospective witness of a party be taken and preserved for use at trial, the court may upon motion of such party and notice to the parties order that testimony of such witness be taken by deposition and that any designated book, paper, document, record, recording, or other material not privileged, be produced at the same time and place. If a witness is detained pursuant to section 3144 of title 18, United States Code, the court on written motion of the witness and upon notice to the parties may direct that the witness' deposition be taken. After the deposition has been subscribed the court may discharge the witness.

(b) Notice of Taking. The party at whose instance a deposition is to be taken shall give to every party reasonable written notice of the time and place for taking the deposition. The notice shall state the name and address of each person to be examined. On motion of a party upon whom the notice is served, the court for cause shown may extend or shorten the time or change the place for taking the deposition. The officer having custody of a defendant shall be notified of the time and place set for the examination and shall, unless the defendant waives in writing the right to be present, produce the defendant at the examination and keep the defendant in the presence of the witness during the examination, unless, after being warned by the court that disruptive conduct will cause the defendant's removal from the place of the taking of the deposition, the defendant persists in conduct which is such as to justify exclusion from that place. A defendant not in custody shall have the right to be present at the examination upon request subject to such terms as may be fixed by the court, but a failure, absent good cause shown, to appear after notice and tender of expenses in accordance with subdivision (c) of this rule shall constitute a waiver of that right and of any objection to the taking and use of the deposition based upon that right.

(c) Payment of Expenses. Whenever a deposition is taken at the instance of the government, or whenever a deposition is taken at the instance of a defendant who is unable to bear the expenses of the taking of the deposition, the court may direct that the expense of travel and subsistence of the defendant and the defendant's attorney for attendance at the examination and the cost of the transcript of the deposition shall be paid by the government.

(d) How Taken. Subject to such additional conditions as the court shall provide, a deposition shall be taken and filed in the manner provided in civil actions except as otherwise provided in these rules, provided that (1) in no event shall a deposition be taken of a party defendant without that defendant's consent, and (2) the scope and manner of examination and cross-examination shall be such as would be allowed in the trial itself. The government shall make available to the defendant or the defendant's counsel for examination and use at the taking of the deposition any statement of the witness being deposed which is in the possession of the government and to which the defendant would be entitled at the trial.

(e) Use. At the trial or upon any hearing, a part or all of a deposition, so far as otherwise admissible under the rules of evidence, may be used as substantive evidence if the witness is unavailable, as unavailability is defined in Rule 804(a) of the Federal Rules of Evidence, or the witness gives testimony at the trial or hearing inconsistent with that witness' deposition. Any deposition may also be used by any party for the purpose of contradicting or impeaching the testimony of the deponent as a witness. If only a part of a deposition is offered in evidence by a party, an adverse party may require the offering of all of it which is relevant to the part offered and any party may offer other parts.

(f) Objections to Deposition Testimony. Objections to deposition testimony or evidence or parts thereof and the grounds for the objection shall be stated at the time of the taking of the deposition.

(g) Deposition by Agreement Not Precluded. Nothing in this rule shall preclude the taking of a deposition, orally or upon written questions, or the use of a deposition, by agreement of the parties with the consent of the court.

Rule 16. Discovery and Inspection

(a) Disclosure of Evidence by the Government.

(1) Information Subject to Disclosure.

(A) Statement of Defendant. Upon request of a defendant the government shall permit the defendant to inspect and copy or photograph: any relevant written or recorded statements made by the defendant, or copies thereof, within the possession, custody or control of the government, the existence of which is known, or by the exercise of due diligence may become known, to the attorney for the government; the substance of any oral statement which the government intends to offer in evidence at the trial made by the defendant whether before or after arrest in response to interrogation by any person then known to the defendant to be a government agent; and recorded testimony of the defendant before a grand jury which relates to the offense charged. Where the defendant is a corporation, partnership, association or labor union, the court may grant the defendant, upon its motion, discovery of relevant recorded testimony of any witness before a grand jury who (1) was, at the time of that testimony, so situated as an officer or employee as to have been able legally to bind the defendant in respect to conduct constituting the offense, or (2) was, at the time of the offense, personally involved in the alleged conduct constituting the offense and so situated as an officer or employee as to have been able legally to bind the defendant in respect to that alleged conduct in which the witness was involved.

(B) Defendant's Prior Record. Upon request of the defendant, the government shall furnish to the defendant such copy of the defendant's prior criminal record, if any, as is within the possession, custody, or control of the government, the existence of which is known, or by the exercise of due diligence may become known, to the attorney for the government.

(C) Documents and Tangible Objects. Upon request of the defendant the government shall permit the defendant to inspect and copy or photograph books, papers, documents, photographs, tangible objects, buildings or places, or copies or portions thereof, which are within the possession, custody or control of the government, and which are material to the preparation of the defendant's defense or are intended for use by the government as evidence in chief at the trial, or were obtained from or belong to the defendant.

(D) Reports of Examinations and Tests. Upon request of a defendant the government shall permit the defendant to inspect and copy or photograph any results or reports of physical or mental examinations, and of scientific tests or experiments, or copies thereof, which are within the possession, custody, or control of the government, the existence of which is known, or by the exercise of due diligence may become known, to the attorney for the government, and which are material to the preparation of the defense or are intended for use by the government as evidence in chief at the trial.

(2) Information Not Subject to Disclosure. Except as provided in paragraphs (A), (B), and (D) of subdivision (a)(1), this rule does not authorize the discovery or inspection of reports, memoranda, or other internal government documents made by the attorney for the government or other government agents in connection with the investigation or prosecution of the case, or of statements made by government witnesses or prospective government witnesses except as provided in 18 U.S.C. § 3500.

(3) Grand Jury Transcripts. Except as provided in Rules 6, 12(i) and 26.2, and subdivision (a)(1)(A) of this rule, these rules do not relate to discovery or inspection of recorded proceedings of a grand jury.

[(4) Failure to Call Witness.] (Deleted Dec. 12, 1975)

(b) Disclosure of Evidence by the Defendant.

(1) Information Subject to Disclosure.

(A) Documents and Tangible Objects. If the defendant requests disclosure under subdivision (a)(1)(C) or (D) of this rule, upon compliance with such request by the government, the defendant, on request of the government, shall permit the government to inspect and copy or photograph books, papers, documents, photographs, tangible objects, or copies or portions thereof, which are within the possession, custody, or control of the defendant and which the defendant intends to introduce as evidence in chief at the trial.

(B) Reports of Examinations and Tests. If the defendant requests disclosure under subdivision (a)(1)(C) or (D) of this rule, upon compliance with such request by the government, the defendant, on request of the government, shall permit the government to inspect and copy or photograph any results or reports of physical or mental examinations and of scientific tests or experiments made in connection with the particular case, or copies thereof, within the possession or control of the defendant, which the defendant intends to introduce as evidence in chief at the trial or which were prepared by a witness whom the defendant intends to call at the trial when the results or reports relate to that witness' testimony.

(2) Information Not Subject To Disclosure. Except as to scientific or medical reports, this subdivision does not authorize the discovery or inspection of reports, memoranda, or other internal defense documents made by the defendant, or the defendant's attorneys or agents in connection with the investigation or defense of the case, or of statements made by the defendant, or by government or defense witnesses, or by prospective government or defense witnesses, to the defendant, the defendant's agents or attorneys.

[**(3) Failure to Call Witness.**] (Deleted Dec. 12, 1975)

(c) Continuing Duty to Disclose. If, prior to or during trial, a party discovers additional evidence or material previously requested or ordered, which is subject to discovery or inspection under this rule, such party shall promptly notify the other party or that other party's attorney or the court of the existence of the additional evidence or material.

(d) Regulation of Discovery.

(1) Protective and Modifying Orders. Upon a sufficient showing the court may at any time order that the discovery or inspection be denied, restricted, or deferred, or make such other order as is appropriate. Upon motion by a party, the court may permit the party to make such showing, in whole or in part, in the form of a written statement to be inspected by the judge alone. If the court enters an order granting relief following such an ex parte showing, the entire text of the party's statement shall be sealed and preserved in the records of the court to be made available to the appellate court in the event of an appeal.

(2) Failure To Comply With a Request. If at any time during the course of the proceedings it is brought to the attention of the court that a party has failed to comply with this rule, the court may order such party to permit the discovery or inspection, grant a continuance, or prohibit the party from introducing evidence not disclosed, or it may enter such other order as it deems just under the circumstances. The court may specify the time, place and manner of making the discovery and inspection and may prescribe such terms and conditions as are just.

(e) Alibi Witnesses. Discovery of alibi witnesses is governed by Rule 12.1.

Rule 17. Subpoena

(a) For Attendance of Witnesses; Form; Issuance. A subpoena shall be issued by the clerk under the seal of the court. It shall state the name of the court and the title, if any, of the proceeding, and shall command each person to whom it is directed to attend and give testimony at the time and place specified therein. The clerk shall issue a subpoena, signed and sealed but otherwise in blank to a party requesting it, who shall fill in the blanks before it is served. A subpoena shall be issued by a United States magistrate in a proceeding before that magistrate, but it need not be under the seal of the court.

(b) Defendants Unable to Pay. The court shall order at any time that a subpoena be issued for service on a named witness upon an *ex parte* application of a defendant upon a satisfactory showing that the defendant is financially unable to pay the fees of the witness and that the presence of the witness is necessary to an adequate defense. If the court orders the subpoena to be issued the costs incurred by the process and the fees of the witness so subpoenaed shall be paid in the same manner in which similar costs and fees are paid in case of a witness subpoenaed in behalf of the government.

(c) For Production of Documentary Evidence and of Objects. A subpoena may also command the person to whom it is directed to produce the books, papers, documents or other objects designated therein. The court on motion made promptly may quash or modify the subpoena if compliance would be unreasonable or oppressive. The court may direct that books, papers, documents or objects designated in the subpoena be produced before the court at a time prior to the trial or prior to the time when they are to be offered in evidence and may upon their production permit the books, papers, documents or objects or portions thereof to be inspected by the parties and their attorneys.

(d) Service. A subpoena may be served by the marshal, by a deputy marshal or by any other person who is not a party and who is not less than 18 years of age. Service of a subpoena shall be made by delivering a copy thereof to the person named and by tendering to that person the fee for 1 day's attendance and the mileage allowed by law. Fees and mileage need not be tendered to the witness upon service of a subpoena issued in behalf of the United States or an officer or agency thereof.

(e) Place of Service.

(1) In United States. A subpoena requiring the attendance of a witness at a hearing or trial may be served at any place within the United States.

(2) Abroad. A subpoena directed to a witness in a foreign country shall issue under the circumstances and in the manner and be served as provided in Title 28, U.S.C., § 1783.

(f) For Taking Deposition; Place of Examination.

(1) Issuance. An order to take a deposition authorizes the issuance by the clerk of the court for the district in which the deposition is to be taken of subpoenas for the persons named or described therein.

(2) Place. The witness whose deposition is to be taken may be required by subpoena to attend at any place designated by the trial court, taking into account the convenience of the witness and the parties.

(g) Contempt. Failure by any person without adequate excuse to obey a subpoena served upon that person may be deemed a contempt of the court from which the subpoena issued or of the court for the district in which it issued if it was issued by a United States magistrate.

(h) Information Not Subject to Subpoena. Statements made by witnesses or prospective witnesses may not be subpoenaed from the government or the defendant under this rule, but shall be subject to production only in accordance with the provisions of Rule 26.2.

Rule 17.1. Pretrial Conference

At any time after the filing of the indictment or information the court upon motion of any party or upon its own motion may order one or more conferences to consider such matters as will promote a fair and expeditious trial. At the conclusion of a conference the court shall prepare and file a memorandum of the matters agreed upon. No admissions made by the defendant or the defendant's attorney at the conference shall be used against the defendant unless the admissions are reduced to writing and signed by the defendant and the defendant's attorney. This rule shall not be invoked in the case of a defendant who is not represented by counsel.

V. VENUE

Rule 18. Place of Prosecution and Trial

Except as otherwise permitted by statute or by these rules, the prosecution shall be had in a district in which the offense was committed. The court shall fix the place of trial within the district with due regard to the convenience of the defendant and the witnesses and the prompt administration of justice.

Rule 19.   Rescinded Feb. 28, 1966, eff. July 1, 1966

Rule 20.   Transfer From the District for Plea and Sentence

(a) **Indictment or Information Pending.** A defendant arrested, held, or present in a district other than that in which an indictment or information is pending against that defendant may state in writing a wish to plead guilty or nolo contendere, to waive trial in the district in which the indictment or information is pending, and to consent to disposition of the case in the district in which that defendant was arrested, held, or present, subject to the approval of the United States attorney for each district. Upon receipt of the defendant's statement and of the written approval of the United States attorneys, the clerk of the court in which the indictment or information is pending shall transmit the papers in the proceeding or certified copies thereof to the clerk of the court for the district in which the defendant is arrested, held, or present, and the prosecution shall continue in that district.

(b) **Indictment or Information Not Pending.** A defendant arrested, held, or present, in a district other than the district in which a complaint is pending against that defendant may state in writing a wish to plead guilty or nolo contendere, to waive venue and trial in the district in which the warrant was issued, and to consent to disposition of the case in the district in which that defendant was arrested, held, or present, subject to the approval of the United States attorney for each district. Upon filing the written waiver of venue in the district in which the defendant is present, the prosecution may proceed as if venue were in such district.

(c) **Effect of Not Guilty Plea.** If after the proceeding has been transferred pursuant to subdivision (a) or (b) of this rule the defendant pleads not guilty, the clerk shall return the papers to the court in which the prosecution was commenced, and the proceeding shall be restored to the docket of that court. The defendant's statement that the defendant wishes to plead guilty or nolo contendere shall not be used against that defendant.

(d) **Juveniles.** A juvenile (as defined in 18 U.S.C. § 5031) who is arrested, held, or present in a district other than that in which the juvenile is alleged to have committed an act in violation of a law of the United States not punishable by death or life imprisonment may, after having been advised by counsel and with the approval of the court and the United States attorney for each district, consent to be proceeded against as a juvenile delinquent in the district in which the juvenile is arrested, held, or present. The consent shall be given in writing before the court but only after the court has apprised the juvenile of the juvenile's rights, including the right to be returned to the district in which the juvenile is alleged to have committed the act, and of the consequences of such consent.

Rule 21.   Transfer From the District for Trial

(a) **For Prejudice in the District.** The court upon motion of the defendant shall transfer the proceeding as to that defendant to another district whether or not such district is specified in the defendant's motion if the court is satisfied that there exists in the district where the prosecution is pending so great a prejudice against the defendant that the defendant cannot obtain a fair and impartial trial at any place fixed by law for holding court in that district.

(b) **Transfer in Other Cases.** For the convenience of parties and witnesses, and in the interest of justice, the court upon motion of the defendant may transfer the proceeding as to that defendant or any one or more of the counts thereof to another district.

(c) Proceedings on Transfer. When a transfer is ordered the clerk shall transmit to the clerk of the court to which the proceeding is transferred all papers in the proceeding or duplicates thereof and any bail taken, and the prosecution shall continue in that district.

Rule 22.   Time of Motion to Transfer

A motion to transfer under these rules may be made at or before arraignment or at such other time as the court or these rules may prescribe.

VI.   TRIAL

Rule 23.   Trial by Jury or by the Court

(a) Trial by Jury. Cases required to be tried by jury shall be so tried unless the defendant waives a jury trial in writing with the approval of the court and the consent of the government.

(b) Jury of Less Than Twelve. Juries shall be of 12 but at any time before verdict the parties may stipulate in writing with the approval of the court that the jury shall consist of any number less than 12 or that a valid verdict may be returned by a jury of less than 12 should the court find it necessary to excuse one or more jurors for any just cause after trial commences. Even absent such stipulation, if the court finds it necessary to excuse a juror for just cause after the jury has retired to consider its verdict, in the discretion of the court a valid verdict may be returned by the remaining 11 jurors.

(c) Trial Without a Jury. In a case tried without a jury the court shall make a general finding and shall in addition, on request made before the general finding, find the facts specially. Such findings may be oral. If an opinion or memorandum of decision is filed, it will be sufficient if the findings of fact appear therein.

Rule 24.   Trial Jurors

(a) Examination. The court may permit the defendant or the defendant's attorney and the attorney for the government to conduct the examination of prospective jurors or may itself conduct the examination. In the latter event the court shall permit the defendant or the defendant's attorney and the attorney for the government to supplement the examination by such further inquiry as it deems proper or shall itself submit to the prospective jurors such additional questions by the parties or their attorneys as it deems proper.

(b) Peremptory Challenges. If the offense charged is punishable by death, each side is entitled to 20 peremptory challenges. If the offense charged is punishable by imprisonment for more than one year, the government is entitled to 6 peremptory challenges and the defendant or defendants jointly to 10 peremptory challenges. If the offense charged is punishable by imprisonment for not more than one year or by fine or both, each side is entitled to 3 peremptory challenges. If there is more than one defendant, the court may allow the defendants additional peremptory challenges and permit them to be exercised separately or jointly.

(c) Alternate Jurors. The court may direct that not more than 6 jurors in addition to the regular jury be called and impanelled to sit as alternate jurors. Alternate jurors in the order in which they are called shall replace jurors who, prior to the time the jury retires to consider its verdict, become or are found to be unable or disqualified to perform their duties. Alternate jurors shall be drawn in the same manner, shall have the same qualifications, shall be subject to the same examination and challenges, shall take the same oath and shall have the same functions, powers, facilities and privileges as the regular jurors. An alternate juror who does not replace a regular juror shall be discharged after the jury retires to consider its verdict. Each side is entitled to 1 peremptory challenge in addition to those otherwise allowed by law if 1 or 2 alternate jurors are to be impanelled, 2 peremptory challenges if 3 or 4 alternate jurors are to be impanelled, and 3 peremptory challenges if 5 or 6 alternate jurors are to be impanelled. The additional peremptory challenges may be used against an alternate juror only, and the other peremptory challenges allowed by these rules may not be used against an alternate juror.

Rule 25. Judge; Disability

(a) During Trial. If by reason of death, sickness or other disability the judge before whom a jury trial has commenced is unable to proceed with the trial, any other judge regularly sitting in or assigned to the court, upon certifying familiarity with the record of the trial, may proceed with and finish the trial.

(b) After Verdict or Finding of Guilt. If by reason of absence, death, sickness or other disability the judge before whom the defendant has been tried is unable to perform the duties to be performed by the court after a verdict or finding of guilt, any other judge regularly sitting in or assigned to the court may perform those duties; but if that judge is satisfied that a judge who did not preside at the trial cannot perform those duties or that it is appropriate for any other reason, that judge may grant a new trial.

Rule 26. Taking of Testimony

In all trials the testimony of witnesses shall be taken orally in open court, unless otherwise provided by an Act of Congress or by these rules, the Federal Rules of Evidence, or other rules adopted by the Supreme Court.

Rule 26.1. Determination of Foreign Law

A party who intends to raise an issue concerning the law of a foreign country shall give reasonable written notice. The court, in determining foreign law, may consider any relevant material or source, including testimony, whether or not submitted by a party or admissible under the Federal Rules of Evidence. The court's determination shall be treated as a ruling on a question of law.

Rule 26.2. Production of Statements of Witnesses

(a) Motion for Production. After a witness other than the defendant has testified on direct examination, the court, on motion of a party who did not call the witness, shall order the attorney for the government or the defendant and the defendant's attorney, as the case may be, to produce, for the examination and use of the moving party, any statement of the witness that is in their possession and that relates to the subject matter concerning which the witness has testified.

(b) Production of Entire Statement. If the entire contents of the statement relate to the subject matter concerning which the witness has testified, the court shall order that the statement be delivered to the moving party.

(c) Production of Excised Statement. If the other party claims that the statement contains matter that does not relate to the subject matter concerning which the witness has testified, the court shall order that it be delivered to the court in camera. Upon inspection, the court shall excise the portions of the statement that do not relate to the subject matter concerning which the witness has testified, and shall order that the statement, with such material excised, be delivered to the moving party. Any portion of the statement that is withheld from the defendant over the defendant's objection shall be preserved by the attorney for the government, and, in the event of a conviction and an appeal by the defendant, shall be made available to the appellate court for the purpose of determining the correctness of the decision to excise the portion of the statement.

(d) Recess for Examination of Statement. Upon delivery of the statement to the moving party, the court, upon application of that party, may recess proceedings in the trial for the examination of such statement and for preparation for its use in the trial.

(e) Sanction for Failure to Produce Statement. If the other party elects not to comply with an order to deliver a statement to the moving party, the court shall order that the testimony of the witness be stricken from the record and that the trial proceed, or, if it is the attorney for the government who elects not to comply, shall declare a mistrial if required by the interest of justice.

(f) Definition. As used in this rule, a "statement" of a witness means:

(1) a written statement made by the witness that is signed or otherwise adopted or approved by the witness;

(2) a substantially verbatim recital of an oral statement made by the witness that is recorded contemporaneously with the making of the oral statement and that is contained in a stenographic, mechanical, electrical, or other recording or a transcription thereof; or

(3) a statement, however taken or recorded, or a transcription thereof, made by the witness to a grand jury.

Rule 27. Proof of Official Record

An official record or an entry therein or the lack of such a record or entry may be proved in the same manner as in civil actions.

Rule 28. Interpreters

The court may appoint an interpreter of its own selection and may fix the reasonable compensation of such interpreter. Such compensation shall be paid out of funds provided by law or by the government, as the court may direct.

Rule 29. Motion for Judgment of Acquittal

(a) Motion Before Submission to Jury. Motions for directed verdict are abolished and motions for judgment of acquittal shall be used in their place. The court on motion of a defendant or of its own motion shall order the entry of judgment of acquittal of one or more offenses charged in the indictment or information after the evidence on either side is closed if the evidence is insufficient to sustain a conviction of such offense or offenses. If a defendant's motion for judgment of acquittal at the close of the evidence offered by the government is not granted, the defendant may offer evidence without having reserved the right.

(b) Reservation of Decision on Motion. If a motion for judgment of acquittal is made at the close of all the evidence, the court may reserve decision on the motion, submit the case to the jury and decide the motion either before the jury returns a verdict or after it returns a verdict of guilty or is discharged without having returned a verdict.

(c) Motion After Discharge of Jury. If the jury returns a verdict of guilty or is discharged without having returned a verdict, a motion for judgment of acquittal may be made or renewed within 7 days after the jury is discharged or within such further time as the court may fix during the 7–day period. If a verdict of guilty is returned the court may on such motion set aside the verdict and enter judgment of acquittal. If no verdict is returned the court may enter judgment of acquittal. It shall not be necessary to the making of such a motion that a similar motion has been made prior to the submission of the case to the jury.

(d) Same: Conditional Ruling on Grant of Motion. If a motion for judgment of acquittal after verdict of guilty under this Rule is granted, the court shall also determine whether any motion for a new trial should be granted if the judgment of acquittal is thereafter vacated or reversed, specifying the grounds for such determination. If the motion for a new trial is granted conditionally, the order thereon does not affect the finality of the judgment. If the motion for a new trial has been granted conditionally and the judgment is reversed on appeal, the new trial shall proceed unless the appellate court has otherwise ordered. If such motion has been denied conditionally, the appellee on appeal may assert error in that denial, and if the judgment is reversed on appeal, subsequent proceedings shall be in accordance with the order of the appellate court.

Rule 29.1. Closing Argument

After the closing of evidence the prosecution shall open the argument. The defense shall be permitted to reply. The prosecution shall then be permitted to reply in rebuttal.

Rule 30. Instructions

At the close of the evidence or at such earlier time during the trial as the court reasonably directs, any party may file written requests that the court instruct the jury on the law as set forth in the requests. At the same time copies of such requests shall be furnished to all parties. The court shall inform counsel of its proposed action upon the requests prior to their arguments to the jury. The court may instruct the jury before or after the arguments are completed or at both times. No party may assign as error any portion of the charge or omission therefrom unless that party objects thereto before the jury retires to consider its verdict, stating distinctly the matter to which that party objects and the grounds of the objection. Opportunity shall be given to make the objection out of the hearing of the jury and, on request of any party, out of the presence of the jury.

Rule 31. Verdict

(a) Return. The verdict shall be unanimous. It shall be returned by the jury to the judge in open court.

(b) Several Defendants. If there are two or more defendants, the jury at any time during its deliberations may return a verdict or verdicts with respect to a defendant or defendants as to whom it has agreed; if the jury cannot agree with respect to all, the defendant or defendants as to whom it does not agree may be tried again.

(c) Conviction of Less Offense. The defendant may be found guilty of an offense necessarily included in the offense charged or of an attempt to commit either the offense charged or an offense necessarily included therein if the attempt is an offense.

(d) Poll of Jury. When a verdict is returned and before it is recorded the jury shall be polled at the request of any party or upon the court's own motion. If upon the poll there is not unanimous concurrence, the jury may be directed to retire for further deliberations or may be discharged.

(e) Criminal Forfeiture. If the indictment or the information alleges that an interest or property is subject to criminal forfeiture, a special verdict shall be returned as to the extent of the interest or property subject to forfeiture, if any.

VII. JUDGMENT

Rule 32. Sentence and Judgment

(a) Sentence.

(1) Imposition of Sentence. Sentence shall be imposed without unnecessary delay, but the court may, when there is a factor important to the sentencing determination that is not then capable of being resolved, postpone the imposition of sentence for a reasonable time until the factor is capable of being resolved. Prior to the sentencing hearing, the court shall provide the counsel for the defendant and the attorney for the Government with notice of the probation officer's determination, pursuant to the provisions of subdivision (c)(2)(B), of the sentencing classifications and sentencing guideline range believed to be applicable to the case. At the sentencing hearing, the court shall afford the counsel for the defendant and the attorney for the Government an opportunity to comment upon the probation officer's determination and on other matters relating to the appropriate sentence. Before imposing sentence, the court shall also—

(A) determine that the defendant and defendant's counsel have had the opportunity to read and discuss the presentence investigation report made available pursuant to subdivision (c)(3)(A) or summary thereof made available pursuant to subdivision (c)(3)(B);

(B) afford counsel for the defendant an opportunity to speak on behalf of the defendant; and

(C) address the defendant personally and determine if the defendant wishes to make a statement and to present any information in mitigation of the sentence.

The attorney for the Government shall have an equivalent opportunity to speak to the court. Upon a motion that is jointly filed by the defendant and by the attorney for the Government, the court may hear in camera such a statement by the defendant, counsel for the defendant, or the attorney for the Government.

(2) Notification of Right to Appeal. After imposing sentence in a case which has gone to trial on a plea of not guilty, the court shall advise the defendant of the defendant's right to appeal, including any right to appeal the sentence, and of the right of a person who is unable to pay the cost of an appeal to apply for leave to appeal in forma pauperis. There shall be no duty on the court to advise the defendant of any right of appeal after sentence is imposed following a plea of guilty or nolo contendere, except that the court shall advise the defendant of any right to appeal his sentence. If the defendant so requests, the clerk of the court shall prepare and file forthwith a notice of appeal on behalf of the defendant.

(b) Judgment.

(1) In General. A judgment of conviction shall set forth the plea, the verdict or findings, and the adjudication and sentence. If the defendant is found not guilty or for any other reason is entitled to be discharged, judgment shall be entered accordingly. The judgment shall be signed by the judge and entered by the clerk.

(2) Criminal Forfeiture. When a verdict contains a finding of property subject to a criminal forfeiture, the judgment of criminal forfeiture shall authorize the Attorney General to seize the interest or property subject to forfeiture, fixing such terms and conditions as the court shall deem proper.

(c) Presentence Investigation.

(1) When Made. A probation officer shall make a presentence investigation and report to the court before the imposition of sentence unless the court finds that there is in the record information sufficient to enable the meaningful exercise of sentencing authority pursuant to 18 U.S.C. 3553, and the court explains this finding on the record.

Except with the written consent of the defendant, the report shall not be submitted to the court or its contents disclosed to anyone unless the defendant has pleaded guilty or nolo contendere or has been found guilty.

(2) **Report.** The report of the presentence investigation shall contain—

(A) information about the history and characteristics of the defendant, including prior criminal record, if any, financial condition, and any circumstances affecting the defendant's behavior that may be helpful in imposing sentence or in the correctional treatment of the defendant;

(B) the classification of the offense and of the defendant under the categories established by the Sentencing Commission pursuant to section 994(a) of title 28, that the probation officer believes to be applicable to the defendant's case; the kinds of sentence and the sentencing range suggested for such a category of offense committed by such a category of defendant as set forth in the guidelines issued by the Sentencing Commission pursuant to 28 U.S.C. 994(a)(1); and an explanation by the probation officer of any factors that may indicate that a sentence of a different kind or of a different length from one within the applicable guideline would be more appropriate under all the circumstances;

(C) any pertinent policy statement issued by the Sentencing Commission pursuant to 28 U.S.C. 994(a)(2);

(D) verified information stated in a nonargumentative style containing an assessment of the financial, social, psychological, and medical impact upon, and cost to, any individual against whom the offense has been committed;

(E) unless the court orders otherwise, information concerning the nature and extent of nonprison programs and resources available for the defendant; and

(F) such other information as may be required by the court.

(3) **Disclosure.**

(A) At least 10 days before imposing sentence, unless this minimum period is waived by the defendant the court shall provide the defendant and the defendant's counsel with a copy of the report of the presentence investigation, including the information required by subdivision (c)(2) but not including any final recommendation as to sentence, and not to the extent that in the opinion of the court the report contains diagnostic opinions which, if disclosed, might seriously disrupt a program of rehabilitation; or sources of information obtained upon a promise of confidentiality; or any other information which, if disclosed, might result in harm, physical or otherwise, to the defendant or other persons. The court shall afford the defendant and the defendant's counsel an opportunity to comment on the report and, in the discretion of the court, to introduce testimony or other information relating to any alleged factual inaccuracy contained in it.

(B) If the court is of the view that there is information in the presentence report which should not be disclosed under subdivision (c)(3)(A) of this rule, the court in lieu of making the report or part thereof available shall state orally or in writing a summary of the factual information contained therein to be relied on in determining sentence, and shall give the defendant and the defendant's counsel an opportunity to comment thereon. The statement may be made to the parties in camera.

(C) Any material which may be disclosed to the defendant and the defendant's counsel shall be disclosed to the attorney for the government.

(D) If the comments of the defendant and the defendant's counsel or testimony or other information introduced by them allege any factual inaccuracy in the presentence investigation report or the summary of the report or part thereof, the court shall, as to each matter controverted, make (i) a finding as to the allegation, or (ii) a determination that no such finding is necessary because the matter controverted will not be taken into account in sentencing. A written record of such findings and determinations shall be appended to and accompany any copy of the presentence investigation report thereafter made available to the Bureau of Prisons.

(E) The reports of studies and recommendations contained therein made by the Director of the Bureau of Prisons pursuant to 18 U.S.C. § 3552(b) shall be considered a presentence investigation within the meaning of subdivision (c)(3) of this rule.

(d) Plea Withdrawal. If a motion for withdrawal of a plea of guilty or nolo contendere is made before sentence is imposed, the court may permit withdrawal of the plea upon a showing by the defendant of any fair and just reason. At any later time, a plea may be set aside only on direct appeal or by motion under 28 U.S.C. § 2255.

(e) Probation. After conviction of an offense not punishable by death or by life imprisonment, the defendant may be placed on probation if permitted by law.

(f) [Revocation of Probation.] (Abrogated Apr. 30, 1979, eff. Dec. 1, 1980)

Rule 32.1. Revocation or Modification of Probation or Supervised Release

(a) Revocation of Probation or Supervised Release.

(1) Preliminary Hearing. Whenever a person is held in custody on the grounds that the person has violated a condition of probation or supervised release, the person shall be afforded a prompt hearing before any judge, or a United States magistrate who has been given authority pursuant to 28 U.S.C. § 636 to conduct such hearings, in order to determine whether there is probable cause to hold the person for a revocation hearing. The person shall be given

(A) notice of the preliminary hearing and its purpose and of the alleged violation;

(B) an opportunity to appear at the hearing and present evidence in the person's own behalf;

(C) upon request, the opportunity to question witnesses against the person unless, for good cause, the federal magistrate decides that justice does not require the appearance of the witness; and

(D) notice of the person's right to be represented by counsel.

The proceedings shall be recorded stenographically or by an electronic recording device. If probable cause is found to exist, the person shall be held for a revocation hearing. The person may be released pursuant to Rule 46(c) pending the revocation hearing. If probable cause is not found to exist, the proceeding shall be dismissed.

(2) Revocation Hearing. The revocation hearing, unless waived by the person, shall be held within a reasonable time in the district of jurisdiction. The person shall be given

(A) written notice of the alleged violation;

(B) disclosure of the evidence against the person;

(C) an opportunity to appear and to present evidence in the person's own behalf;

(D) the opportunity to question adverse witnesses; and

(E) notice of the person's right to be represented by counsel.

(b) Modification of Probation or Supervised Release. A hearing and assistance of counsel are required before the terms or conditions of probation or supervised release can be modified, unless the relief to be granted to the person on probation or supervised release upon the person's request or the court's own motion is favorable to the person, and the attorney for the government, after having been given notice of the proposed relief and a reasonable opportunity to object, has not objected. An extension of the term of probation or supervised release is not favorable to the person for the purposes of this rule.

Rule 33. New Trial

The court on motion of a defendant may grant a new trial to that defendant if required in the interest of justice. If trial was by the court without a jury the court on motion of a defendant for a new trial may vacate the judgment if entered, take additional testimony and direct the entry of a new judgment. A motion for a new trial based on the ground of newly discovered evidence may be made only before or within two years after final judgment, but if an appeal is pending the court may grant the motion only on remand of the case. A motion for a new trial based on any other grounds shall be made within 7 days after verdict or finding of guilty or within such further time as the court may fix during the 7-day period.

Rule 34. Arrest of Judgment

The court on motion of a defendant shall arrest judgment if the indictment or information does not charge an offense or if the court was without jurisdiction of the offense charged. The motion in arrest of judgment shall be made within 7 days after verdict or finding of guilty, or after plea of guilty or *nolo contendere,* or within such further time as the court may fix during the 7-day period.

Rule 35. Correction of Sentence

(a) Correction of a Sentence on Remand. The court shall correct a sentence that is determined on appeal under 18 U.S.C. 3742 to have been imposed in violation of law, to have been imposed as a result of an incorrect application of the sentencing guidelines, or to be unreasonable, upon remand of the case to the court—

(1) for imposition of a sentence in accord with the findings of the court of appeals; or

(2) for further sentencing proceedings if, after such proceedings, the court determines that the original sentence was incorrect.

(b) Correction of Sentence for Changed Circumstances. The court, on motion of the Government, may within one year after the imposition of a sentence, lower a sentence to reflect a defendant's subsequent, substantial assistance in the investigation or prosecution of another person who has committed an offense, in accordance with the guidelines and policy statements issued by the Sentencing Commission pursuant to section 994 of title 28, United States Code. The court's authority to lower a sentence under this subdivision includes the authority to lower such sentence to a level below that established by statute as a minimum sentence.

Rule 36. Clerical Mistakes

Clerical mistakes in judgments, orders or other parts of the record and errors in the record arising from oversight or omission may be corrected by the court at any time and after such notice, if any, as the court orders.

[VIII.   APPEAL] (Abrogated Dec. 4, 1967, eff. July 1, 1968)

[Rule 37.   Taking Appeal; and Petition for Writ of Certiorari.] (Abrogated Dec. 4, 1967, Eff. July 1, 1968)

Rule 38.   Stay of Execution

(a) Death. A sentence of death shall be stayed if an appeal is taken from the conviction or sentence.

(b) Imprisonment. A sentence of imprisonment shall be stayed if an appeal is taken from the conviction or sentence and the defendant is released pending disposition of appeal pursuant to Rule 9(b) of the Federal Rules of Appellate Procedure. If not stayed, the court may recommend to the Attorney General that the defendant be retained at, or transferred to, a place of confinement near the place of trial or the place where an appeal is to be heard, for a period reasonably necessary to permit the defendant to assist in the preparation of an appeal to the court of appeals.

(c) Fine. A sentence to pay a fine or a fine and costs, if an appeal is taken, may be stayed by the district court or by the court of appeals upon such terms as the court deems proper. The court may require the defendant pending appeal to deposit the whole or any part of the fine and costs in the registry of the district court, or to give bond for the payment thereof, or to submit to an examination of assets, and it may make any appropriate order to restrain the defendant from dissipating such defendant's assets.

(d) Probation. A sentence of probation may be stayed if an appeal from the conviction or sentence is taken. If the sentence is stayed, the court shall fix the terms of the stay.

(e) Criminal Forfeiture, Notice to Victims, and Restitution. A sanction imposed as part of the sentence pursuant to 18 U.S.C. 3554, 3555, or 3556 may, if an appeal of the conviction or sentence is taken, be stayed by the district court or by the court of appeals upon such terms as the court finds appropriate. The court may issue such orders as may be reasonably necessary to ensure compliance with the sanction upon disposition of the appeal, including the entering of a restraining order or an injunction or requiring a deposit in whole or in part of the monetary amount involved into the registry of the district court or execution of a performance bond.

(f) Disabilities. A civil or employment disability arising under a Federal statute by reason of the defendant's conviction or sentence, may, if an appeal is taken, be stayed by the district court or by the court of appeals upon such terms as the court finds appropriate. The court may enter a restraining order or an injunction, or take any other action that may be reasonably necessary to protect the interest represented by the disability pending disposition of the appeal.

[Rule 39.   Supervision of Appeal.]   (Abrogated Dec. 4, 1967, Eff. July 1, 1968)

IX.   SUPPLEMENTARY AND SPECIAL PROCEEDINGS

Rule 40.   Commitment to Another District

(a) Appearance Before Federal Magistrate. If a person is arrested in a district other than that in which the offense is alleged to have been committed, that person shall be taken without unnecessary delay before the nearest available federal magistrate. Preliminary proceedings concerning the defendant shall be conducted in accordance with Rules 5 and 5.1, except that if no preliminary examination is held because an indictment has been returned or an information filed or because the defendant elects to have the preliminary examination conducted in the district in which the prosecution is pending, the person shall be held to answer upon a finding that such person is the person named in the indictment, information or warrant. If held to answer, the defendant shall be held to answer in the district court in which the prosecution is pending, provided that a warrant is issued in that district if the arrest was made without a warrant, upon production of the warrant or a certified copy thereof.

(b) Statement by Federal Magistrate. In addition to the statements required by Rule 5, the federal magistrate shall inform the defendant of the provisions of Rule 20.

(c) Papers. If a defendant is held or discharged, the papers in the proceeding and any bail taken shall be transmitted to the clerk of the district court in which the prosecution is pending.

(d) Arrest of Probationer or Supervised Releasee. If a person is arrested for a violation of probation or supervised release in a district other than the district having jurisdiction, such person shall be taken without unnecessary delay before the nearest available federal magistrate. The federal magistrate shall:

(1) Proceed under Rule 32.1 if jurisdiction over the person is transferred to that district;

(2) Hold a prompt preliminary hearing if the alleged violation occurred in that district, and either (i) hold the person to answer in the district court of the district having jurisdiction or (ii) dismiss the proceedings and so notify that court; or

(3) otherwise order the person held to answer in the district court of the district having jurisdiction upon production of certified copies of the judgment, the warrant, and the application for the warrant, and upon a finding that the person before the magistrate is the person named in the warrant.

(e) Arrest for Failure to Appear. If a person is arrested on a warrant in a district other than that in which the warrant was issued, and the warrant was issued because of the failure of the person named therein to appear as required pursuant to a subpoena or the terms of that person's release, the person arrested shall be taken without unnecessary delay before the nearest available federal magistrate. Upon production of the warrant or a certified copy thereof and upon a finding that the person before the magistrate is the person named in the warrant, the federal magistrate shall hold the person to answer in the district in which the warrant was issued.

(f) Release or Detention. If a person was previously detained or conditionally released, pursuant to chapter 207 of title 18, United States Code, in another district where a warrant, information, or indictment issued, the federal magistrate shall take into account the decision previously made and the reasons set forth therefor, if any, but will not be bound by that decision. If the federal magistrate amends the release or detention decision or alters the conditions of release, the magistrate shall set forth the reasons therefore [1] in writing.

Rule 41.   Search and Seizure

(a) Authority to Issue Warrant. A search warrant authorized by this rule may be issued by a federal magistrate or a judge of a state court of record within the district wherein the property or person sought is located, upon request of a federal law enforcement officer or an attorney for the government.

(b) Property or Persons Which May Be Seized With a Warrant. A warrant may be issued under this rule to search for and seize any (1) property that constitutes

---

[1] So in original.

evidence of the commission of a criminal offense; or (2) contraband, the fruits of crime, or things otherwise criminally possessed; or (3) property designed or intended for use or which is or has been used as the means of committing a criminal offense; or (4) person for whose arrest there is probable cause, or who is unlawfully restrained.

(c) Issuance and Contents.

(1) Warrant Upon Affidavit. A warrant other than a warrant upon oral testimony under paragraph (2) of this subdivision shall issue only on an affidavit or affidavits sworn to before the federal magistrate or state judge and establishing the grounds for issuing the warrant. If the federal magistrate or state judge is satisfied that grounds for the application exist or that there is probable cause to believe that they exist, that magistrate or state judge shall issue a warrant identifying the property or person to be seized and naming or describing the person or place to be searched. The finding of probable cause may be based upon hearsay evidence in whole or in part. Before ruling on a request for a warrant the federal magistrate or state judge may require the affiant to appear personally and may examine under oath the affiant and any witnesses the affiant may produce, provided that such proceeding shall be taken down by a court reporter or recording equipment and made part of the affidavit. The warrant shall be directed to a civil officer of the United States authorized to enforce or assist in enforcing any law thereof or to a person so authorized by the President of the United States. It shall command the officer to search, within a specified period of time not to exceed 10 days, the person or place named for the property or person specified. The warrant shall be served in the daytime, unless the issuing authority, by appropriate provision in the warrant, and for reasonable cause shown, authorizes its execution at times other than daytime. It shall designate a federal magistrate to whom it shall be returned.

(2) Warrant Upon Oral Testimony.

(A) General Rule. If the circumstances make it reasonable to dispense with a written affidavit, a Federal magistrate may issue a warrant based upon sworn oral testimony communicated by telephone or other appropriate means.

(B) Application. The person who is requesting the warrant shall prepare a document to be known as a duplicate original warrant and shall read such duplicate original warrant, verbatim, to the Federal magistrate. The Federal magistrate shall enter, verbatim, what is so read to such magistrate on a document to be known as the original warrant. The Federal magistrate may direct that the warrant be modified.

(C) Issuance. If the Federal magistrate is satisfied that the circumstances are such as to make it reasonable to dispense with a written affidavit and that grounds for the application exist or that there is probable cause to believe that they exist, the Federal magistrate shall order the issuance of a warrant by directing the person requesting the warrant to sign the Federal magistrate's name on the duplicate original warrant. The Federal magistrate shall immediately sign the original warrant and enter on the face of the original warrant the exact time when the warrant was ordered to be issued. The finding of probable cause for a warrant upon oral testimony may be based on the same kind of evidence as is sufficient for a warrant upon affidavit.

(D) Recording and Certification of Testimony. When a caller informs the Federal magistrate that the purpose of the call is to request a warrant, the Federal magistrate shall immediately place under oath each person whose testimony forms a basis of the application and each person applying for that warrant. If a voice recording device is available, the Federal magistrate shall record by means of such device all of the call after the caller informs the Federal magistrate that the purpose of the call is to request a warrant. Otherwise a stenographic or longhand verbatim record shall be made. If a voice recording device is used or a stenographic record made, the Federal magistrate shall have the record transcribed, shall certify the accuracy of the transcription, and shall file a copy of the original record and the transcription with the court. If a longhand verbatim record is made, the Federal magistrate shall file a signed copy with the court.

(E) Contents. The contents of a warrant upon oral testimony shall be the same as the contents of a warrant upon affidavit.

(F) Additional Rule for Execution. The person who executes the warrant shall enter the exact time of execution on the face of the duplicate original warrant.

(G) Motion to Suppress Precluded. Absent a finding of bad faith, evidence obtained pursuant to a warrant issued under this paragraph is not subject to a motion to suppress on the ground that the circumstances were not such as to make it reasonable to dispense with a written affidavit.

(d) Execution and Return with Inventory. The officer taking property under the warrant shall give to the person from whom or from whose premises the property was taken a copy of the warrant and a receipt for the property taken or shall leave the copy and receipt at the place from which the property was taken. The return shall be made promptly and shall be accompanied by a written inventory of any property taken. The inventory shall be made in the presence of the applicant for the warrant and the person from whose possession or premises the property was taken, if they are present, or in the presence of at least one credible person other than the applicant for the warrant or the person from whose possession or premises the property was taken, and shall be verified by the officer. The federal magistrate shall upon request deliver a copy of the inventory to the person from whom or from whose premises the property was taken and to the applicant for the warrant.

(e) Motion for Return of Property. A person aggrieved by an unlawful search and seizure or by the deprivation of property may move the district court for the district in which the property was seized for the return of the property on the ground that such person is entitled to lawful possession of the property. The court shall receive evidence on any issue of fact necessary to the decision of the motion. If the motion is granted, the property shall be returned to the movant, although reasonable conditions may be imposed to protect access and use of the property in subsequent proceedings. If a motion for return of property is made or comes on for hearing in the district of trial after an indictment or information is filed, it shall be treated also as a motion to suppress under Rule 12.

(f) Motion to Suppress. A motion to suppress evidence may be made in the court of the district of trial as provided in Rule 12.

(g) Return of Papers to Clerk. The federal magistrate before whom the warrant is returned shall attach to the warrant a copy of the return, inventory and all other papers in connection therewith and shall file them with the clerk of the district court for the district in which the property was seized.

(h) Scope and Definition. This rule does not modify any act, inconsistent with it, regulating search, seizure and the issuance and execution of search warrants in circumstances for which special provision is made. The term "property" is used in this rule to include documents, books, papers and any other tangible objects. The term "daytime" is used in this rule to mean the hours from 6:00 a.m. to 10:00 p.m. according to local time. The phrase "federal law enforcement officer" is used in this rule to mean any government agent, other than an attorney for the government as defined in Rule 54(c), who is engaged in the enforcement of the criminal laws and is within any category of officers authorized by the Attorney General to request the issuance of a search warrant.

Rule 42. Criminal Contempt

(a) Summary Disposition. A criminal contempt may be punished summarily if the judge certifies that the judge saw or heard the conduct constituting the contempt and that it was committed in the actual presence of the court. The order of contempt shall recite the facts and shall be signed by the judge and entered of record.

(b) Disposition Upon Notice and Hearing. A criminal contempt except as provided in subdivision (a) of this rule shall be prosecuted on notice. The notice shall state the time and place of hearing, allowing a reasonable time for the preparation of the defense, and shall state the essential facts constituting the criminal contempt charged and describe it as such. The notice shall be given orally by the judge in open court in the presence of the defendant or, on application of the United States attorney or of an attorney appointed by the court for that purpose, by an order to show cause or an order of arrest. The defendant is entitled to a trial by jury in any case in which an act of Congress so provides. The defendant is entitled to admission to bail as provided in these rules. If the contempt charged involves disrespect to or criticism of a judge, that judge is disqualified from presiding at the trial or hearing except with the defendant's consent. Upon a verdict or finding of guilt the court shall enter an order fixing the punishment.

X. GENERAL PROVISIONS

Rule 43. Presence of the Defendant

(a) Presence Required. The defendant shall be present at the arraignment, at the time of the plea, at every stage of the trial including the impaneling of the jury and the return of the verdict, and at the imposition of sentence, except as otherwise provided by this rule.

(b) Continued Presence Not Required. The further progress of the trial to and including the return of the verdict shall not be prevented and the defendant shall be considered to have waived the right to be present whenever a defendant, initially present,

(1) is voluntarily absent after the trial has commenced (whether or not the defendant has been informed by the court of the obligation to remain during the trial), or

(2) after being warned by the court that disruptive conduct will cause the removal of the defendant from the courtroom, persists in conduct which is such as to justify exclusion from the courtroom.

(c) Presence Not Required. A defendant need not be present in the following situations:

(1) A corporation may appear by counsel for all purposes.

(2) In prosecutions for offenses punishable by fine or by imprisonment for not more than one year or both, the court, with the written consent of the defendant, may permit arraignment, plea, trial, and imposition of sentence in the defendant's absence.

(3) At a conference or argument upon a question of law.

(4) At a reduction of sentence under Rule 35.

Rule 44. Right to and Assignment of Counsel

(a) Right to Assigned Counsel. Every defendant who is unable to obtain counsel shall be entitled to have counsel assigned to represent that defendant at every stage of the proceedings from initial appearance before the federal magistrate or the court through appeal, unless that defendant waives such appointment.

(b) Assignment Procedure. The procedures for implementing the right set out in subdivision (a) shall be those provided by law and by local rules of court established pursuant thereto.

(c) Joint Representation. Whenever two or more defendants have been jointly charged pursuant to Rule 8(b) or have been joined for trial pursuant to Rule 13, and are represented by the same retained or assigned counsel or by retained or assigned counsel who are associated in the practice of law, the court shall promptly inquire with respect to such joint representation and shall personally advise each defendant of the right to the effective assistance of counsel, including separate representation. Unless it appears that there is good cause to believe no conflict of interest is likely to arise, the court shall take such measures as may be appropriate to protect each defendant's right to counsel.

Rule 45.   Time

(a) Computation. In computing any period of time the day of the act or event from which the designated period of time begins to run shall not be included. The last day of the period so computed shall be included, unless it is a Saturday, a Sunday, or a legal holiday, or, when the act to be done is the filing of some paper in court, a day on which weather or other conditions have made the office of the clerk of the district court inaccessible, in which event the period runs until the end of the next day which is not one of the aforementioned days. When a period of time prescribed or allowed is less than 11 days, intermediate Saturdays, Sundays and legal holidays shall be excluded in the computation. As used in these rules, "legal holiday" includes New Year's Day, Birthday of Martin Luther King, Jr., Washington's Birthday, Memorial Day, Independence Day, Labor Day, Columbus Day, Veterans Day, Thanksgiving Day, Christmas Day, and any other day appointed as a holiday by the President or the Congress of the United States, or by the state in which the district court is held.

(b) Enlargement. When an act is required or allowed to be done at or within a specified time, the court for cause shown may at any time in its discretion (1) with or without motion or notice, order the period enlarged if request therefor is made before the expiration of the period originally prescribed or as extended by a previous order or (2) upon motion made after the expiration of the specified period permit the act to be done if the failure to act was the result of excusable neglect; but the court may not extend the time for taking any action under Rules 29, 33, 34 and 35, except to the extent and under the conditions stated in them.

[(c) Unaffected by Expiration of Term.] (Rescinded Feb. 28, 1966, eff. July 1, 1966.)

(d) For Motions; Affidavits. A written motion, other than one which may be heard *ex parte,* and notice of the hearing thereof shall be served not later than 5 days before the time specified for the hearing unless a different period is fixed by rule or order of the court. For cause shown such an order may be made on *ex parte* application. When a motion is supported by affidavit, the affidavit shall be served with the motion; and opposing affidavits may be served not less than 1 day before the hearing unless the court permits them to be served at a later time.

(e) Additional Time After Service by Mail. Whenever a party has the right or is required to do an act within a prescribed period after the service of a notice or other paper upon that party and the notice or other paper is served by mail, 3 days shall be added to the prescribed period.

Rule 46. Release from Custody

(a) Release Prior to Trial. Eligibility for release prior to trial shall be in accordance with 18 U.S.C. §§ 3142 and 3144.

(b) Release During Trial. A person released before trial shall continue on release during trial under the same terms and conditions as were previously imposed unless the court determines that other terms and conditions or termination of release are necessary to assure such person's presence during the trial or to assure that such person's conduct will not obstruct the orderly and expeditious progress of the trial.

(c) Pending Sentence and Notice of Appeal. Eligibility for release pending sentence or pending notice of appeal or expiration of the time allowed for filing notice of appeal, shall be in accordance with 18 U.S.C. § 3143. The burden of establishing that the defendant will not flee or pose a danger to any other person or to the community rests with the defendant.

(d) Justification of Sureties. Every surety, except a corporate surety which is approved as provided by law, shall justify by affidavit and may be required to describe in the affidavit the property by which the surety proposes to justify and the encumbrances thereon, the number and amount of other bonds and undertakings for bail entered into by the surety and remaining undischarged and all the other liabilities of the surety. No bond shall be approved unless the surety thereon appears to be qualified.

(e) Forfeiture.

(1) Declaration. If there is a breach of condition of a bond, the district court shall declare a forfeiture of the bail.

(2) Setting Aside. The court may direct that a forfeiture be set aside in whole or in part, upon such conditions as the court may impose, if a person released upon execution of an appearance bond with a surety is subsequently surrendered by the surety into custody or if it otherwise appears that justice does not require the forfeiture.

(3) Enforcement. When a forfeiture has not been set aside, the court shall on motion enter a judgment of default and execution may issue thereon. By entering into a bond the obligors submit to the jurisdiction of the district court and irrevocably appoint the clerk of the court as their agent upon whom any papers affecting their liability may be served. Their liability may be enforced on motion without the necessity of an independent action. The motion and such notice of the motion as the court prescribes may be served on the clerk of the court, who shall forthwith mail copies to the obligors to their last known addresses.

(4) Remission. After entry of such judgment, the court may remit it in whole or in part under the conditions applying to the setting aside of forfeiture in paragraph (2) of this subdivision.

(f) Exoneration. When the condition of the bond has been satisfied or the forfeiture thereof has been set aside or remitted, the court shall exonerate the obligors and release any bail. A surety may be exonerated by a deposit of cash in the amount of the bond or by a timely surrender of the defendant into custody.

(g) Supervision of Detention Pending Trial. The court shall exercise supervision over the detention of defendants and witnesses within the district pending trial for the purpose of eliminating all unnecessary detention. The attorney for the government shall make a biweekly report to the court listing each defendant and witness who has been held in custody pending indictment, arraignment or trial for a period in excess of ten days. As to each witness so listed the attorney for the government shall make a statement of the reasons why such witness should not be released with or without the taking of a deposition pursuant to Rule 15(a). As to each defendant so listed the attorney for the government shall make a statement of the reasons why the defendant is still held in custody.

(h) Forfeiture of Property. Nothing in this rule or in chapter 207 of title 18, United States Code, shall prevent the court from disposing of any charge by entering an order directing forfeiture of property pursuant to 18 U.S.C. 3142(c)(2)(K) if the value of the property is an amount that would be an appropriate sentence after conviction of the offense charged and if such forfeiture is authorized by statute or regulation.

Rule 47. Motions

An application to the court for an order shall be by motion. A motion other than one made during a trial or hearing shall be in writing unless the court permits it to be made orally. It shall state the grounds upon which it is made and shall set forth the relief or order sought. It may be supported by affidavit.

Rule 48. Dismissal

(a) By Attorney for Government. The Attorney General or the United States attorney may by leave of court file a dismissal of an indictment, information or complaint and the prosecution shall thereupon terminate. Such a dismissal may not be filed during the trial without the consent of the defendant.

(b) By Court. If there is unnecessary delay in presenting the charge to a grand jury or in filing an information against a defendant who has been held to answer to the district court, or if there is unnecessary delay in bringing a defendant to trial, the court may dismiss the indictment, information or complaint.

Rule 49. Service and Filing of Papers

(a) Service: When Required. Written motions other than those which are heard ex parte, written notices, designations of record on appeal and similar papers shall be served upon each of the parties.

(b) Service: How Made. Whenever under these rules or by an order of the court service is required or permitted to be made upon a party represented by an attorney, the service shall be made upon the attorney unless service upon the party personally is ordered by the court. Service upon the attorney or upon a party shall be made in the manner provided in civil actions.

(c) Notice of Orders. Immediately upon the entry of an order made on a written motion subsequent to arraignment the clerk shall mail to each party a notice thereof and shall make a note in the docket of the mailing. Lack of notice of the entry by the clerk does not affect the time to appeal or relieve or authorize the court to relieve a party for failure to appeal within the time allowed, except as permitted by Rule 4(b) of the Federal Rules of Appellate Procedure.

(d) Filing. Papers required to be served shall be filed with the court. Papers shall be filed in the manner provided in civil actions.

(e) Filing of Dangerous Offender Notice. A filing with the court pursuant to 18 U.S.C. § 3575(a) or 21 U.S.C. § 849(a) shall be made by filing the notice with the clerk of the court. The clerk shall transmit the notice to the chief judge or, if the chief judge is the presiding judge in the case, to another judge or United States magistrate in the district, except that in a district having a single judge and no United States magistrate, the clerk shall transmit the notice to the court only after the time for disclosure specified in the aforementioned statutes and shall seal the notice as permitted by local rule.

Rule 50. Calendars; Plan for Prompt Disposition

(a) Calendars. The district courts may provide for placing criminal proceedings upon appropriate calendars. Preference shall be given to criminal proceedings as far as practicable.

(b) Plans for Achieving Prompt Disposition of Criminal Cases. To minimize undue delay and to further the prompt disposition of criminal cases, each district court shall conduct a continuing study of the administration of criminal justice in the district court and before United States magistrates of the district and shall prepare plans for the prompt disposition of criminal cases in accordance with the provisions of Chapter 208 of Title 18, United States Code.

Rule 51. Exceptions Unnecessary

Exceptions to rulings or orders of the court are unnecessary and for all purposes for which an exception has heretofore been necessary it is sufficient that a party, at the time the ruling or order of the court is made or sought, makes known to the court the action which that party desires the court to take or that party's objection to the action of the court and the grounds therefor; but if a party has no opportunity to object to a ruling or order, the absence of an objection does not thereafter prejudice that party.

Rule 52. Harmless Error and Plain Error

(a) Harmless Error. Any error, defect, irregularity or variance which does not affect substantial rights shall be disregarded.

(b) Plain Error. Plain errors or defects affecting substantial rights may be noticed although they were not brought to the attention of the court.

Rule 53. Regulation of Conduct in the Court Room

The taking of photographs in the court room during the progress of judicial proceedings or radio broadcasting of judicial proceedings from the court room shall not be permitted by the court.

Rule 54. Application and Exception

(a) Courts. These rules apply to all criminal proceedings in the United States District Courts; in the District Court of Guam; in the District Court for the Northern Mariana Islands, except as otherwise provided in articles IV and V of the covenant provided by the Act of March 24, 1976 (90 Stat. 263); in the District Court of the Virgin Islands; and (except as otherwise provided in the Canal Zone Code) in the United States District Court for the District of the Canal Zone; in the United States Courts of Appeals; and in the Supreme Court of the United States; except that all offenses shall continue to be prosecuted in the District Court of Guam and in the District Court of the Virgin Islands by information as heretofore except such as may be required by local law to be prosecuted by indictment by grand jury.

(b) Proceedings.

(1) Removed Proceedings. These rules apply to criminal prosecutions removed to the United States district courts from state courts and govern all procedure after removal, except that dismissal by the attorney for the prosecution shall be governed by state law.

(2) Offenses Outside a District or State. These rules apply to proceedings for offenses committed upon the high seas or elsewhere out of the jurisdiction of any particular state or district, except that such proceedings may be had in any district authorized by 18 U.S.C. § 3238.

(3) Peace Bonds. These rules do not alter the power of judges of the United States or of United States magistrates to hold to security of the peace and for good behavior under Revised Statutes, § 4069, 50 U.S.C. § 23, but in such cases the procedure shall conform to these rules so far as they are applicable.

(4) Proceedings Before United States Magistrates. Proceedings involving misdemeanors before United States magistrates are governed by the Rules of Procedure for the Trial of Misdemeanors before United States Magistrates.

(5) Other Proceedings. These rules are not applicable to extradition and rendition of fugitives; civil forfeiture of property for violation of a statute of the United States; or the collection of fines and penalties. Except as provided in Rule 20(d) they do not apply to proceedings under 18 U.S.C., Chapter 403—Juvenile Delinquency—so far as they are inconsistent with that chapter. They do not apply to summary trials for offenses against the navigation laws under Revised Statutes §§ 4300–4305, 33 U.S.C. §§ 391–396, or to proceedings involving disputes between seamen under Revised Statutes, §§ 4079–4081, as amended, 22 U.S.C. §§ 256–258, or to proceedings for fishery offenses under the Act of June 28, 1937, c. 392, 50 Stat. 325–327, 16 U.S.C. §§ 772–772i, or to proceedings against a witness in a foreign country under 28 U.S.C. § 1784.

(c) Application of Terms. As used in these rules the following terms have the designated meanings.

"Act of Congress" includes any act of Congress locally applicable to and in force in the District of Columbia, in Puerto Rico, in a territory or in an insular possession.

"Attorney for the government" means the Attorney General, an authorized assistant of the Attorney General, a United States Attorney, an authorized assistant of a United States Attorney, when applicable to cases arising under the laws of Guam the Attorney General of Guam or such other person or persons as may be authorized by the laws of Guam to act therein, and when applicable to cases arising under the laws of the Northern Mariana Islands the Attorney General of the Northern Mariana Islands or any other person or persons as may be authorized by the laws of the Northern Marianas to act therein.

"Civil action" refers to a civil action in a district court.

The words "demurrer," "motion to quash," "plea in abatement," "plea in bar" and "special plea in bar," or words to the same effect, in any act of Congress shall be construed to mean the motion raising a defense or objection provided in Rule 12.

"District court" includes all district courts named in subdivision (a) of this rule.

"Federal magistrate" means a United States magistrate as defined in 28 U.S.C. §§ 631–639, a judge of the United States or another judge or judicial officer specifically empowered by statute in force in any territory or possession, the Commonwealth of Puerto Rico, or the District of Columbia, to perform a function to which a particular rule relates.

"Judge of the United States" includes a judge of a district court, court of appeals, or the Supreme Court.

"Law" includes statutes and judicial decisions.

"Magistrate" includes a United States magistrate as defined in 28 U.S.C. §§ 631–639, a judge of the United States, another judge or judicial officer specifically empowered by statute in force in any territory or possession, the Commonwealth of Puerto Rico, or the District of Columbia, to perform a function to which a particular rule relates, and a state or local judicial officer, authorized by 18 U.S.C. § 3041 to perform the functions prescribed in Rules 3, 4, and 5.

"Oath" includes affirmations.

"Petty offense" has the meaning set forth in 18 U.S.C. 19.

"State" includes District of Columbia, Puerto Rico, territory and insular possession.

"United States magistrate" means the officer authorized by 28 U.S.C. §§ 631–639.

Rule 55. Records

The clerk of the district court and each United States magistrate shall keep records in criminal proceedings in such form as the Director of the Administrative Office of the United States Courts may prescribe. The clerk shall enter in the records each order or judgment of the court and the date such entry is made.

Rule 56. Courts and Clerks

The district court shall be deemed always open for the purpose of filing any proper paper, of issuing and returning process and of making motions and orders. The clerk's office with the clerk or a deputy in attendance shall be open during business hours on all days except Saturdays, Sundays, and legal holidays, but a court may provide by local rule or order that its clerk's office shall be open for specified hours on Saturdays or particular legal holidays other than New Year's Day, Birthday of Martin Luther King, Jr., Washington's Birthday, Memorial Day, Independence Day, Labor Day, Columbus Day, Veterans Day, Thanksgiving Day, and Christmas Day.

Rule 57. Rules by District Courts

Each district court by action of a majority of the judges thereof may from time to time, after giving appropriate public notice and an opportunity to comment, make and amend rules governing its practice not inconsistent with these rules. A local rule so adopted shall take effect upon the date specified by the district court and shall remain in effect unless amended by the district court or abrogated by the judicial council of the circuit in which the district is located. Copies of the rules and amendments so made by any district court shall upon their promulgation be furnished to the judicial council and the Administrative Office of the United States Courts and be made available to the public. In all cases not provided for by rule, the district judges and magistrates may regulate their practice in any manner not inconsistent with these rules or those of the district in which they act.

[Rule 58. Forms.] (Abrogated Apr. 28, 1983, Eff. Aug. 1, 1983)

Rule 59. Effective Date

These rules take effect on the day which is 3 months subsequent to the adjournment of the first regular session of the 79th Congress, but if that day is prior to September 1, 1945, then they take effect on September 1, 1945. They govern all criminal proceedings thereafter commenced and so far as just and practicable all proceedings then pending.

Rule 60. Title

These rules may be known and cited as the Federal Rules of Criminal Procedure.

Appendix D

PROPOSED AMENDMENTS TO FEDERAL RULES OF CRIMINAL PROCEDURE

[NOTE: The following amendments were approved by the Supreme Court on May 1, 1990, to take effect on December 1, 1990. New material is underlined; material to be deleted is lined through.]

Rule 5. Initial Appearance Before the Magistrate

* * *

(b) MISDEMEANORS AND OTHER PETTY OFFENSES.

If the charge against the defendant is a misdemeanor or other petty offense triable by a United States magistrate under 18 U.S.C. § 3401, the magistrate shall proceed in accordance with the Rule 58. the Rules of Procedure for the Trial of Misdemeanors Before United States Magistrates.

Rule 41. Search and Seizure

(a) AUTHORITY TO ISSUE WARRANT.

A search warrant authorized by this rule may be issued by a federal magistrate or a judge of a state court of record within the district wherein the property or person sought is located, upon request of a federal law enforcement officer or an attorney for the government. Upon the request of a federal law enforcement officer or an attorney for the government, a search warrant authorized by this rule may be issued (1) by a federal magistrate, or a state court of record within the federal district, for a search of property or for a person within the district, (2) by a federal magistrate for a search of property or for a person either within or outside the district if the property or person is within the district when the warrant is sought but might move outside the district before the warrant is executed, and (3) by a federal magistrate for a search of property outside the United States if the property is lawfully subject to search and seizure by the United States and is relevant to a criminal investigation in the district in which the warrant is sought.

* * *

Rule 54. Application and Exception

* * *

(b) PROCEEDINGS.

* * *

(4) Proceedings Before United States Magistrates. Proceedings involving misdemeanors and other petty offenses are governed by Rule 58 the Rules of Procedure for the Trial of Misdemeanors before United States Magistrates.

* * *

148

(c) APPLICATION OF TERMS.

*   *   *

"Petty offense" is defined in 18 U.S.C. § ~~1(3)~~ 19.

Rule 58. Procedure for Misdemeanors and Other Petty Offenses

(a) SCOPE.

(1) In General. This rule governs the procedure and practice for the conduct of proceedings involving misdemeanors and other petty offenses, and for appeals to judges of the district courts in such cases tried by magistrates.

(2) Applicability of Other Federal Rules of Criminal Procedure. In proceedings concerning petty offenses for which no sentence of imprisonment will be imposed the court may follow such provisions of these rules as it deems appropriate, to the extent not inconsistent with this rule. In all other proceedings the other rules govern except as specifically provided in this rule.

(3) Definition. The term "petty offenses for which no sentence of imprisonment will be imposed" as used in this rule, means any petty offenses as defined in 18 U.S.C. § 19 as to which the court determines, that, in the event of conviction, no sentence of imprisonment will actually be imposed.

(b) PRETRIAL PROCEDURES.

(1) Trial Document. The trial of a misdemeanor may proceed on an indictment, information, or complaint or, in the case of a petty offense, on a citation or violation notice.

(2) Initial Appearance. At the defendant's initial appearance on a misdemeanor or other petty offense charge, the court shall inform the defendant of:

(A) The charge, and the maximum possible penalties provided by law, including payment of a special assessment under 18 U.S.C. § 3013, and restitution under 18 U.S.C. § 3663;

(B) the right to retain counsel;

(C) unless the charge is a petty offense for which appointment of counsel is not required, the right to request the assignment of counsel if the defendant is unable to obtain counsel;

(D) the right to remain silent and that any statement made by the defendant may be used against the defendant;

(E) the right to trial, judgment, and sentencing before a judge of the district court, unless the defendant consents to trial, judgment, and sentencing before a magistrate;

(F) unless the charge is a petty offense, the right to trial by jury before either a magistrate or a judge of the district court; and

(G) if the defendant is held in custody and charged with a misdemeanor other than a petty offense, the right to a preliminary examination in accordance with 18 U.S.C. § 3060, and the general circumstances under with the defendant may secure pretrial release.

(3) Consent and Arraignment.

(a) Trial Before a Magistrate. If the defendant signs a written consent to be tried before the magistrate which specifically waives trial before a judge of the district court, the magistrate shall take the defendant's plea. The defendant may plead not guilty, guilty or with the consent of the magistrate, nolo contendere.

(b) **Failure to Consent.** If the defendant does not consent to trial before the magistrate, the defendant shall be ordered to appear before a judge of the district court for futher proceedings on notice.

(c) **ADDITIONAL PROCEDURES APPLICABLE ONLY TO PETTY OFFENSES FOR WHICH NO SENTENCE OF IMPRISONMENT WILL BE IMPOSED.**

With respect to petty offenses for which no sentence of imprisonment will be imposed, the following additional procedures are applicable:

(1) **Plea of Guilty or Nolo Contendere.** No plea of guilty or nolo contendere shall be accepted unless the court is satisfied that the defendant understands the nature of the charge and the maximum possible penalties provided by law.

(2) **Waiver of Venue for Plea and Sentence.** A defendant who is arrested, held, or present in a district other than that in which the indictment, information, complaint, citation or violation notice is pending against that defendant may state in writing a wish to plead guilty or nolo contendere, to waive venue and trial in the district in which the proceeding is pending, and to consent to disposition of the case in the district in which that defendant was arrested, is held, or is present. Unless the defendant thereafter pleads not guilty, the prosecution shall be had as if venue were in such district, and notice of the same shall be given to the magistrate in the district where the proceeding was originally commenced. The defendant's statement of a desire to plead guilty or nolo contendere is not admissible against the defendant.

(3) **Sentence.** The court shall afford the defendant an opportunity to be heard in mitigation. The court shall then immediately proceed to sentence the defendant, except that in the discretion of the court, sentencing may be continued to allow an investigation by the probation service or submission of additional information by either party.

(4) **Notification of Right to Appeal** After imposing sentence in a case which has gone to trial on a plea of not guilty, the court shall advise the defendant of the defendant's right to appeal including any right to appeal the sentence. There shall be no duty on the court to advise the defendant of any right of appeal after sentence is imposed following a plea of guilty or nolo contendere, except that the court shall advise the defendant of any right to appeal the sentence.

(d) **SECURING THE DEFENDANT'S APPEARANCE; PAYMENT IN LIEU OF APPEARANCE.**

(1) **Forfeiture of Collateral.** When authorized by local rules of the district court, payment of a fixed sum may be accepted in suitable cases in lieu of appearance and as authorizing the termination of the proceedings. Local rules may make provision for increases in fixed sums not to exceed the maximum fine which could be imposed.

(2) **Notice to Appear.** If a defendant fails to pay a fixed sum, request a hearing, or appear in response to a citation or violation notice, the clerk or a magistrate may issue a notice for the defendant to appear before the court on a date certain. The notice may also afford the defendant an additional opportunity to pay a fixed sum in lieu of appearance, and shall be served upon the defendant by mailing a copy to the defendant's last known address.

(3) **Summons or Warrant.** Upon an indictment or a showing by one of the other documents specified in (b)(1) of probable cause to believe that an offense has been committed and that the defendant has committed it, the court may issue an arrest warrant or, if no warrant is requested by the attorney for the prosecution, a summons. The showing of probable cause shall be made in writing upon oath or under penalty for perjury, but the affiant need not appear before the court. If the defendant fails to appear before the court in response to a summons, the court may

summarily issue a warrant for the defendant's immediate arrest and appearance before the court.

(e) RECORD.

Proceedings under this rule shall be taken down by a reporter or recorded by suitable sound equipment.

(f) NEW TRIAL.

The provisions of Rule 33 shall apply.

(g) APPEAL.

(1) Decision, Order, Judgment or Sentence by a District Judge. An appeal from a decision, order, judgment or conviction or sentence by a judge of the district court shall be taken in accordance with the Federal Rules of Appellate Procedure.

(2) Decision, Order, Judgment or Sentence by a Magistrate.

(a) Interlocutory Appeal. A decision or order by a magistrate which, if made by a judge of the district court, could be appealed by the government or defendant under any provision of law, shall be subject to an appeal to a judge of the district court provided such appeal is taken within 10 days of the entry of the decision or order. An appeal shall be taken by filing with the clerk of court a statement specifying the decision or order from which an appeal is taken and by serving a copy of the statement upon the adverse party, personally or by mail, and by filing a copy with the magistrate.

(b) Appeal From Conviction or Sentence. An appeal from a judgment of conviction or sentence by a magistrate to a judge of the district court shall be taken within 10 days after entry of the judgment. An appeal shall be taken by filing with the clerk of court a statement specifying the judgment from which an appeal is taken, and by serving a copy of the statement upon the United States Attorney, personally or by mail, and by filing a copy with the magistrate.

(c) Record. The record shall consist of the original papers and exhibits in the case together with any transcript, tape, or other recording of the proceedings and a certified copy of the docket entries which shall be transmitted promptly to the clerk of court. For purposes of the appeal, a copy of the record of such proceedings shall be made available at the expense of the United States to a person who establishes by affidavit the inability to pay or give security therefor, and the expense of such copy shall be paid by the Director of the Administrative Office of the United States Courts.

(d) Scope of Appeal. The defendant shall not be entitled to a trial de novo by a judge of the district court. The scope of the appeal shall be the same as an appeal from a judgment of a district court to a court of appeals.

(3) Stay of Execution; Release Pending Appeal. The provisions of Rule 38 relating to stay of execution shall be applicable to a judgment of conviction or sentence. The defendant may be released pending appeal in accordance with the provisions of law relating to release pending appeal from a judgment of a district court to a court of appeals.

†